Enterprise iPhone and iPad Administrator's Guide

Charles Edge

Apress®

Enterprise iPhone and iPad Administrator's Guide

ISBN-13 (pbk): 978-1-4302-3009-0

ISBN-13 (electronic): 978-1-4302-3010-6

Printed and bound in the United States of America 9 8 7 6 5 4 3 2 1

President and Publisher: Paul Manning
Lead Editor: Clay Andres
Development Editor: James Markham
Technical Reviewer: Edward Marczak
Editorial Board: Steve Anglin, Mark Beckner, Ewan Buckingham, Gary Cornell, Jonathan Gennick, Jonathan Hassell, Michelle Lowman, Matthew Moodie, Duncan Parkes, Jeffrey Pepper, Frank Pohlmann, Douglas Pundick, Ben Renow-Clarke, Dominic Shakeshaft, Matt Wade, Tom Welsh
Coordinating Editor: Kelly Moritz
Copy Editors: Sharon Wilkey, Heather Lang, Mary Ann Fugate
Compositor: MacPS, LLC
Indexer: BIM Indexing & Proofreading Services
Artist: April Milne
Cover Designer: Anna Ishchenko

Distributed to the book trade worldwide by Springer Science+Business Media, LLC., 233 Spring Street, 6th Floor, New York, NY 10013. Phone 1-800-SPRINGER, fax (201) 348-4505, e-mail orders-ny@springer-sbm.com, or visit www.springeronline.com.

For information on translations, please e-mail rights@apress.com, or visit www.apress.com.

Apress and friends of ED books may be purchased in bulk for academic, corporate, or promotional use. eBook versions and licenses are also available for most titles. For more information, reference our Special Bulk Sales–eBook Licensing web page at www.apress.com/info/bulksales.

To my darling wife and my sweet little girl

Contents at a Glance

Contents

About the Authors

 **Charles S. Edge, Jr.** is the director of technology at 318, the nation's largest Mac consultancy. At 318, Charles leads a team of the finest gunslingers to have ever been assembled for the Mac platform, working on network architecture, security, storage, and deployment for various vertical and horizontal markets. Charles maintains the 318 blog at www.318.com/techjournal as well as a personal site at www.krypted.com and is the author of several titles on Mac OS X Server and systems administration topics. He has spoken at conferences around the world, including DEF CON, Black Hat, LinuxWorld, MacWorld, MacSysAdmin, and the Apple Worldwide Developers Conference. Charles is the developer of the SANS course on Mac OS X Security and the author of its best practices guide to securing Mac OS X as well. Charles is also the author of many white papers, including a guide on mass-deploying virtualization on the Mac platform for VMware. Charles lives in Minneapolis, Minnesota with his wife, Lisa, and sweet little bucket of a daughter, Emerald.

About the Technical Reviewer

 **Edward Marczak** is a frequent speaker at technology conferences and the co-founder of MacTech Conference. He writes a monthly column for, and is the Executive Editor of MacTech Magazine. His days are currently spent on the Mac team at Google. Past the technology, Ed is a husband and father and enjoys travelling and playing music.

Acknowledgments

I'd like to first and foremost thank the iOS and Mac OS X communities. This includes everyone from the people who design these beautiful devices and the OS that sits atop them, to the people who dissect them and then help others learn further. I truly stand on the shoulders of giants. Of those at Apple who need to be thanked specifically: Eric Wheetley, Schoun Regan, Nathan Haggard, Terry Walker, David Starr, Josh Inman, Jeff Walling, Joel Rennich, Josh Wisenbaker, Greg Smith, JD Mankovsky, Drew Tucker, Stale Bjorndal, Cawan Starks, Eric Senf, Jennifer Jones, and everyone on the Mac OS X Server, Xsan, and Final Cut Server development team. Outside of Apple, thanks to Arek Dreyer and the other Peachpit Press authors for paving the way to build another series of Mac and iOS systems administration books by producing such quality content.

The third-party vendors who took their valuable time to work with me on preparing some of the content have made the book a far better title. Special thanks to all of them, but primarily to AirWatch and the team at JAMF!

The crew at 318 also deserves a lot of credit. It's their hard work that led to having the time to complete yet another book! Special thanks to JJ and to KK for holding everything together in such wild times! Also a special thanks to Zack Smith, Beau Hunter and Chris Barker for their help in various areas of this book.

And finally, a special thanks to Apress for letting me continue to write books for them. They fine-tune the dribble I provide into a well-oiled machine of mature prose. This especially includes Clay Andres for getting everything in motion not only for this book but also for the entire series and, of course, to Kelly Moritz for pulling it all together in the end with her amazing cracks of the whhhip (yes, that's a *Family Guy* reference). Also to Ryan Faas, who wrote the original outline of the book, much of which is still intact. And it wouldn't be prudent to forget the technical editor, Ed Marczak, one of the most talented engineers I've ever had the good fortune to work with.

Introduction

Is the iPhone ready for the enterprise? How about the iPad or iPod Touch? What can you do to create value for your users and environments? What are some of the things currently being done with these devices? How do you deploy them in large quantities, and once deployed, how do you make changes to the configurations? What about applications? In this book, we look at many of the questions that systems administrators have and answer them in a practical manner, to guide you through deployments and management of devices.

In *Chapter 1* we look at strategy. This is the big picture. Here, we introduce the larger concepts for integrating iOS into the enterprise.

Chapter 2 looks at procurement: how do you purchase the devices? What options are available for manual configuration (although we won't discuss the actual manual configuration until Chapter 3)? Do you really need iTunes on all the computers with mobile devices? If so, how can you manage what users are able to do with iTunes?

In *Chapter 3*, we look mostly at how to perform the basic tasks on the devices manually. Here, we look at setting up access to the corporate virtual private network (VPN) and network. We will look at other basic setup and configuration tasks that are built right into the device without the need for third-party tools.

Chapter 4 is all about groupware. Although the focus is on Microsoft Exchange integration, we will look at other solutions and options for everyone else. Because most environments will also configure a number of policies from their Exchange servers, we'll also take this opportunity to discuss doing so and cover the options available to deployments from Exchange 2003 to Exchange 2010.

One of the biggest differences between a mobile device and a full desktop computer is how they interact with files. In *Chapter 5* we will look at various options for getting files onto the portable devices. This includes sharing to the device, sharing from the device, and manually synchronizing to the device. But we also look at some of the more popular cloud-based solutions and what to do with files after you have them on the devices.

Our users don't stay put. That's what we address in *Chapter 6*. Secure communications are critical in an enterprise. Not because we don't trust our users, but mostly we don't trust the threat of unsavory characters taking advantage of our users. (OK, so many don't trust the users either, but that is a whole other book just waiting to happen.) In this chapter we will look at VPNs, proxies, and other forms of remote access (and the strategy we use to provide services remotely). If your groupware strategy involves using Mac OS X Server to remotely access services, chances are you will leverage the Mobile Access service to proxy incoming connection requests into your environment. Using Mobile Access services will require that your users use Mac OS X Server for their groupware services, including accessing calendars and contacts. But in addition to looking at Mac OS X Server, we'll look at accessing standard protocols that enterprises use to provide access to data for end users.

Developing web applications for the iPhone is simple for existing web development teams in most enterprise environments. An application native to the device, or a *fat client*, is not as simple. In *Chapter 7* we will look at getting your web application to run on the mobile devices and also look at the basics for building your own fat client.

In *Chapter 8* we look at building profiles for iOS. This chapter primarily focuses on using the iPhone Configuration Utility to build a profile, push the profile to a mobile device using a wired connection, and then programmatically build iPhone configuration profiles so they can be deployed en masse.

In *Chapter 9*, we move to looking at the various methods to push profiles to devices. Our approach includes doing so without the use of third-party software; however, the focus is on using third-party software because there are more features available in doing so.

In *Chapter 10* we switch gears a bit and focus our attention on the third-party applications that do not provide a file service or fulfill a basic IT infrastructure objective. This includes a number of applications that make an employee's life easier, such as those used for controlling presentations, interacting with social networks, and fulfilling other work duties. This book is not a rehash of the App store, though, and so our focus is on enterprise-level productivity applications.

Finally, in *Chapter 11* we look at how to support these devices. This includes the tools available to your service desk, the training available to your support staff, and the processes that work most fluidly with the Information Technology Infrastructure Library (ITIL), a bible for how many IT departments do business) and other management frameworks.

Managing iOS devices is changing rapidly. New third-party tools are available all the time, iOS updates are being released more frequently than updates to even Mac OS X, and Apple is innovating the marketplace with new and exciting applications for their mobile devices. While this book includes information for iOS 4, a lot will change in the next few months, and you should search and verify that the information is up-to-date on Apple.com at each step of the way of your integration.

These mobile devices are powerful and sexy. The power gives you a wealth of information at your fingertips, but the design of the devices, including their usability, and their increasing adoption is paving the way for future generations of tools that are more and more useful and relevant. The devices are innovative, and the strategy for integration should be equally as innovative! Have a plan, but be able to react to changes in the market. If there is an innovative idea behind how your organization is going to use iOS-based devices, then everything else will just sell itself!

## Chapter 1

The Inevitability of the iPhone in the Enterprise

Practically every conversation about integrating Mac OS X into enterprise environments tends to include the iPhone (Figure 1–1). iPhones are cool, feature rich, extensible, and can integrate with practically any existing enterprise solution. The iPhone also has many features developed almost specifically for satisfying the needs of large organizations, most notably its capability to integrate into Microsoft Exchange Server. Although the iPhone can also be used to support other messaging solutions, its native Exchange support provides seamless integration without requiring third-party software. Many of the policies that you use to manage devices via Exchange also function on the iPhone, making it a complement to many an existing mobile device paradigm.

Figure 1–1. *iPhone*

Three Devices, One Platform

But wait, this book isn't about just the iPhone. It's really about iOS, the operating system that runs on the iPhone, the iPod Touch, and the iPad. The iPhone is one of the most popular phones on the market today. But the iPhone itself is really just what the name indicates, a phone. As with many other modern-day cellular phones, it also has a camera, a speaker, a microphone, an antenna (the publicity for the iPhone 4 antenna is much to Apple's chagrin), and of course, a data plan. The iPod Touch (Figure 1–2) is similar to the iPhone but lacks some of its core features. Most notable is the fact that it is not a phone—it's an iPod. Physically, the iPod Touch does not have a microphone, camera, or Bluetooth. The iPod Touch also comes with a different dock, has a headphone jack on the bottom, and older models didn't have a built-in speaker. The iPod Touch is otherwise very similar to the iPhone; they are spec'd similarly performance-wise, and both run the same software stack.

Figure 1–2. *iPod Touch*

On the outside, the iPad (Figure 1–3) is most similar to the iPod Touch. It does not come with a camera, but it is larger and able to perform any task an iPod Touch can, with more screen real estate showing at greater resolution. On the inside, the iPad couldn't be more different: it has a completely different chipset. Most applications that run on the iPod Touch and the iPhone can run on an iPad, but not all have yet been formatted for the larger screen and therefore may have distorted text on the iPad.

Figure 1–3. *iPad*

Not all features or tools are available on all of the devices. Throughout this book, I note when referencing a feature or application available exclusively for one model or specifically not available for a given model. I also refrain from discussing iPod models that are not an iPod Touch (for example, the Nano), given that they will run very different software from those most often integrated into the enterprise.

The devices all take advantage of a rich development framework, which is built on a subset of Mac OS X's Cocoa development platform, Cocoa Touch. This is a mobile, optimized development environment that allows for the creation of feature-rich, user-friendly applications using a program called Xcode to develop software. As you can see in Figure 1–4, Xcode is the same tool used to write applications for all Apple platforms.

Figure 1–4. *Xcode's Project Gallery*

The number of applications that have been published to the App Store, Apple's online marketplace, are a testament to the extensibility of the underlying language. But there is definitely a learning curve to writing applications for the iPhone for those without previous development experience. Those with OS X development experience, or experience with other object-oriented languages, should be able to familiarize themselves with the environment quickly. In some cases, it will be easier to develop applications that can be leveraged using a web browser, thus enabling various platforms to connect to the application and rapid development of portals customized for each type of device that may be supported.

Welcoming Change While Protecting the Enterprise

Being in the information technology field in an enterprise means constant change. It means that new gadgets come and go on an almost annual basis and that we frequently have to look at industrywide changes. Many IT departments are built around the idea that a solid command and control structure must be developed to keep users from harming their devices and therefore keep support costs down.

The iPhone is cool. Apple has spent a lot of time developing a device that is both a feature-rich platform and simple to use. The iPod Touch enables you to use many of the same features as with the iPhone, but you can use it without the monthly charges from a cellular provider. And then there is the iPad. The iPad goes above and beyond anything available on the iPod Touch or iPhone by giving you a faster processer and a larger screen, allowing for more productivity and even cooler applications. But if you are reading this book, you aren't likely interested in cool; you are likely more interested in productivity.

Sandbox

One of the main differences between the iPhone and other platforms is the implementation of application sandboxing. *Application sandboxing* means that applications are not able to communicate with one another. The most recent release of iOS—version 4—provides more options for developers to integrate solutions that can work with one another. However, the options are still few, and many are still untapped. What this means is that each application is almost always a silo (memory, processing, and data) unto itself. That sandbox protects the device from many of the problems plaguing other platforms, such as malware.

The sandbox extends to multitasking. Although iOS 4 also introduces more options for developers to determine how their application runs in the background, it is still best to use push technologies to communicate with applications that are not the foreground application. Most applications ask servers for data, but *push* means that data is sent to the application instead. A great example of this is any application that can put a red number over its icon, or *badge,* even when the application is not open. This number represents data that is waiting for the user to use. Push technology means that applications do not have to be open to receive data, limiting the resource intensity that the application has.

> **NOTE:** Although one of the promises of push is that it will lessen the load on your battery, in actuality it can increase the load on the battery and should be tested in each environment before deciding to leverage push en masse.

Long-Term Implications

Every device that is used in an enterprise comes with its own total cost of ownership. Depending on the size of your deployment, you will likely spend as much time planning the deployment as you will spend on the deployment itself (if not more). As the old saying goes, measure twice, cut once. But consider the recent adoption in the enterprise of these devices and know that you need to maintain a certain level of agility with your infrastructure.

Before you deploy your mobile devices, there are some considerations that you will want to address (even if your design requirements will change drastically over the course of the next 18 months), including the following:

- What settings will go on each device?

- How much automation will we leverage?

- How will policies be managed?

- How will our assets be tracked?

- What written policies do we need to ratify in anticipation of our deployment?

- How much user interaction will be required, and what kind of zero-tier assets can we provide to users for that interaction?

- What kind of data will users need to access, and how will they access that data when they are in the office?

- How will users access data remotely?

> **NOTE:** *Zero-tier assets* are any assets that enable you to stop problems before an end user needs to contact your service desk. These often include wikis and written documentation, for example.

Every iOS device that gets deployed in an environment has an amount of automation that can simplify and streamline the deployment. For each click that can be saved, you will reduce the deployment time by a number of seconds. The more devices that you will be pushing out, the more significant these click-saving automations will be. Devices also need support, and the traditional thought behind support is that the more freedom you give users, the more per user you will pay in support. But given that Apple has a different way of doing things than you may be used to with other solutions, prepare to think a little differently!

Mobile Integration Strategies

Each mobile platform is unique and so requires a unique integration strategy. For example, the BlackBerry from Research In Motion has BlackBerry Enterprise Server, capable of managing a fleet of BlackBerrys. Android, iPhone, iPod Touch, and Windows Mobile devices are capable of using ActiveSync for connecting to an Exchange server. From the Exchange server, policies can be applied and users can access mail, contacts, and calendars.

All of these devices will need to be activated, and all will need to be configured to work with your server. Of these, the BlackBerry is likely one of the easiest to deploy en masse for an enterprise. However, the gap narrows each year and can become even narrower with some of the strategies and third-party software discussed throughout this book. But one of the core concepts in this book is the idea of user choice. And if you are going to be supporting different types of devices, look for commonalities across platforms. Many support policies are handed down from ActiveSync, most come with a standard web browser, and almost all support groupware access through Microsoft Exchange or Google Apps.

By focusing on how you can provide the maximum number of services to devices with the least amount of integration, you will most likely maximize the return on investment of every dime of your infrastructure. This may seem obvious, but keep in mind that most devices are compliant to certain standards. This compliance enables you to extend support to additional platforms in some cases with absolutely no additional infrastructure.

Although device standards are important, each device will have its own specific design requirements, in many cases because most have their own unique development environment. This book focuses on minimizing these, and when possible provides recommendations for things you can do with infrastructure built for iOS that will also allow for tighter integration with other mobile devices.

The Paradigm Shift

The unique development environment is only one way that iOS-based devices are different from what you encounter with other platforms. The iPad and iPhone represent a new challenge to many environments. Many of the devices are owned by end users. There isn't a historical evolution of products and processes around iOS given its rapid adoption in many an enterprise. In addition, the management options (including third-party options) aren't yet as mature as those for many other brands and operating systems of mobile devices. iOS-based devices aren't waiting for most enterprises or the systems administration community to come up with a solid plan, though, because—to put it simply—users love them.

Impact to Infrastructure

Users love iOS-based devices (and many of those users sit in the C-level suites of enterprises) because they are powerful. Most enterprises already have such devices, whether the devices are officially acknowledged or not. Many organizations support these devices, and others do not. Either way, the enterprise needs to formulate a plan of embracing the devices, before business units split the centralized support structure of your organization and do so themselves.

For many organizations, centralized management is one of the most critical aspects when deploying any device to the enterprise en masse. Apple has not yet communicated a comprehensive strategy for centrally managing these devices. However, several third-party products have emerged to allow for centralized management of them. For example, JAMF Software has built management features for iOS-based devices into their Casper Suite of products for centrally managing Mac OS X. The companies Equinux (TARMAC) and Dell (KACE) have released management tools as well. All of these tools will allow for deployment, management, and reporting, providing a granular level of control over the devices that is not available using Apple tools alone.

We cover these tools in Chapter 8; most look like Figure 1–5, which shows a dedicated mechanism for managing the devices.

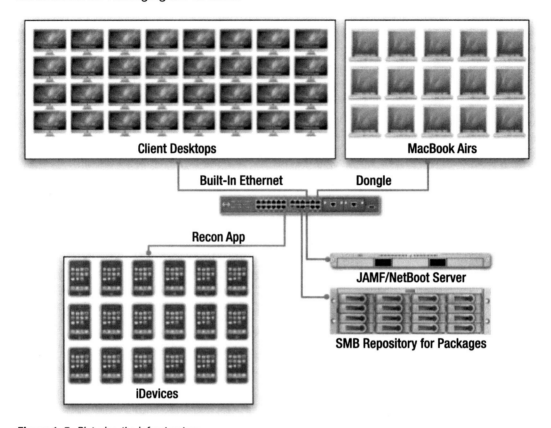

Figure 1–5. *Picturing the infrastructure*

NOTE: There is a debate in IT over whether personally owned devices need any form of centralized management. This is more of a religious debate than I would prefer to get into in this book, but it is worth noting that many organizations do require centralized management of these devices because they have corporate data on them.

All of the third-party products for deploying the iPhone, iPad, and iPod Touch use the same basic underlying technology that is provided by Apple. Basically, you start with creating a configuration profile in the iPhone Configuration Utility (Chapter 7). You attach those profiles to groups of devices. You then load the application from the App Store or push the applications on each device, and you finally deploy the profiles to the devices. Given that all of the devices share an affinity for profiles generated using the iPhone Configuration Utility, it is critical to understand how to use the utility, how the profiles are interpreted and—according to the size of the deployment—how to tap into some of the options that can be manually added to profiles that have not yet been exposed.

Not that you have to use third-party products. Apple has produced sample code for leveraging an environment's existing directory service to generate profiles on the fly. The code is written in Ruby and does not have a support contract; therefore, many environments will not want to use it for one of those reasons. If your enterprise has a large number of Mac OS X–based computers, it may be cost-effective to leverage this code. However, for most environments, it will be cost prohibitive to do so given the steep learning and development curves.

The policy and patch management aspects of the iPhone are currently not as easy a process. After a device is deployed, policy management is handled from within Google Apps, Microsoft Exchange, or another solution that supports policy management. This allows for remote wiping, assigning password requirements, and so forth. The third-party applications do not yet support loading software onto devices over the air, and so many systems administrators will be frustrated when they run reports and find that a number of applications on devices are out-of-date. Third-party vendors list application deployment as a feature in their road map, and so this is likely a situation that will resolve itself for the platform in due time.

Finally, reporting can still be done from JAMF Software's Recon Mobile app (a component of the Casper Suite), AirWatch, or other third-party solutions that support reporting on mobile devices. Overall, the policies that are used for the devices and their configuration are influenced by multiple factors, without a tool such as the Resultant Set of Policies, which many Active Directory administrators are familiar with and which can show how overlapping policies are interpreted to a Windows client. But the maturity of the third-party products will likely make up for this at some point.

Integration with the Enterprise

Most IT departments are going to be concerned about the items listed in the previous section: deployment, patch management, reporting, groupware, and so forth. But most important is user productivity. In order to maximize the return on investment in these devices, users need to use them to access the various services offered in the enterprise. These include file services, application publishing, web services, and logging into the network (on-site and remotely).

Accessing files is the most common need most people have when interacting with networks. With a standard computer, you can read, edit, save, copy, e-mail, and delete many types of files out of the box. You can also purchase more software to allow you to interact with other types of files, such as Microsoft Office, the Adobe Creative Suite, and iWork. With iOS-based devices, most file types can be accessed in a read-only capacity by default. Third-party applications (and iWork for iOS) step in to fill this void by allowing you to edit documents. Those third-party applications can be purchased, or even built if you have a team capable of such a task.

The larger screen and keyboard on the iPad can enable you to have a similar experience to the one that you have with a desktop. However, editing documents on the iPod Touch and iPhone is going to be difficult without a high level of frustration. By using third-party applications, editing documents can be more easily accomplished. iWork from Apple contains some of the best tools currently available, but those can be used only with files using the iWork formats. There are other applications, which are covered in Chapter 5.

Most third-party applications allow you to synchronize documents to devices by using a wire or another specific application, such as Google. However, for most applications, getting the documents to the devices can also be a challenge over the air. Applications cannot communicate with one another. In Chapter 5, you will look at some tools that enable you to access documents as files. But you cannot then edit them with another application unless you copy them to the local device, which can be done with the clipboard or through an application. This requires an almost scripted workflow design, rather than allowing users to interact with files through the Finder or Windows Explorer, as they would traditionally do in Mac OS X or Microsoft Windows. Although Google Apps and Dropbox have made this process much more seamless, not all organizations maintain their data in the cloud. Also, the devices will drain battery power and be under high CPU load with what would be a minor operation on an actual computer. Although accessing files and augmenting them in a manner that is meaningful is a challenge, you will learn about doing so in Chapter 5 to ease the burden many an enterprise will feel.

Although working with documents represents a common aspect of computer use, it is obviously not the only thing that computers are used for. In many enterprises, people also need to access intranets and business applications—most of which have no client specific to iOS. Many that are web based also will not work with the devices, given browser incompatibilities. Of those that do work with the devices, you then have issues with screen resolution, size of the text on the screen, and accessing data remotely. But the lion's share of IT budgets are geared toward building these enterprise-line business tools, such as Enterprise Resource Planning (ERP), Customer Relationship Management (CRM), and Human Resources (HR) applications.

Luckily, many of these tools (after all, that's what ERP, CRM and other business applications are: tools to help people do their jobs more efficiently) will have an application programming interface, or API. An API enables developers to effectively build custom solutions that work with their tools. One such custom solution could be a web portal that aggregates content from various business tools, or allows end users to interact with data aggregated from those tools—for example, a portal that pulls certain fields from databases to show an executive a dashboard for a company's performance. Another would be a custom application that allows for meaningful interaction with this data built in Objective-C, the native programming language for iOS. That tool would then be sending data back up to the database, rather than just displaying figures from it.

Finally, applications can be provided to iOS-based devices via a thin client. In the context of this book, a thin client is an application that runs on iOS and allows access to a client application or to a full operating system environment running on Microsoft Windows or on Mac OS X. In this book, you will look at leveraging the following standards for communicating with iOS-based devices:

Remote Desktop Protocol (RDP): The proprietary Microsoft protocol for providing a remote graphical user interface (GUI) to another computer

Virtual Network Computing (VNC): A cross-platform desktop-sharing system, more common in Mac OS X and Linux

Independent Computing Architecture (ICA): The proprietary Citrix Systems client for accessing their application server environment

Although there are other tools that will allow you to leverage a thin-client environment, these are the most common in use in the enterprise and will complete our look at application development in Chapter 11. Thin-client solutions offer a method to access applications remotely without developing software, but can be the quickest solution to deploy when you need to stand up an application infrastructure quickly.

Summary

This chapter has focused on addressing the challenges that you will face when trying to integrate iOS-based devices into an enterprise. We discussed how this unique mobile platform fits into most environments and the burning questions that need to be answered quickly and up front.

Through the rest of the book, we will shift our focus to more of a tactical description of carrying out what we have covered here. We will cover the questions that an enterprise-level organization might ask, given an upcoming mass deployment and integration project. Up next, though, we're going to look at how we bring a solutions-oriented approach to addressing these issues.

NOTE: Before you get started with the technical parts of this book, if you are using an iPhone, you will need to make sure that the subscriber identity module (SIM) card has been installed and that the iPhone has been activated. If your organization uses Microsoft Exchange or VPN connectivity, you will also need to make sure you have an enterprise data plan, or the iPhone will not be able to leverage ActiveSync.

## Chapter 2

Purchasing and Activating

One of the most frustrating aspects of deploying a large fleet of iOS-based devices is just getting them all set up and configured. As mentioned in Chapter 1, this involves configuring the device with each setting for the user, installing the applications, and configuring each of those with the settings required. Before you can do any of this, you must first plug each device into iTunes and activate it. And before you can do that, you have to buy the devices.

As with everything involving computing en masse, purchasing can be a nightmare, because buying even small items can mean that you just overspent by a sum magnified by the number of units being acquired. Therefore, this chapter starts by having you look at details around purchasing to prepare for a pilot or a large deployment. You will also look at considerations around application purchasing.

Because you cannot use the device until it is activated, I've combined purchasing with activation in this chapter. If you will be activating a large number of devices in a row, there are some things you can do to be efficient with your time, and these are covered in the "Managing Activations" section of this chapter. After a device is activated, if it is used on another computer (running a different copy of iTunes), then it will need to be reset.

In large organizations, multiple people can often use the same device over the course of its lifetime. I consider the repurposing of a device similar to purchasing a new device and therefore present options for purchasing, activating, and then purchasing applications during this chapter as well in subsequent sections.

By the end of the chapter, you will be able to buy, activate, buy applications for, and ultimately retire or repurpose iOS-based devices to complete their life cycle. Hopefully, plenty of planning goes into the process as well. After plans have been made, though, the process begins with buying those sexy mobile devices.

Making Large-Purchase Considerations

Apple looks at enterprise environments in one of two ways: as large educational environments or corporate enterprises (and government is considered a subset of enterprise). According to the size and scale of your corporate enterprise, you may already have a dedicated account executive or systems engineer. You may also work with the business units at one of the retail outlets, Apple Online, or various resellers. If you are currently purchasing Apple hardware, you should be able to use any of the aforementioned sources to obtain mobile devices as well, with the exception of some resellers.

Educational environments can have an enterprise scale (and often have a larger scale than their corporate counterparts as far as Mac OS X and iOS are concerned). Therefore, they are handled as corporate enterprises would be. Most educational institutions have an account executive and a systems engineer. You should continue to use these resources when purchasing mobile devices.

In other words, treat purchasing Apple's mobile devices as you would their desktop counterparts. Unless of course you get sweetheart licensing from one of the wireless providers. Then do what makes the most fiscal sense, while providing a clear channel of support. Apple, or its approved vendors, is sure to verify that you get good pricing, provide varying amounts of assistance in the planning and deployment (where needed), and work with you to minimize your mass deployment's potential for a packaging nightmare.

Finally, it is worth more to your organization to purchase equipment in packaging designed for multiple units. It just so happens that purchasing is typically less spendy when you buy products in bulk, but more important, it saves time during deployment. There is a fixed amount of time associated with unboxing the product during a large deployment, no matter the platform. If you are using packaging that is designed for mass deployment, your project will likely be more environmentally friendly, save on the required man-hours (an indirect cost savings), and save on cost.

Preparing the Pilot

By the time you've purchased your mobile devices, you should have a plan in place for what you will do with them. The failed pilot program is one with no purpose. You may feel that if you simply place devices into the hands of people, they may or may not figure out how to maximize the potential of those devices. But in order to provide some modicum of guidance, decide before you put the devices into the hands of users how you are going to deploy them, whether users can use their standard enterprise messaging account to purchase software and register devices, how they will be distributed, how patch management will be handled, and of course, what business objective the devices are there to meet.

Strategizing for your deployment and patch management is covered from a bird's-eye, or cursory, view in Chapter 1 and then further in Chapters 8 and 9. In this chapter, you're mostly going to look at preparing the devices to be able to carry out whichever strategy you proceed with. Doing so often involves placing software on the mobile devices prior to placing them into production.

Because every device must be plugged into iTunes and activated, either the IT staff or the user is going to need to touch each device. That touch ranges from 1 minute to 10 minutes per device. You also need to unbox all of the equipment, which requires from 1 to 3 minutes per device (assuming you can keep up a grueling schedule). Therefore, if you are deploying 1,000 devices, you will need 2,000 to 13,000 minutes before you put an asset tag on a device, install a management agent, or personalize it whatsoever. That is the difference between about 34 and 217 hours worth of labor. When you are preparing for a pilot, you are likely looking at an initial batch of about only 100 devices. However, when you project out during the pilot, this is a metric often overlooked.

After the hardware has been purchased, shipped, unboxed, and then activated, your pilot will be ready to proceed. Before you move on to figuring out what to put on all those devices and how to hook them into your back-end infrastructure, let's first take a look at how to streamline the actual activation process.

Purchasing Applications

One strength of iOS devices is in the bevy of applications available to the platform. As of the writing of this book, more than 250,000 unique applications are in the App Store. Most of those applications are purchased one by one, by individuals.

Understanding the License Agreement

Each application, or *app*, for short, can be used in a variety of ways. Figure 2–1 shows the licensing agreement for the App Store.

NOTE: Apple routinely updates the licensing agreement for App Store access. You will occasionally need to accept the new agreement when attempting to use the store.

What this seems to mean (to a non-lawyer) is that you can either use an app in such a way that it follows a user from device to device or in such a way that it is tied to the device. Mac OS X is a multiuser operating system, but although the underpinnings are there to house multiple accounts on a single iOS-based device, the iOS does not currently have an option for multiple users, making iOS-based devices very much one-person devices. Therefore, the licensing agreement can mean that if you have a single user who purchases an application, that person can use the application on their iPhone, iPad, or iPod Touch provided that user does not exceed the limit of five devices. However, if you have an iOS-based device that is used as somewhat of a kiosk (for example, in a lab in an educational environment), you instead can use the license for all users who use that system.

End User License Agreements, or EULAs, can be interesting to read. To quote the App Store EULA:

APP STORE PRODUCT USAGE RULES

(i) You may download and sync a Product for personal, noncommercial use on any device You own or control.

(ii) If You are a commercial enterprise or educational institution, You may download and sync a Product for use by either (a) a single individual on one or more devices You own or control or (b) multiple individuals, on a single shared device You own or control. For example, a single employee may use the Product on both the employee's iPhone and iPad, or multiple students may serially use the Product on a single iPad located at a resource center or library.

(iii) You shall be able to store App Store Products from up to five different Accounts at a time on compatible iOS-based devices.

(iv) You shall be able to store App Store Products on five iTunes-authorized devices at any time.

(v) You shall be able to manually sync App Store Products from at least one iTunes-authorized device to devices that have manual sync mode, provided that the App Store Product is associated with an Account on the primary iTunes-authorized device, where the primary iTunes-authorized device is the one that was first synced with the device or the one that you subsequently designate as primary using iTunes.

Figure 2–1. *App Store EULA*

Purchasing in Bulk

Although acquiring applications using iTunes is straightforward enough, many institutions will have a problem with users buying software on accounts that are in many cases tied to personal accounts. Acquiring software applications one at a time can also be time-consuming. Finally, depending on how devices are to be used, you may find it more economical to purchase software in bulk.

Educational environments can use the Volume Purchase program, which allows buying a large number of applications and then using Volume Vouchers to put the applications onto devices. To quote Apple:

The Volume Purchase Program allows educational institutions to purchase multiple copies of the same app at once. Developers may also offer a discount for these multiple purchases. To use this program, you must have a Program Facilitator account, which can be obtained by any Authorized Purchaser from your institution. To get started, redeem a Volume Voucher by clicking Redeem Voucher, below.

For more on the Volume Purchase Program, see `http://volume.itunes.apple.com/us/store`.

Managing Activations

Now that you have seen the importance of having a streamlined activation process, let's move on to managing the activations. If you are setting up a large number of mobile devices, activating them can be a tedious process. When you start talking about thousands of them, it can be downright overwhelming. However, you can reduce the number of clicks, taps, and touches by telling iTunes not to synchronize devices with the iTunes Library following activation (synchronizing effectively binds the mobile device to a computer).

To block the synchronizing, you use what is commonly referred to as *iTunes Activation mode*. Activation mode instructs iTunes to eject a device after it's been activated rather than trying to synchronize music, photos, and other media that may be on your system. By setting iTunes to Activation mode, you cut out a couple of clicks from the activation process and don't attempt a lengthy sync.

NOTE: iTunes still needs to be running on a computer that has an active Internet connection, even when in Activation mode. In order to be activated, an iPhone needs a valid SIM card.

Using StoreActivationMode

To enable activation-only mode on a Mac, you need only to write a 1 to the StoreActivationMode key in `com.apple.iTunes`. This can be done using the following command:

```
defaults write com.apple.iTunes StoreActivationMode -integer 1
```

When you open iTunes and click the About iTunes item in the iTunes menu, you should see a notice indicating that the device is in Activation mode, as seen in Figure 2–2.

Figure 2–2. *iTunes version and mode information*

Windows is even more common than Mac OS X for users of iTunes. To enable iTunes
Activation mode for Windows, you would run the iTunes executable, using the
/setPrefInt option to set StoreActivationMode to 1. If you change to the C:\Program
Files\iTunes directory, you can run the following command:

```
iTunes.exe /setPrefInt StoreActivationMode 1
```

You cannot sync an iPhone, iPad, or iPod Touch while Activation mode is enabled.
Therefore, if you are activating devices from your desktop machine and you have one of
Apple's mobile devices that you then want to sync to, you'll need to disable Activation
mode to sync to it. To disable activation-only mode on a Mac, use the defaults
command to delete the StoreActivationMode key from com.apple.iTunes.plist:

```
defaults delete com.apple.iTunes StoreActivationMode
```

Or to disable Activation mode on Windows, cd back into C:\Program Files\iTunes and
then run iTunes.exe with the /setPrefInt option to change StoreActivationMode back
to 0:

```
iTunes.exe /setPrefInt StoreActivationMode 0
```

Using StoreGeniusMode

In addition to Activation mode, there is also a restore-only mode called Genius mode,
which essentially allows only backup and restoration of the devices as opposed to
allowing only activation as Activation mode does. To enable Genius mode on a Mac, you
can run the following command, creating a key called StoreGeniusMode in
com.apple.iTunes that is set to true (or integer 1) to accomplish this:

```
defaults write com.apple.iTunes StoreGeniusMode -integer 1
```

This mode is also available in Windows by cd'ing into the C:\Program Files\iTunes directory and running the following:

```
iTunes.exe /setPrefInt StoreGeniusMode 1
```

You can then disable restore-only mode with this command:

```
defaults write com.apple.iTunes StoreGeniusMode -integer 0
```

Or for Windows, cd to C:\Program Files\iTunes and run the iTunes executable, setting the StoreGeniusMode option to 0:

```
iTunes.exe /setPrefInt StoreGeniusMode 0
```

Activating Devices

Whether you choose to use iTunes Activation mode, need to back up devices, or just want to use iTunes to get started, the next step is to activate some devices.

Getting Started

When you first turn on a new iOS-based device, you will see a screen like that in Figure 2–3. The imagery indicates that you cannot do anything with the device until, as mentioned earlier in this chapter, you plug the iOS-based device into a computer with iTunes installed. At this point, go ahead and plug the device into a computer that has iTunes open and running.

Figure 2–3. *A device waiting for activation*

As soon as you plug the device in, you will hear a chime and the screen will turn black. If you press the center button of the device, you can then use the device. If your only goal is to activate the device, you are finished. It can now be used normally. Simply slide the Slide to Unlock slider (Figure 2–4) from left to right and you will be placed at the home screen (more on the home screen in Chapter 3). If you will be using the iPhone Configuration Utility to configure devices, you can find more on the next step in a typical "imaging" scenario there, which is to say, deploying the configuration and applications.

Figure 2–4. *Unlocking the slider*

Synchronizing for the First Time

Although you can go ahead and start using the devices, if iTunes is not in Activation mode, you can also first perform an initial synchronization. If you are doing a very small pilot or plugging the device into the computer that the end user will use it with, you can actually download applications via iTunes, put music on the devices, subscribe to podcasts, and synchronize photos with applications that iTunes can link to the device. At this point, with the device still plugged into the machine, look at iTunes. You will see that iTunes is attempting to name the device based on the name of the user who has iTunes open (Figure 2–5).

Figure 2–5. *Setting up a new mobile device*

NOTE: You can also restore the device from a previously made backup at this point, part of many a support path. Although Chapter 11 covers supporting iOS-based devices, that topic is also covered at the end of this chapter because it is often part of placing devices back into production.

Choosing Synchronization Options

If this is a new device and you will not be restoring a backup to the unit, then set the radio button to Setup as New. Next, click the Continue button to be taken to the Setup screen. Here you can make some basic configuration options for the features you will synchronize to the device. As you can see in Figure 2–6, you have the options to Automatically Sync Songs to My Device, Automatically Add Photos to My Device, and Automatically Sync Applications to My Device. These check boxes will synchronize your iTunes Library, iPhoto Library, and applications that were purchased from the iTunes App Store (discussed further in the "Using the App Store" section of this chapter).

Figure 2–6. *Choosing basic configuration options for new devices*

When you are satisfied with your choices, click the Done button. At this point, you will be asked whether iTunes should open automatically when it is connected. If you want a computer to only charge a device or have a plan for the iOS devices that does not include iTunes on client computers, you should not use this option. Otherwise, simply click the Yes button to proceed (Figure 2–7).

Figure 2–7. *Configuring devices for automatic connections to iTunes*

The device will then restart. When it comes back up, iTunes will immediately begin to synchronize the data that you have elected to be synchronized. At this point, the devices can be personalized. But before handing them to end users, first consider what policies, both written and digital, that you wish to have for the devices.

Developing Organizational Policies

Most enterprises have a set of policies that define how, why, and sometimes even when a device can be used. iOS-enabled devices tend to be about choice. However, most organizations require some form of agreement that users must accept before issuing the devices. This agreement can include requirements from insurance, assurance that the device is recoverable, acknowledgement of policies (especially if you plan to possibly remotely wipe devices), or even a list of allowable applications/sites.

Not all organizations will leverage policies for these mobile devices, especially if the devices are not officially supported by the IT department. However, if you do, there is no reason to reinvent the wheel. You can use policies that are similar (if not the same) as your organization's policies for other aspects of the IT operation, such as those a user may have signed when initially being given a desktop computer. These policies may require a small amount of tailoring to cover insurance and other possible requirements, but for the most part they are somewhat interchangeable.

If your organization does not yet have an acceptable use policy, consider using the one in Appendix A of this book as a starting point. Make sure to have your legal representation review the policy and/or supply one more suited to your needs prior to putting the policy out to your general user base.

> **NOTE:** When you log into Mac OS X, Windows, and some other operating systems, you might be prompted with an acceptable use policy. The same cannot be said for iOS-enabled devices. These need to have acceptance applied in another fashion, such as the old standby of having a user sign a physical document.

Using the App Store

After a device is put in front of a user, one of the first things that will be done is that the user will access the App Store. At the iPhone App Store, users can purchase and/or download applications for their iPhone.

Application development can be a fairly complicated task. If you are looking for a specific function outside of the iPhone's default software, it's never a bad idea to see whether such a tool is already on the market before committing development resources to the task. The App Store should be the first place you look, rather than simply starting a large development project.

To access the App Store, open iTunes and click the iTunes Store listing under Store. Then click the link for App Store (Figure 2–8).

Figure 2–8. *The iTunes App Store*

You will now be able to browse, buy, and download applications. However, as mentioned in the "Purchasing Applications" section of this chapter, you will need to come up with a way to allow users to acquire applications (some use gift cards/codes purchased for the purpose, some have staff expense the purchase, and others use bulk-purchasing programs). After the app is purchased, the applications will automatically sync to the devices (provided that option was selected during setup).

NOTE: You can also purchase applications directly from the devices, which is covered in Chapter 3.

Managing iTunes

Many environments will try to deploy iOS-based devices without iTunes. But iTunes provides a seamless interface for users who use an iPhone, iPad, or iPod Touch. Deployment without iTunes will be very complicated. You don't have to use iTunes to interact with a device, but it sure makes life much easier. If you choose to deploy iTunes as part of your mass deployment, whether it is to Windows or to Mac OS X clients (where it would be installed by default), there are some features that many organizations will certainly want to limit. Luckily, Apple allows you to manage various iTunes features for both Windows and Mac OS X clients. For Windows, Registry keys can be used, and for Mac OS X, there is the ~/Library/Preferences/com.apple.iTunes.plist file.

Using the `com.apple.iTunes.plist` file, you will have the ability to add the preference domain into the Workgroup Manager Managed Preferences (as covered in Chapter 7). After the domain is added, you will be able to set options to manage, including the following keys (which are self-explanatory for the most part):

- `allowiTunesUAccess`
- `disableAppleTV`
- `disableAutomaticDeviceSync`
- `disableCheckForUpdates`
- `disableDeviceRegistration`
- `disableGeniusSidebar`
- `disableGetAlbumArtwork`
- `disableMusicStore`
- `disableOpenStream`
- `disablePlugins`
- `disablePodcasts`
- `disableRadio`
- `disableSharedMusic`
- `gamesLimit`
- `moviesLimit`
- `ratingSystemID`
- `restrictExplicit`
- `restrictGames`
- `restrictMovies`
- `restrictTVshows`
- `tvShowsLimit`

If you have not been allowing your users to use iTunes because of a specific feature having been abused (for example, radio), you can now limit many individual features of iTunes and therefore allow users to still have access to less-intrusive capabilities, such as iTunesU and podcasts. If you don't have a managed environment and are considering pushing out a new `com.apple.iTunes.plist` file to your users, beware. The feat will be a little tricky if you want to make sure to preserve any paired devices. Information about iPhones and Apple TVs can be found in this file, so it's best not to perform file drop (common with package management tools, such as Composer from JAMF Software). If you do wish to push a preference into the file directly, rather than use managed preferences, it will be best to utilize a shell script and the `defaults` command. For example, to disable iTunes Radio, you could use the following:

```
defaults write ~/Library/Preferences/com.apple.iTunes disableRadio -bool true
```

If you are using a Microsoft Windows-based environment, the Registry keys are covered in the following Apple Kbase article: `http://support.apple.com/kb/ht2102`.

Registering Devices

After the devices are activated, you will need to support them. If you have problems, especially those that are covered under the warranty (no, dropping your iPhone into the toilet or accidentally running over it with your car is not covered under the warranty—I wish it were, though, and applaud you for trying to convince the guys at the Genius Bar that you didn't do anything to it). In order to activate the warranty, you will need to do so manually at `www.apple.com/support/applecare/overview`.

> **NOTE:** If you are registering a large number of devices, you should work with the entity that you purchased the devices from to register them en masse.

Backing Up and Restoring Devices

Every asset that your organization has that has data on it should at least be considered during a backup plan. iPhones, iPads, and iPod Touches usually have more data that resides in a cloud, but other than that, they are no different from desktop computers. However, the number of iOS-based devices not being backed up is somewhat staggering when compared to other types of devices.

If your organization provides users access to iTunes, backup and restoration is a fairly straightforward process. Otherwise, you may want to provide a shared system running iTunes in kiosk mode, or simply deploy iTunes in kiosk mode, or look at some of the options mentioned earlier in the "Managing iTunes" section in order to reduce the security or resource utilization concerns that certain features of iTunes can cause.

> **NOTE:** There are other reasons for providing access to iTunes. As covered in the "Upgrading the Software" section later in this chapter, you also need access to iTunes in order to keep the version of the operating system up-to-date.

To back up an iOS-based device using iTunes, first plug the device into the computer as you would do for any standard sync. Then click the device name and go through the tabs, making sure all of the data that you want to synchronize from (and to) the device is selected (Figure 2–9).

Figure 2-9. *iTunes synchronization*

Next, right-click (or Control+click if you have a one-button mouse) on the name of the device listed in the Devices section of iTunes and then click Sync. You can also back up the settings by clicking Back Up (Figure 2–10), effectively replacing the current backup file that is already present and used with restorations. This option backs up only settings, though, as data is backed up during synchronizations.

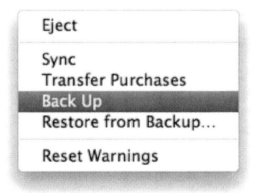

Figure 2-10. *Choosing the Back Up option*

Restoring settings and data is also straightforward. Clicking the Restore button at the main iTunes screen (shown earlier in Figure 2–9) will bring up a confirmation screen. Here you can simply click the Restore button to confirm that you actually want to overwrite the data on the device, and iTunes will restore the settings to the device based on the latest backup of settings. After the settings have been restored, the synchronization process will kick in, and the data will then be put back on the device. You can also restore settings to a device as part of a reset process for the unit. In the next section, you will look at resetting devices and then restoring data to a recently reset unit.

Placing Devices Back into Production

Chances are that you will have staff, student, or customer turnover, no matter the type of organization you have. As such, when devices are pulled out of service, you will find that you often want to reset them prior to putting them back into service. That may mean just clearing out the settings, or performing a reset back to factory default settings, or sending a remote wipe to the device (which you will look at further in Chapter 4). Either way, prior to giving the device to another user, you will need to wipe it clean.

NOTE: When you reset a device, you will need to recomplete the activation process.

The easiest way to wipe a device clean is to plug it into another computer running iTunes. Doing so erases the data and pairs the device with a new computer. This can be seen in Figure 2–11, which shows a device that has been plugged into a different computer and is prompting that it needs to be erased to be synchronized with that computer. Although this provides a quick and easy way of repurposing devices, it can also be challenging, because it means that when you provide a new desktop to users, you also need to wipe their device if they will be connecting to it via iTunes. Doing so means transferring the data prior to repurposing the device.

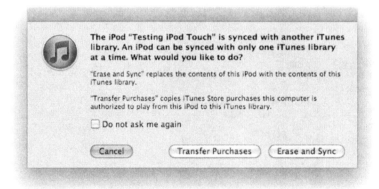

Figure 2–11. *Erasing a device from iTunes*

Upgrading the Software

New versions of software come out all the time. There will probably be a new version of iOS between the time I type these words and you open the book (although, hopefully, the screenshots and walk-throughs still look the same). Chapter 3 covers basic use of the devices and upgrading applications through the App Store. In this section, you are going to look at upgrading the actual operating system.

To upgrade Apple's iOS operating system, you need to plug the device into iTunes. Then click the device name in the Devices list and click the Update button, as seen in Figure 2–12.

Figure 2–12. *Upgrading software from iTunes*

You are then notified that the operating system will be updated, with an indication as to the type of device and the version being updated (Figure 2–13). If you indeed want to update the device, click the Update button.

Figure 2–13. *Accepting the update*

The Important Information screen will then show you an installer for the software being placed onto the device. Click the Next button at this point (Figure 2–14).

Figure 2–14. *The Important Information screen*

At the Software License Agreement screen of the installer, you will need to agree to the license agreement, as shown in Figure 2–15. Provided that you agree with the agreement, click the Agree button, and the device will then be updated.

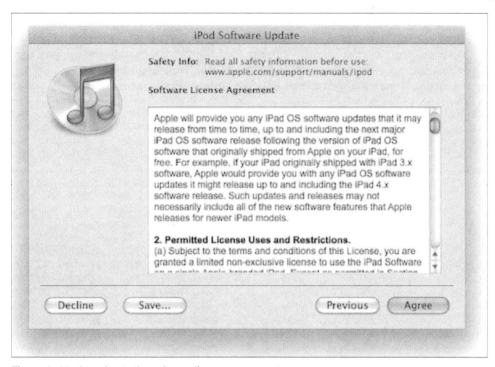

Figure 2–15. *Agreeing to the software license agreement*

The updates will download and then install on the device. If you do not see an update that you know you should see in iTunes, you can run a standard software update, and the update will likely be an option to install.

> **NOTE:** If you will not be distributing iTunes to your users, you might need to have each user come in to your service desk for software updates.

Summary

iTunes is not an absolute requirement for a large deployment of iPads, iPhones, or iPod Touches. But as you have seen throughout this chapter, a lot of issues will come up if users do not have access to iTunes. In addition, the service desk at your organization will very likely have to complete tasks on behalf of users without iTunes. Many third-party software packages will mitigate the need for iTunes, but few will completely remove the need.

In this chapter, we picked up after the planning that was done in Chapter 1. At the beginning of this chapter, you looked at the first tasks involved in unboxing, activating, and registering systems. You also looked at other tasks that are often related to placing systems that were outside your jurisdiction back into a known state, thus remediating your existing deployment or providing a mechanism to reassign devices to new users.

At this point, you have a plan and you have devices that are ready to be used. Now it's time to fine-tune your plan and pick exactly which settings and applications you want to deploy. In Chapter 3, you will get started with the basic functionality, navigation, and use of the iOS-based devices so you can find the settings that work best for your organization and begin generating support documentation and processes.

Applying Basic Configurations to Mobile Devices

Before you can start to mass-deploy a device and manage it with policies, you need to understand how various settings will impact the device and how to set those same settings manually. Several policies can be manually configured for the iPad, iPhone, and iPod Touch that affect the security of the devices and the experience that end users will have with them. These devices also have basic configuration choices, which are not policy based, that you can set to make them easier to work with based on the logic of your organization.

This chapter is about manually configuring basic settings for a mobile device. You will learn about the basic use of iPhone, iPod Touch, and iPad; configuring wireless network connections; configuring basic network settings such as proxies; securing devices with basic settings; and deploying and manually setting up non-Exchange-based e-mail accounts. This chapter does not cover configuring devices for Microsoft Exchange, virtual private networks (VPNs), or mass deployment (these features are covered in Chapters 4, 6, and 7, respectively).

This chapter is meant to be a primer on basic administrative tasks for iOS-based devices. Because many pilot programs at enterprises require only a small deployment of devices, mass deployment often does not make sense given the added costs of having to build out infrastructure for deployment. This chapter covers many of the tasks that most administrators will need to do when dealing with that first batch of devices on their networks.

Self-service will not eliminate support requests. However, it will enable you to give end users an outline for supporting themselves in your environment. If iOS-based devices are supported in your environment, you can give end users the ability to deploy their own devices and to call the service desk at your organization only if they need help. This gives users fast access to support (which they provide themselves) and reduces call volume, freeing your staff to more quickly respond to other requests.

Getting Familiar with iOS 4

One of the most important aspects of any device is navigating around the darn thing. So let's go ahead and get acclimated with the *home screen*, which is the initial screen that you see when you are using an iOS-based device. Figure 3–1 shows the default home screen on an iPad, along with some key items to know.

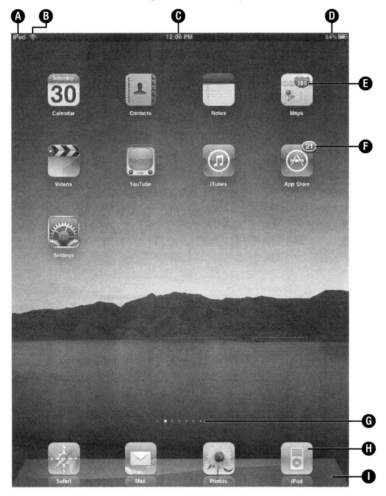

Figure 3–1. *The iPad home screen*

> **NOTE:** The iPod Touch and iPhone home screens are identical to the iPad's, except for their smaller size.

The areas of interest that you will see on the screen include the following:

(A) *Device indicator*: Shows the type of device that you are using.

(B) *Wi-Fi indicator*: Shows the strength of your Wi-Fi connection to the wireless network that you have joined.

(C) *Time indicator*: Shows the current time on the device.

(D) *Battery indicator*: Shows the remaining charge on the battery (the percentage can be removed in preferences).

(E) *Application badges*: Indicate applications that can be opened on the device. A badge can also be created by users for a web site. Finally, applications can be nested within folders that appear as application badges with multiple applications inside them.

(F) *Application alert*: Indicates that an application has an alert. For example, the App Store application will show the number of applications that need an update, the Mail application can show the number of unread e-mail messages, and the Calendar application will show the number of new schedule requests.

(G) *Page selector*: The iPad can have multiple pages of applications. This selector enables you to switch (or *swipe*) between them.

(H) *Dock applications*: Applications that are located in your dock and that are static across page swipes.

(I) *The dock*: A bar with four static applications that are consistent through the various screens of applications.

These devices have several other interesting options, but these are the ones that you will most likely need to know to access the features discussed throughout this chapter.

Setting Wireless Network Connections

Because storage on an iPhone, iPod Touch, and iPad is somewhat limited, one of the most important features of the device is its capability to go online (whether you are accessing the Internet or an intranet). All iOS-based devices support connecting to standards-compliant wireless access points that support Wired Equivalent Privacy (WEP), Wi-Fi Protected Access (WPA), WPA2, WPA Enterprise, or WPA2 Enterprise. The access that the device has to these wireless access points is similar to that of many other platforms. However, because some iOS-based devices can stream data over those connections (for example, with FaceTime), the devices are less apt to switch between wireless access points, which has led to some environments not allowing them. Still, the strain created on a network backbone that is caused by roaming between access points pales in comparison to the strain on networks everywhere as people are increasingly interacting on a daily basis with content that is online (most notable is streaming radio and video).

Configuring Wireless Network Settings

To configure wireless network settings to access a wireless network, start by opening the Settings application, found on the device's home screen. (The Settings application can be moved, so if it is not on your initial screen, scroll until you find it.) Next, click Wi-Fi, bringing up a screen similar to that in Figure 3–2 when using the iPad.

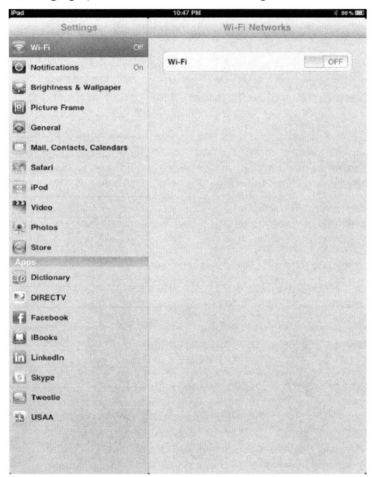

Figure 3–2. *Enabling Wi-Fi*

If Wi-Fi is set to the Off position (and therefore grayed out), slide it to the On position to the right, as shown in Figure 3–3.

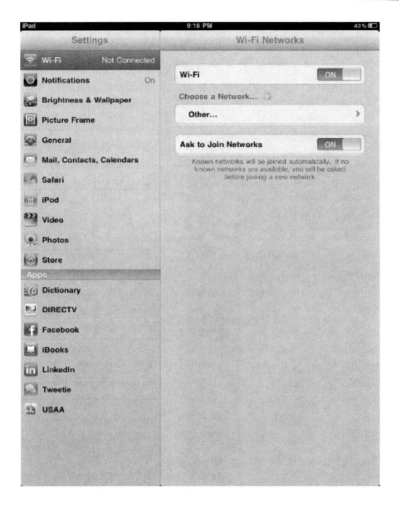

Figure 3–3. *Wi-Fi options*

NOTE: The iPod Touch and iPhone have a similar Settings screen, although the Wi-Fi option is listed in a single column and when tapped brings up a settings view rather than continuing to show all of the applications along the left sidebar, or column.

Joining a Wireless Network

After Wi-Fi is enabled, you will want to join a particular network from a presented list of discovered wireless network names. Select the appropriate network and then enter the required information to connect to it (typically a password for WEP, or a username and password combination for WPA Enterprise). Alternatively, if you want to connect to a hidden network (one with suppression of the service set identifier, or SSID, enabled), tap

Other and then specify the SSID, security type, and credentials. As you can see in Figure 3–3, the network connection appears similar to how you would connect to the same type of network from within Mac OS X or another desktop operating system.

Next, enter the wireless network name and then the type of security that is guarding the environment. According to the type of security (WEP vs. WPA or WPA2 Enterprise), you will be asked for a password or for a username and password, as shown in Figure 3–4.

Figure 3–4. *Configuring wireless access*

After you have joined a wireless network, you should test the network connection. This is easily done by opening mobile Safari, the native web browser that comes with all iOS-based devices, and verifying that a web site can load. We cover mobile Safari in the next section of this chapter.

Leveraging the Mobile Web Browser

iOS-based devices come with the mobile Safari web browser, which is based on the increasingly popular open source WebKit engine and is a cousin to the Safari application that runs on Mac OS X. Most web sites that function properly in Safari for Mac OS X will also function appropriately in the mobile edition of the browser, provided they do not leverage plug-ins that the browser supports, such as Flash. However, a few key technologies have not been implemented at the time of this writing. For example, Security Assertion Markup Language (SAML), the single sign-on framework used by many large Microsoft SharePoint Server installations, is not supported on the iPhone or iPod Touch.

I recommend that if you are going to be using web applications such as software as a service (SaaS) providers or internal portals, you thoroughly test each business function (and field of each screen) to determine what may or may not need some fine-tuning to work seamlessly for the iPhone and iPod Touch. For that matter, I recommend the same thing for all of your supported mobile platforms where possible, because back-end code can be more easily repurposed for other devices by changing the size of the web page to that of each platform.

Configuring the Browser (Mobile Safari)

Whatever the strategy for leveraging the web browser, Safari is there by default, and users are likely to use it unless you restrict access to the application. If users are going to use the browser, you have some control over what the browser can do. In order to configure the settings for the browser, tap the Settings application and then click Safari in the Settings column, bringing up the screen shown in Figure 3–5.

Figure 3–5. *Safari options*

Here you have the ability to configure various settings, including the following:

Search Engine: Enables you to indicate whether you would prefer to use Google or Yahoo! for the search engine. When searching, use the Search field in the upper-right corner of Safari.

AutoFill: Brings up the AutoFill view, which enables users to set the following:

- *Use Contact Info*: Fills fields in a site with information obtained from the My Info field.

- *My Info*: Prompts to select a contact, which is used to AutoFill fields in sites (for example, physical address, e-mail address, and so forth).

- *Names and Passwords*: When set to On, this option enables the device to cache usernames and passwords to sites.

- *Clear All*: Clears the cache of AutoFill information.

Always Show Bookmarks Bar: When set to On, shows a bar with a listing of bookmarked sites.

Fraud Warning: When set to On, prompts users with a warning when they are visiting a site that is suspected of being a phishing site or otherwise harmful.

JavaScript: When set to the default position On, enables all JavaScript code run from web sites visited by the device.

Block Pop-Ups: When set to On, this option disables the capability of a site to bring up a new page.

Accept Cookies: Enables you to block all cookies, to allow all cookies, or to allow cookies only from sites that are visited (and therefore not cache cookies from other domains).

Clear History: When tapped, clears the history of visited sites from Safari (prompts to verify choice).

Clear Cookies: When tapped, removes cached cookies from Safari (prompts to verify choice).

Clear Cache: When tapped, clears cached images and content from Safari (prompts to verify choice).

Developer: Allows you to enable the Debug Console, which is useful for obtaining more-verbose error messages when fine-tuning web sites to run on iOS.

Navigating Through the Browser Environment

After configuring Safari, you can access it by using the Safari icon located in the dock on the home screen. From here, you are in a browser environment similar to that of most popular browsers. However, the environment is somewhat limited given the nature of the device. Safari in iOS is meant to be a simple browser, meaning that you cannot open standard URIs (file paths), export or import items (such as bookmarks), or print a web page. Instead, the simple user experience is meant to be a pleasure to browse with, conserve screen real estate, and still provide many of the features that a browser on a desktop computer would. In Figure 3–6, you can see what Safari looks like and the basic functionality available.

> **NOTE:** Icons can be moved and altered, so if one is not where you think it should be, make sure to scroll through the screens until you find it!

Figure 3–6. *Browsing the Web by using Safari*

From the home page, you can use the Search field to search for content on the Web or click in the address bar, as seen in Figure 3–7, to bring up a page manually.

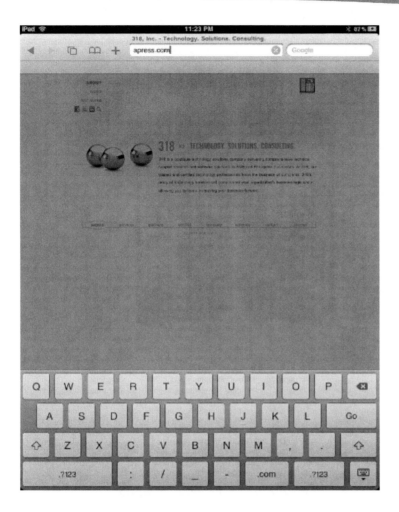

Figure 3–7. *Manually entering a URL in Safari*

You can then bookmark sites that users in your organization will likely need access to so they can access those sites most easily. Earlier, we noted that you cannot import or export bookmarks. However, you can bookmark sites within the device. Those bookmarks will be backed up when you back up the device, but they cannot be exported from the backup (nor the device) or interacted with from a desktop machine. To bookmark a site, browse to a site and then click the plus sign (+). On the iPad, you will see a menu asking whether you would like to Add Bookmark (which will show under the address bar if enabled earlier in this section), Add to Home Screen (which will create a bookmark to the site on the main screen of the iPad, on the last page), or Mail Link to This Page (Figure 3–8). Click the Add Bookmark option and you will then see the site bookmarked in Safari (and from that point on, you can autocomplete the site's address by using the address bar whether the site is resident in the cache or not).

Figure 3–8. *Bookmarking a site in Safari*

Although Safari has other options, the ones defined in this chapter should provide a support staff with a solid foundation to be able to troubleshoot, manage, and maintain the browser aspect of an iOS-based device. In Chapter 7, you will take a more in-depth look at developing a site specifically for Safari, and in Chapters 8 and 9, you will learn how to set the configuration options referenced in this chapter en masse.

Installing SSL Certificates

A Secure Sockets Layer (SSL) certificate is used to sign various forms of digital communication. When you visit a web site and the URL changes from http to https, you are switching to a secure mode, whereby the communications are signed with a certificate. Each certificate is issued from a *certificate authority*, or CA. The CA follows certain rules to verify that the vendor is indeed legitimate before giving that vendor a certificate for the server in question.

There are a several ways to obtain a certificate. Many organizations use self-signed certificates. A *self-signed certificate* is one that is signed from the server that it is hosted on, rather than a third party. Many organizations also use a *wildcard certificate*, which enables them to use the certificate on more than one server.

These certificates can be installed on iOS-based devices through various means. The easiest way to install a new certificate on an iPhone or iPod Touch is by providing the certificate via a web site, or by e-mailing the certificate to the user. In both scenarios, the user needs to either visit the web site, or tap the certificate attached in an e-mail. After you have reached this point, you will be presented with the Install Profile interface. In Figure 3–9, I accessed our organization's root CA certificate by opening the example URL http://myco.com/myco_ca.cer in Safari, which installs our LBC Certificate Authority root certificate.

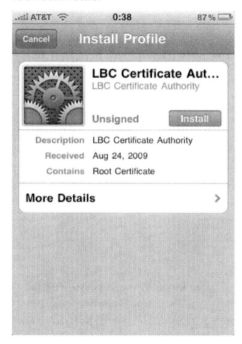

Figure 3–9. *The Install Profile screen*

At this point, you can verify that it is the appropriate certificate, and then tap the Install button to install it. If you are using an internally signed CA (unless your organization happens to be a CA), you will be presented with an error, as seen in Figure 3–10.

Figure 3–10. *Unverified root certificate*

Click Install Now to add the certificate to the device's local trust. You will be prompted to enter your device password, if one has been configured. The certificate will then be added, and from now on accessing SSL services signed by your CA will function without warning.

To modify certificates that have been installed, and remove them from the trust, you must use the General pane found under the Settings app. In this interface, certificates will be listed under the Profile section, as seen in Figure 3–11.

Figure 3–11. *Installed profiles*

You can click each installed profile to view more information. In this interface, profiles can simply be imported certificates, but they can also be configurations created using the iPhone Configuration Utility, discussed extensively later in this book. Using this interface, you can remove any installed restrictions, provided you can supply the phone's passcode when prompted.

Setting up E-Mail Accounts

The iPhone's built-in mail client, Mail, supports numerous services and protocols. Compatible with the industry-standard Internet Message Access Protocol (IMAP), Post Office Protocol (POP), and Simple Mail Transfer Protocol (SMTP), the device also has support for Microsoft Exchange Server, MobileMe, Gmail, Yahoo! Mail, and AOL. Of these services, push notifications are available for Exchange, Yahoo!, and MobileMe. Configuring the e-mail client is a very straightforward process.

E-mail account creation is handled on the iPhone through the Mail, Contacts, Calendars settings pane. To access this, from the iPhone home screen, click the Settings app. After the Settings app has launched, scroll down to Mail, Contacts, Calendars, found directly below General. Similarly (as shown in Figure 3–12), the iPad can launch the Settings application and then enable you to click the Mail, Contacts, Calendars view to see settings for groupware options.

Figure 3–12. *The Mail, Contacts, Calendars screen*

Next, we're going to add an account by tapping Add Account. At the Add Account screen, you have to select which type of account you will be setting up, as seen in Figure 3–13. Now you are ready to configure the app for your specific account type.

NOTE: You can install only one Exchange and one MobileMe account at any given time.

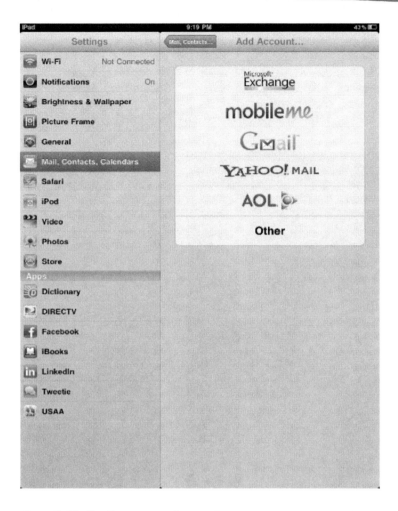

Figure 3–13. *Creating a new mail account*

TIP: If no e-mail account is configured, you can access the Add Account screen by directly opening the Mail app.

Leveraging the Cloud

A popular alternative to maintaining your own infrastructure is to leverage the infrastructure of an organization that can provide services to large quantities of users for less money (per capita) than you can. When doing so, you will need little to no infrastructure and you can easily provision resources based on need. You can also easily install these services, because your users need only usernames and passwords. In fact, provided these services are compatible, you can safely assume that users are already using them via their iOS-based devices and will occasionally call in for support on them.

If you are using a Google Apps, Yahoo!, AOL, or MobileMe (which contains Apple's cloud-based mail solution) account, you can easily add any of those accounts by selecting the type of account in the screen shown in Figure 3–13. After making the selection, you will fill out the appropriate settings (that is, username and password), as shown in Figure 3–14.

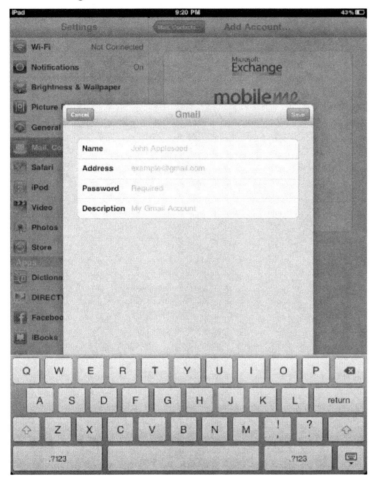

Figure 3–14. *Creating a Gmail account*

Using IMAP, POP, and SMTP

If your environment uses standard POP and IMAP protocols to access mail, and SMTP to send mail, you will tap Other to bring up a screen similar to that in Figure 3–15.

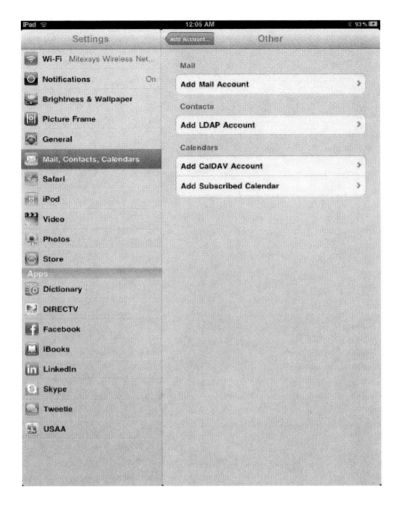

Figure 3–15. *Adding a mail account*

Next, tap the Add Mail Account button. At the New Account screen, type the full name of the user whose e-mail you are configuring in the Name field. This represents the name that will be shown in the From field when sending e-mails. After specifying a full name, type the user's e-mail address in the Address field. Next, type the Password and a short description of the account into the Password and Description fields, respectively, as seen in Figure 3–16. Click Save when you are finished entering the settings into the device.

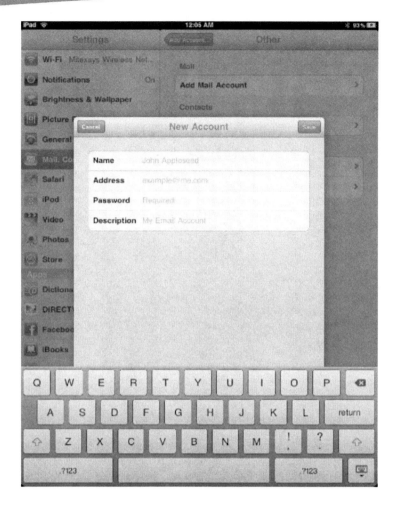

Figure 3–16. *Adding an IMAP or POP account*

At the second New Account screen, select whether the account should be POP or IMAP by using the top bar to select one or the other. Then enter the following settings (Figure 3–17):

■ Provide the server name in the Host Name field.

■ Enter the user ID from your mail host in the User Name field.

■ Type the password used to access your e-mail account in the Password field.

- For Outgoing server, provide the appropriate information, in many cases mirroring the preceding fields. User Name and Password are optional here, given that some mail servers require authentication in order to thwart would-be spammers. For the vast majority of configurations, you will need to supply authentication credentials for your outgoing (SMTP) server as well.

Figure 3–17. *IMAP and POP server information*

When you are satisfied with your settings, tap the Save button in the top-right corner of the screen. The Save button becomes available only after you have entered all of the required fields. The New Account screen should then verify your account information. After you complete the settings, open Mail and test sending and receiving.

Securing the Device

In many environments, locking down an iOS-based device is simply a necessary evil. To lock down an iOS-based device, you have a few options to consider. These include restricting access to applications, setting up a passcode to wake the device from sleep, and configuring the device to automatically lock or go to sleep. These are all done in the Settings application by using the General settings.

Restricting Access to Applications

Restricting access to specific applications limits how applications can behave. In some cases, this could mean disabling access to the applications, such as Safari or the YouTube application that is bundled with the device. In other cases, you might limit the ability to install certain types of applications or watch movies. You can also restrict what access certain applications have to the device. For example, you can set the device to not allow the use of location services from applications (for example, the global positioning system, or GPS). Finally, you can restrict users from being able to install applications or from being able to perform an In-App upgrade (an upgrade from within an installed application).

To restrict access to specific applications, click the Restrictions option on the General screen of the Settings application. Then tap the Enable Restrictions button, as you can see in Figure 3–18.

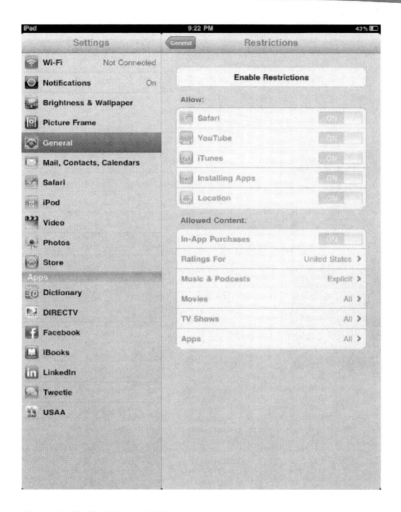

Figure 3–18. *Enabling restrictions*

You will then see a screen overlay the Settings screen that asks you to provide a passcode. A passcode is required to enable restrictions because that passcode will then be used to allow changing the restrictions settings. At the passcode screen (Figure 3–19), you provide a passcode. After you tap the fourth number, you need to provide the passcode again.

Figure 3–19. *Using a passcode for restrictions*

After you tap your fourth number at the verification screen, you will have an unlocked Restrictions view, which you can see in Figure 3–20. By default, all of the options are allowed for end users to access applications and content. Tap the On button for any of the Allow items, and that item will no longer be accessible. These include the following:

Safari: Disables the default web browser on the device.

YouTube: Disables access to the YouTube application.

iTunes: Disables listening to music through the iTunes application.

Installing Apps: Disables the ability to install applications.

Location: Disables access to the GPS on the device for all applications.

You can also configure the type of content that various applications can access. In order to do so, use the following options to indicate which type of content is to be accessible to end users:

In-App Purchases: When set to On, this option enables access to upgrade applications from within applications. If you enable this feature, you will likely want to disable the ability for users without a PIN to install third-party applications with the Apps feature at the bottom of this screen.

Ratings For: Allows access to ratings from various countries.

Music & Podcasts: When set to the Off position, disables access to content that has been marked as Explicit.

Movies: Enables you to specify certain content ratings for movies that are inaccessible on the device. These include G, PG, PG-13, R, and NC-17. For more on movie ratings, see the official site that governs how these are assigned at www.mpaa.org/ratings.

TV Shows: Enables you to specify certain content ratings that are inaccessible on the device. These include TV-Y, TV-Y7, TV-G, TV-PG, TV-14, TV-MA, and Don't Allow TV Shows. For more on ratings, see the the official site that governs how these are assigned at www.fcc.gov/parents/parent_guide.html.

Apps: Enables you to disable all third-party apps or allow all applications that have a minimum rating of 4, 9, 12, or 17. These numbers are derived from the crowd-sourced rating system that Apple employs.

Figure 3–20. *Limiting access on the device*

Authenticating with Passcodes

Although restricting access to content is one way to secure a device, this restriction is mostly used to govern what a user is able to access. However, many organizations are more concerned with protecting content on the device, such as documents, mail, and custom applications. As with a desktop computer, the best way to do this is to require authentication of some sort to unlock the device. iOS-based devices can use a passcode, and if the passcode is entered incorrectly a predetermined number of times, you can reset the device back to factory default settings.

You can trust the remote wipe feature, covered further in Chapter 9 (using MobileMe) and Chapter 4 (using Exchange) to enable you to reset a device in the event that you are aware that the device has fallen out of acceptable use *and* the device has wireless access. However, erasing the device based on invalid passcode attempts is an additional line of defense, given that you cannot guarantee the device will receive the instructions to remotely wipe before someone attempts to launch a brute-force attack on the device by entering every possible combination of numbers. Requiring a passcode enables you to keep a device that has fallen into inappropriate hands safe, even if you have not yet remotely wiped the device (because perhaps you do not yet know it is missing).

To set the passcode, you first configure how quickly a passcode is required from the time the device goes to sleep. Open the Settings application and then tap General. From here, tap Passcode Lock, which brings up the screen shown in Figure 3–21 (or somewhat smaller on an iPhone or iPod Touch, but with the same options). Tapping the Turn Passcode On button prompts you to provide a passcode (unless one has already been assigned to the device).

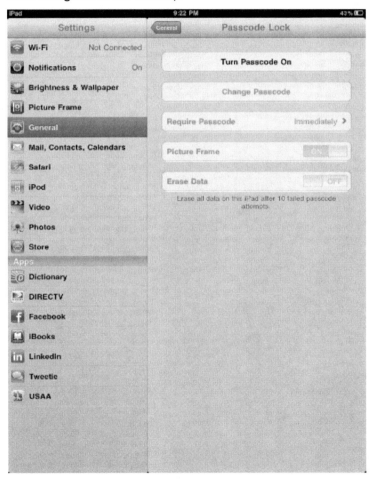

Figure 3–21. *Enabling a passcode to access a device*

You can come back to this screen at any point to change the passcode, which can be done by tapping the Change Passcode button and entering the old and new passcodes.

After you have provided the passcode, tap the Require Passcode button, which brings up a screen that enables you to configure how long a device will sleep before it requires you to enter a passcode to gain access to the device. As you can see in Figure 3–22, the duration can be set to 2, 5, 10, or 15 minutes. Selecting Never effectively disables the feature except when a device is started after being powered off.

Figure 3–22. *Setting time for passcodes*

NOTE: In a recent discussion with an organization that had distributed the iPhone to all employees, an executive was asked whether any confidential data was on the iPhones. The executive said that there was none; but when asked whether confidential information was possibly located in individuals' Exchange mailboxes, he indicated with absolute certainty that confidential data was there. When pressed further, the executive located a list of passwords to key server infrastructure that had been e-mailed to employees. The passcode feature is the bare minimum of security that an enterprise should enforce for devices. Although the current culture in the information technology CIO suite seems to indicate that restrictions are being reduced on devices to help drive innovation, it is arguably still good practice to require passwords. You can also deploy these options en masse, using Microsoft Exchange (Chapter 4) or Profiles (Chapters 8 and 9), enabling you to distribute these devices throughout the enterprise without allowing possibly secure data to be leaked.

After passcodes are set, though, do not forget them, or make certain that your users understand that they should not forget them. Security is not a trivial matter, although in the next section we review some options for obtaining data from a device even without the use of a passcode.

Maintaining Devices

Chapter 11 discusses the infrastructure that you need to build to support these devices. In this section, you're going to look at basic maintenance that most end users perform themselves for iOS-based devices. This is because it seems like no matter what technology you are talking about, certain troubleshooting steps are always appropriate, regardless of the end user's symptom. For example, is the hardware working as intended? Will the iPhone make a phone call? Is the service plan still active for the device?

Performing Basic Startup Maintenance

If a device will not power on, try plugging it into a power source to check the battery. If the device is on and running, but otherwise unresponsive, you can try to force-quit the frontmost application. To accomplish this, press and hold the Lock button until the shutdown slider appears. At this point, press and hold the Home button for a second or two until the frontmost application quits. This is the equivalent of using Control+Opt+Esc in Mac OS X to force-quit an application or Ctrl+Alt+Esc in Windows to bring up the Task Manager.

If that doesn't work, reboot the iPhone or iPod Touch by holding the Sleep button on the top of the device. After a few moments, a red slider appears. Press and slide the slider from left to right to shut down the device, similar to the procedure used to wake an iPhone. Press and hold the Sleep button to power the device back on. You can also reset the device by holding down the Sleep and Home buttons until you see an Apple logo. Finally, you can perform a factory reset on a device from the Settings icon on the home screen: click General ➤ Reset ➤ Reset All Settings (make sure you have a good backup of the device before doing this).

If the device isn't booting at all, you can attempt to boot the device in recovery mode. To do so, first launch iTunes on your admin station. Next, with the device off, press and hold the Home button. With the Home button depressed, plug the device into your admin station via Universal Serial Bus (USB). The iPhone should display that it is in recovery mode, and you can now restore the phone to factory defaults.

Verifying Network Connectivity

When you are troubleshooting network services on the iPhone or iPod Touch, you should always verify network connectivity first. This is critical before you do anything else, because many applications require the ability to open a network connection to an outside host. If you are having trouble accessing specific services but can connect to a network, verify that network connections are available between the device you are connecting to and the device you are connecting from. Outside of checking for network connectivity with Safari, Apple doesn't really provide a good means for this. You can examine network settings found under the Settings application, but those don't give all the data needed to properly confirm external connectivity. Some third-party applications can assist here, providing ping and traceroute capabilities. One such app with great polish is Bjango, though there are a handful of others to choose from.

If you encounter problems deploying profiles via the iPhone Configuration Utility, this can be caused by a few different things. Say, for example, you receive a generic deployment error when attempting to install a profile on a phone. First, verify that the problem is not due simply to a misconfiguration of the device. At times, issues may be device specific. If this is the case, there may be a problem with your device's configuration file, stored in the folder `~/Library/MobileDevices` and named according to the device's identifier. Deleting that file can sometimes resolve your problem. If not, consider deleting the application preferences at `~/Library/Preferences/com.apple.iPhoneConfigurationUtility.plist` (make sure the device is not running).

Obtaining Updates

Software and firmware updates can be deployed to an iPhone or iPod Touch only by using iTunes. To do so, open iTunes, go to the Devices section, and then click the name of the device you are going to update. Click the Check for Update button (as shown in Figure 3–23), following the onscreen instructions to completion. Unfortunately, there are no capabilities for over-the-air updates; it all must be user initiated through iTunes syncing. At the time of this writing, Apple does not provide a solution to mass-deploy or manage updates to your fleet of devices.

Figure 3–23. *iTunes—iPhone sync overview*

Another option for updating the applications on your device is to use the App Store application that comes with the device. The App Store can be used to install new applications and update installed applications. To access the App Store, open the App Store application on a device, which will put you at a screen similar to that in Figure 3–24.

Figure 3–24. *The App Store*

When the App Store is open, you can use the Search field in the upper-right corner of the screen when you are in the Featured, Top Charts, or Categories view of the application (views can be switched by using the black bar along the bottom of the application) to search for applications that you would like to install. After you install an application, you can update it by opening the Updates view of the App Store. Clicking this view brings up a screen similar to that in Figure 3–25. Here you can click the button for each application that indicates the cost (in our example, they are free, so the button is labeled Free). You can also update all of the applications by clicking the Update All button in the upper-right corner of the screen.

Figure 3–25. *Updating applications*

After you have tapped the button to Update All or the button that indicates the cost of an application, you will be taken to a screen that enables you to provide the password for the iTunes account that was previously provided (which can be seen in Figure 3–26). All updates, whether for a free application or one that costs money, will need an iTunes account in order to update them if updating is being done through the App Store.

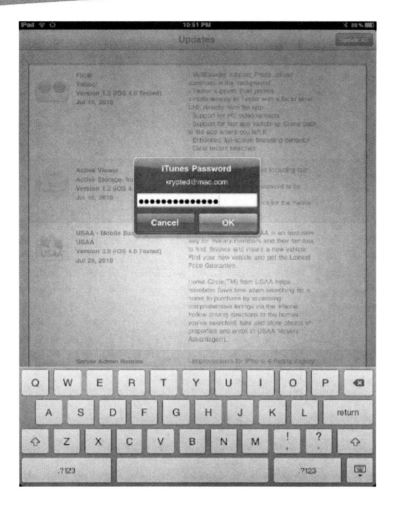

Figure 3–26. *App Store iTunes account*

Organizations should typically strive to keep users running the latest versions of applications on any devices that they have deployed. The iPhone is no different from other devices. Keeping applications up-to-date will mean that they run optimally and that they are as secure as possible. For applications that are distributed internally and so not published to the App Store, keep in mind that a business process needs to be put in place that enables you to distribute these. They can be distributed by sending the compiled project from Xcode (the native development tool for iOS) to the users, who can then install the applications through iTunes.

Leveraging the Logs

The iPhone and iPod Touch store logs that can be useful in troubleshooting the devices. You can access the logs by using the iPhone Configuration Utility. Simply plug the device into the computer you would like to review logs for and then click the device in the Devices list. Next, click the Console tab (as seen in Figure 3–27), and you will see the logs there. You can then use the Case Insensitive Filter field to search for specific entries.

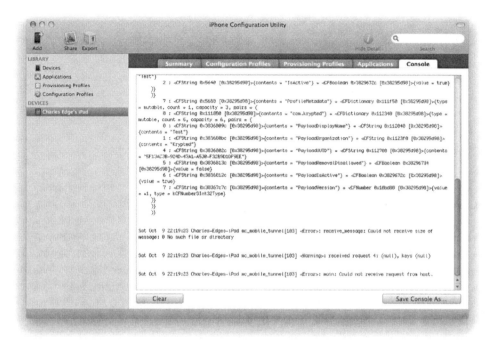

Figure 3–27. *Device console logs*

Performing Backup and Restoration

Backup and restoration of an iPhone is also a function solely fulfilled client-side via USB and iTunes. Unfortunately, there are no centralized management capabilities. A device's configuration, including third-party stored data, is backed up whenever it is plugged into the computer. Device media itself is backed up solely according to the iTunes sync settings. This includes the user's music, movies, and pictures. You can also initiate a backup manually by right-clicking on your iPhone in the iTunes sidebar, listed under Devices. As seen in Figure 3–28, the contextual menu for the device provides several functions, including transferring songs and video that were purchased on the phone to the local computer, backing up, and restoring.

NOTE: Because of the amount of data that can be stored on devices, it can take up to an hour to back them up and restore them.

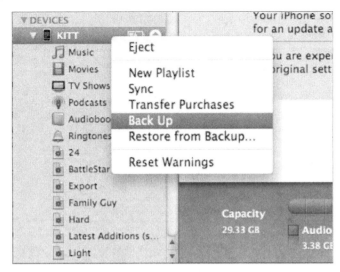

Figure 3–28. *Initiating a device backup in iTunes*

Device backups are stored at ~/Library/Application Support/MobileSync/Backup on Mac OS X machines, and on Windows machines they can be found at C:\ Documents and Settings\username\Application Data\Apple Computer\MobileSync\Backup. Inside this directory, you will see a directory for each device that you have synced with your system, named after the device's identifier, the same identifier utilized by the iPhone Configuration Utility. Each device will have a primary backup folder, as well as incremental backup folders, which are named after the device's identifier and suffixed with a date string. Inside the device's primary folder, you will find mddata, mdinfo, and mdbackup files. Each is a plist file in binary format (see Chapter 7).

Because of the lack of management capabilities and the amount of time required for backups (not to mention that many environments do not use iTunes, thus obviating a backup), ensuring that iPhones are fully backed up largely becomes reliant on users remembering to do so. Therefore, it is recommended to utilize server-side storage whenever possible for data such as documents. For instance, it is highly recommended to utilize IMAP- or ActiveSync-based mail solutions over POP. Shared calendars should be utilized wherever possible, as should contacts. In any case, strong user education is highly encouraged. Users need to be aware of their responsibility to ensure that their iPhones are synced to their computers on a regular basis.

Restoring a device that has previously been synchronized to a Mac OS X computer is a fairly straightforward process, making resetting devices a plausible troubleshooting step. To restore a device, open iTunes and click Device in the Devices section of your list, in the left pane. At the Summary page, you will see a Restore button. Click it and you will then be greeted by a confirmation screen asking whether you really want to do this, because after all, it is going to wipe out anything that was new to the device since the last synchronization. If you are okay with that, click OK, and the restore will begin—and will take as long as the media you have in iTunes will take to synchronize from iTunes to the device.

Bypassing the Passcode

Cellebrite, a tool designed for mobile content transfer and backup, has a solution that can unlock the passcode on an iPhone or iPod (not all models, mind you), but only if you have a computer that has synchronized with it. iTunes generates a security ID for each iPhone or iPod that is synchronized. Cellebrite can use the security ID file from iTunes to gain direct access to the iPhone data and reset the configured passcode.

Cellebrite isn't the only tool, though; there are others as well, many of which will allow you to mount the device with or without actually writing data to it. But what if you don't have the passcode or a machine that the handheld has been synchronized with? Jonathan Zdziarski, in his book *iPhone Forensics* (O'Reilly Media, 2008), provides steps to remove the passcode without a security ID file by doing some fun firmware hacks. Overall, this book is a good read, although it seems that developments with the iPhone are moving so rapidly that many of the steps have changed (or will very shortly).

Prior to the iPhone 3GS, a big component was still missing for the iPhone and iPod Touch—the development of a full disk encryption (FDE) solution for the platform. FDE is a feature that works its magic by encrypting all data written to the device on the fly. Apple's solution with the 3GS, though, is not without its caveats. First and foremost, it has been demonstrated that the encryption key is stored in software on the device, rather than utilizing a hardware-based solution, such as Trusted Platform Module (TPM). This means that though the data itself is encrypted, the key to unlock that encryption can be retrieved from the device. The ramification of this discovery means that the encryption provided by the 3GS is relegated to one primary benefit: fast wipes. Fully wiping an old-generation iPhone or iPod Touch can take several hours, depending on the amount of data stored on the device. That's a lot of time if you are trying to wipe out potentially sensitive data. Because of the iPhone 3GS's full disk encryption, a remote wipe deletes the encryption key in a matter of seconds, rendering all the data on the device irretrievable. This is certainly beneficial, but an iPhone that has had its SIM card removed isn't likely going to receive its remote wipe command. If the attacker has the tool set to extract the key, the whole system can be bypassed.

Summary

You have to understand how to perform basic functions with a device in order to support it. The knowledge of basic functionality is also critical when looking to architect and then manage the devices after they are deployed. In this chapter, you have looked at the basic use of an iOS-based device, picking up where the basic setup instructions were covered in Chapter 2.

You should be taking notes as you encounter settings that your organization will employ. These settings can then be built into profiles, which we cover in Chapter 7. Those profiles can then be mass-deployed to the devices by using the options that we cover in Chapter 8. Understanding which options you will use and how those options will impact the user experience is key to rolling out large quantities of devices.

Now that you can navigate around on the devices and install applications, we are going to move on to one of the most critical aspects of most smart phones in Chapter 4: collaboration.

## Chapter 4

Integrating with Groupware

Everyone loves their iPhone. Most recently, everyone seems to also love their iPad. Many an executive will attend a meeting with an iPad rather than a notebook, something frowned upon with laptops before the advent of the tablet. It seems you cannot have a conversation about how to integrate Apple's mobile devices without discussing how those devices will integrate with the messaging and groupware platform of the organization.

In most of these environments, mail will get in the way of meetings, causing people to pay more attention to the calendar invitations and "emergency" e-mails they receive rather than to the meeting that they are there to attend. Be that as it may, access to various groupware platforms and the advent of the mobile platform in general has changed the game of enterprise communication. As such, iOS-based devices provide access to a plethora of enterprise groupware solutions.

Of these, the ones with the most successful iPhone, iPod Touch, and iPad integration are Microsoft Exchange Server and Google Apps, which uses ActiveSync to provide much of the same functionality that Exchange provides. There is also Mac OS X Server, Kerio Connect, and several other solutions that can be made to resemble the functionality of Exchange. The debate over groupware platforms and whether your data should reside in the cloud or on your own servers is not an argument for this book. Instead, this chapter focuses on the integration that occurs after those decisions have been made, and lays out the technical options so that if the decisions have yet to be made, they can be in as educated a fashion as possible.

Luckily, whether you are using a Windows Exchange server to host your mail, contacts, and calendars, a Kerio server running on Red Hat Enterprise Linux or Google Apps, your client-side configuration will be very much the same. Given that Microsoft Exchange is the leader in the marketplace, I devote most of this chapter to Exchange. That being said, most of the coverage can easily be ported between products because they use mostly the same back-end technologies.

I also use this chapter as a chance to present the topics of using remote wipe and remotely managed policies because those are often deployed from an Exchange server.

Integrating with Microsoft Exchange Servers

Most conversations about groupware integration revolve around Microsoft Exchange Server. Love it or hate it, you need to work with Exchange if your organization leverages the platform for groupware. Your iOS-based devices should be able to plug and play with your Exchange environment. But iOS-based devices can also act as canaries in a coal mine, bringing to light issues that are not otherwise seen when using Microsoft clients to communicate with Exchange. In this section, you will look first at making sure that Exchange is ready to be used and the basic concepts of managing a Microsoft Exchange environment. You will then go on to the topic of using iOS-based devices with Exchange and even using Exchange to manage iOS-based devices.

Ensuring a Proper Exchange Environment

The most important aspect of making sure that your mobile devices of any type will communicate with Microsoft Exchange is to make sure that the ecosystem that is Microsoft Exchange is set up and configured properly. This ecosystem includes IIS, CAS, OWA (or EWS), and a bunch of other acronyms that need to be defined:

Domain Name System (DNS): The DNS server in an Exchange environment is used to locate resources for Microsoft Exchange, Active Directory, and other critical components of the messaging infrastructure. These include records that can be used for finding hosts based on translating names to IP addresses (A records), names based on names (CNAME records), IP addresses to names (PTR records), and for locating resources by using what are known as service records (SRV records).

Active Directory: Active Directory is the directory service that is used in Microsoft environments. Active Directory can store users, passwords, computers, printers, and other data on network objects and make that data available to users and client software in a secure fashion.

Internet Information Services (IIS): The web server built into Windows Server. This is the component of Windows used to publish content for Mac OS X's Mail app and the Mail application for the iPhone, iPad, and iPod Touch mobile devices. IIS is the web server that provides the foundation for OWA and ActiveSync.

Global Address List (GAL): Contacts that are available to all users in an Exchange environment.

Outlook Web Access (OWA): Clients can communicate with Microsoft Exchange in a variety of ways; most notable is its support for OWA from a web browser or for a number of clients.

Exchange ActiveSync (also known as ActiveSync or EAS): Proprietary protocol that uses Extensible Markup Language (XML) over Hypertext Transfer Protocol (HTTP) to synchronize Exchange data to clients. ActiveSync has been licensed to Apple, Google, and other mobile device manufacturers as well as Kerio, Zimbra, and other software manufacturers.

Client Access Server (CAS): The Exchange role used to provide front-end services (OWA, EWS, and so forth) to clients.

Exchange 2007/2010 consists of various roles, each controlling the functionality that a server is able to offer to clients and to other Exchange servers. Most of the integration that will be done with Exchange will be done through the CAS role. For the most part, the technologies included in the CAS role existed in Exchange 2003 and earlier. The idea of breaking Exchange into predefined roles, and the CAS role specifically, is new in Exchange Server 2007/2010. One component of Exchange 2007/2010 that does not exist in previous versions is the Exchange Web Services (EWS) API, which opens up numerous options for developers.

Using Exchange Server Remote Connectivity Analyzer

Making sure that the environment is configured correctly is critical to using ActiveSync to communicate between a mobile device and Exchange Server. Because of how critical this relationship is, Microsoft has developed a tool called the Exchange Remote Connectivity Analyzer that is used specifically to check that the Exchange environment is correctly configured. Given that the devices that synchronize with the server are typically outside of the office, this tool is hosted by Microsoft at www.testexchangeconnectivity.com.

When you visit the site, you will see that you have a few options to choose from (Figure 4–1). You will want to choose the Microsoft Exchange ActiveSync Connectivity Tests option because we need to validate ActiveSync functionality for the iPhone (as well as Google Android and Windows Mobile, for that matter). After you have done so, click the Next button.

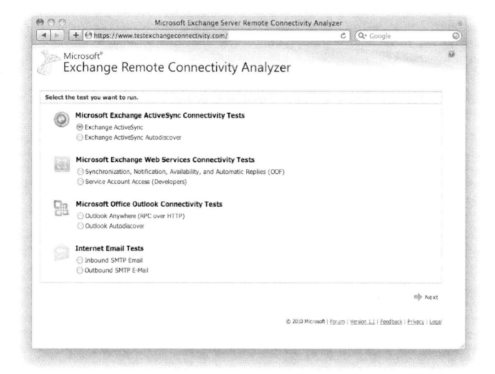

Figure 4–1. *Accessing the Exchange Remote Connectivity Analyzer*

You will then be prompted to provide the following information in order for the tests to run (Figure 4–2). Unless otherwise specified, the following fields are required:

E-Mail Address: The e-mail address to use to run the tests.

Manually Specify Server Settings: Optional setting that enables you to specify which server to use in situations where AutoDiscover is failing (similar to being able to provide your server name if it is not automatically discerned during the account configuration process).

Domain/Username: The username (including the prefixed domain name of your environment) for the user logging in.

Password: The user in the Domain/Username field's password.

Confirm Password: A second password to match the password field.

Synchronize All Items in the Inbox Folder: Optional field that takes a long time to run but checks that all of the data in a user's inbox is able to synchronize.

Ignore Trust for SSL: Because the protocol analyzer is not equipped with an SSL certificate, this option can be used to bypass SSL needs.

I Understand: Legalese from Microsoft.

Verification: CAPTCHA data to keep bots from abusing the site.

Figure 4–2. *Using a valid account with the analyzer*

NOTE: If you wish, you can create a temporary account to use with the analyzer, thus not providing Microsoft a password to log into your environment.

After you have filled in the required fields (e-mail address, username, password, disclaimer, and CAPTCHA), you can click the Run Test button at the bottom of the screen.

As you can see in Figure 4–3, the test failed because AutoDiscover is not configured for the domain in question. AutoDiscover enables the device to enumerate the paths and names for the various aspects of the server environment. Typically, this failure will be caused by a DNS issue (the required names are not associated to the domain), or the failure could be caused by the inaccessibility of specific paths that are required for OWA to function correctly.

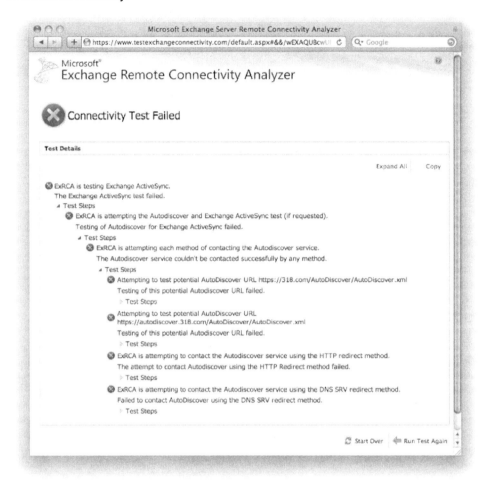

Figure 4–3. *A failed test with the analyzer*

Based on the output of the analyzer, you will be able to at a minimum verify that the environment is ready to function for any Exchange-compatible client and in most cases narrow down the potential cause of any problems.

NOTE: It may seem awkward (from a security perspective) to give your password to a web site. The domain can be validated as being owned by Microsoft by using a standard WHOIS search, but you should still use a temporary account that can be deleted after the analyzer has completed.

Looking at Paths in Exchange

One of the very first tasks to undertake when integrating Mac OS X into Microsoft Exchange is to log into Outlook Web Access. If you can log into OWA without issue, you should also be able to set up the iOS Exchange client.

In order to authenticate into Web-Based Distributed Authoring and Versioning (WebDAV), you should be able to access the server over HTTP or HTTPS. These are the same general paths (often dubbed virtual paths) that can be checked prior to setting up clients (or more to the point, if you have problems setting up clients). In Exchange 2003, the /exchange path handles mailbox access for both OWA and WebDAV, so it may appear as though they're the same protocol stack (they're not). In Exchange 2003, there are two other paths to consider: the /public path handles requests for public folders; the /exchweb path has resources that are used by OWA and WebDAV (and so still need to be accessible even if you don't typically type them in). You can also follow the paths with usernames in the form of the fully qualified e-mail addresses if you're receiving errors that you can't authenticate when you haven't yet been prompted for a password. The following are paths you may need to use to access OWA (which, in an Exchange 2003 environment, typically means you can also access WebDAV). In this example (these URLs are just examples and will not work if you try to access them), we are accessing an Exchange server at the address exchange.krypted.com:

Mailbox access:

- https://exchange.krypted.com/exchange/username@domain.com
- https://exchange.krypted.com/owa
- https://exchange.krypted.com/exchweb
- https://exchange.krypted.com

Public folder access:

- https://exchange.krypted.com/public
- https://exchange.krypted.com/public/username@domain.com

On more-modern Exchange servers, there can be even more paths, because Exchange 2007 and Exchange 2010 have more web-oriented features. This is not to say that the paths already mentioned have been deprecated; in most cases, they have not. Exchange provides support for these by using legacy virtual directories (made possible by davex.dll) that should be able to handle Exchange WebDAV requests. However, the following are the mailbox-access URLs you may run into:

- https://exchange.krypted.com
- https://exchange.krypted.com/owa
- https://exchange.krypted.com/exchange
- https://exchange.krypted.com/exchweb

Overall, WebDAV integration is a safe bet, but there is a newer and better way: EWS. EWS leverages SOAP (originally known as Simple Object Access Protocol) to exchange data through XML, allowing for more developers to interact with Exchange. EWS is faster and chews through less bandwidth, adding synchronization support for categories and tasks (not otherwise provided by WebDAV). Possible URLs that you will see include the following:

- `https://exchange.krypted.com` (More than likely, an administrator used a virtual directory to help shorten the path.)

- `https://exchange.krypted.com/ews` (Exchange should throw a Directory Listing Denied error.)

- `https://exchange.krypted.com/ews/Exchange.asmx` (The default setting)

- `https://exchange.krypted.com/ews/Serivces.wsdl` (A redirect to a blank page)

After you have confirmed your paths, you can move on to setting up the client application.

> **TIP:** Paths may also be followed by a colon and then the port number that the service is running on if a custom port has been used (`https://exchange.krypted.com:8443/ews`).

Troubleshooting Exchange 2007 and 2010 Virtual Directories

In a number of deployments, the iOS Exchange client simply will not work, even though Outlook Web Access will authenticate users. To resolve this, we often use a series of Windows PowerShell commands. PowerShell is the command-line scripting language used for Windows Server 2008, Exchange Server 2007, and Exchange 2010 environments. To start off, we'll get a list of all the virtual directories by using the `Get-OwaVirtualDirectory` commandlet without any operators (on the server):

`Get-OwaVirtualDirectory`

If you are having an issue with a specific virtual directory, you can delete it by using this command:

`Remove-OwaVirtualDirectory "owa (Default Web Site)"`

The preceding command uses the `owa` virtual directory, but it could have used `Exchange`, `Public`, `Exchweb`, or `Exadmin` as well. To re-create the directory, use the following command (again replacing `owa` in the quoted portion of the command with the specified virtual directory you are re-creating:

`New-OwaVirtualDirectory -OwaVersion "Exchange2007 -Name "owa (Default Web Site)"`

Because a virtual directory is just that, virtual, you will not encounter any problems from deleting it, except that while it is offline, your clients who use it will not be able to connect to the server. Note that when you re-create the virtual directory, you will need to go into IIS and customize the permissions as defined by your organization's security policy before using the virtual directory again. The ability to delete virtual directories—or more important, to create new ones—is a great help when troubleshooting connectivity issues. After you've created a new virtual directory, before you customize permissions, test the iOS client for Microsoft Exchange Server. Then, after you customize the permissions, test the iOS client for Microsoft Exchange Server again. Or you may want to create an entirely new virtual directory without deleting the existing one during testing.

Because Exchange, Public, Exchweb, and Exadmin are not native to Microsoft Exchange 2007/2010, you would actually replace Exchange2007 with Exchange2003or2000 for those directories. So if you wanted to re-create Exadmin, for example, you would use the following command:

```
New-OwaVirtualDirectory -OwaVersion "Exchange2003or2000"-Name "Exadmin (Default Web Site)"
```

Configuring iOS for ActiveSync

The iPhone and iPod Touch natively support exchange via the ActiveSync protocol and are officially supported by the Mail app when hosted by Exchange 2003 SP2 or Exchange 2007/2010. However, the client should work with most third-party ActiveSync implementations, such as Kerio Connect and Google Apps. Configuring ActiveSync access on an iPhone is a very straightforward process. Exchange accounts are configured by adding a new account under the Mail, Contacts, Calendars pane in the Settings app (Figure 4–4).

Figure 4–4. *Mail, Contacts, Calendars settings*

From the Add Account screen (Figure 4–5), the very first item in the list is Microsoft Exchange. Select it to create a new Exchange account.

Figure 4–5. *Adding an account in iPhone*

At the next screen, you will see fields for your user account data, which should match information used for logging in through OWA. Enter the Email address, the Domain, the Username, and the Password, as shown in Figure 4–6. Also provide a short description of the account that is being added.

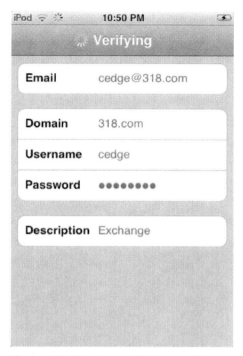

Figure 4–6. *Entering your Exchange settings*

Tap Next after you have entered all of your appropriate settings and you will then see a screen similar to Figure 4–6, while the device is verifying the Exchange account information that was previously provided. It will then often return back to the same screen, but with the addition of a server field (Figure 4–7).

> **NOTE:** This step can be circumvented if all of the appropriate DNS records are present to enumerate the server address.

Figure 4–7. *Adding a server when AutoDiscover fails*

From here the device will try to configure for the environment. If the Exchange server cannot be determined from the provided domain information and DNS, you will be asked to manually specify the DNS name of the Exchange server. Provided that the device can synchronize with the Exchange server, you will see a list of items to potentially synchronize. As you will note in Figure 4–8, these include Mail, Contacts, and Calendars. You can move any of the three to an Off slide position in order to disable synchronization for each specific option. When you're satisfied with the options that will be synchronized, tap the Save button.

Figure 4–8. *Exchange service configuration*

You should now have an Exchange client configured and synchronized on an iOS-based device. Provided that your organization supports Outlook Web Access, configuring synchronization with a Microsoft Exchange environment should occur without much fanfare. Having said this, ActiveSync requires Outlook Web Access to function. If you are in a 2003 environment, this is simple enough, but in 2007/2010 you will need to point your account settings at the server that houses the CAS role for the mailbox in question unless the environment is capable of proxying connections properly.

After your initial synchronization has completed, verify that mail, contacts, and calendars work as they should. If they do, you're ready to start using Exchange accounts with your mobile devices!

> **NOTE:** You can have only one active ActiveSync account configured on an iPhone or iPod Touch at any given time.

Using Exchange to Manage Policies

Microsoft is a master of mobile device management. Owning its own platform provides the company with insight into what most environments want, or need, to have control over at a bare minimum. This includes the features that environments wish to deny access to. This denial is known as a policy. Exchange can manage policies for a number of mobile devices, including those based on iOS.

To assign a policy to a user, when the user is created, click the check box for Exchange ActiveSync Mailbox Policy and then choose the policy that you would like applied to the user, as you can see in Figure 4–9.

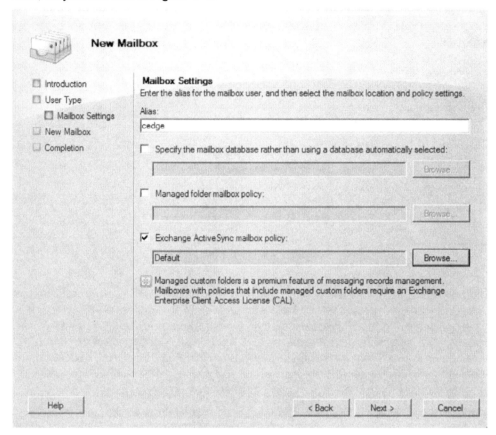

Figure 4–9. *Using a policy with a new Exchange account*

When you have selected the policy, click the Next button to proceed. You can also assign policies to users that are already on the server. To do so, browse to the user in Exchange System Manager and then open the properties pane for that user's account. From the account properties, click the Mailbox Features tab. Then click Exchange ActiveSync in the list of features and click the Properties button. You will then be able to select an ActiveSync policy for the user (Figure 4–10).

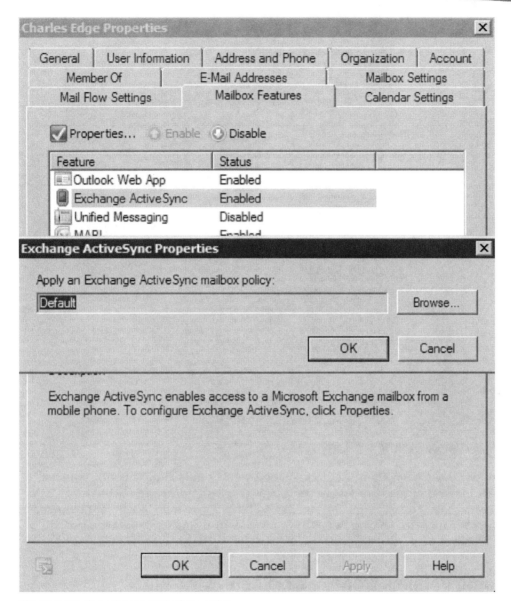

Figure 4–10. *Changing the ActiveSync policy*

You can create a new ActiveSync policy in Exchange System Manager. When you open the tool, click Organization Configuration and then Client Access. This brings up the Exchange ActiveSync Mailbox Policies tab, where you can edit existing policies or create a new policy by clicking New Exchange ActiveSync Mailbox Policy. Several options are available, as shown in Figure 4–11.

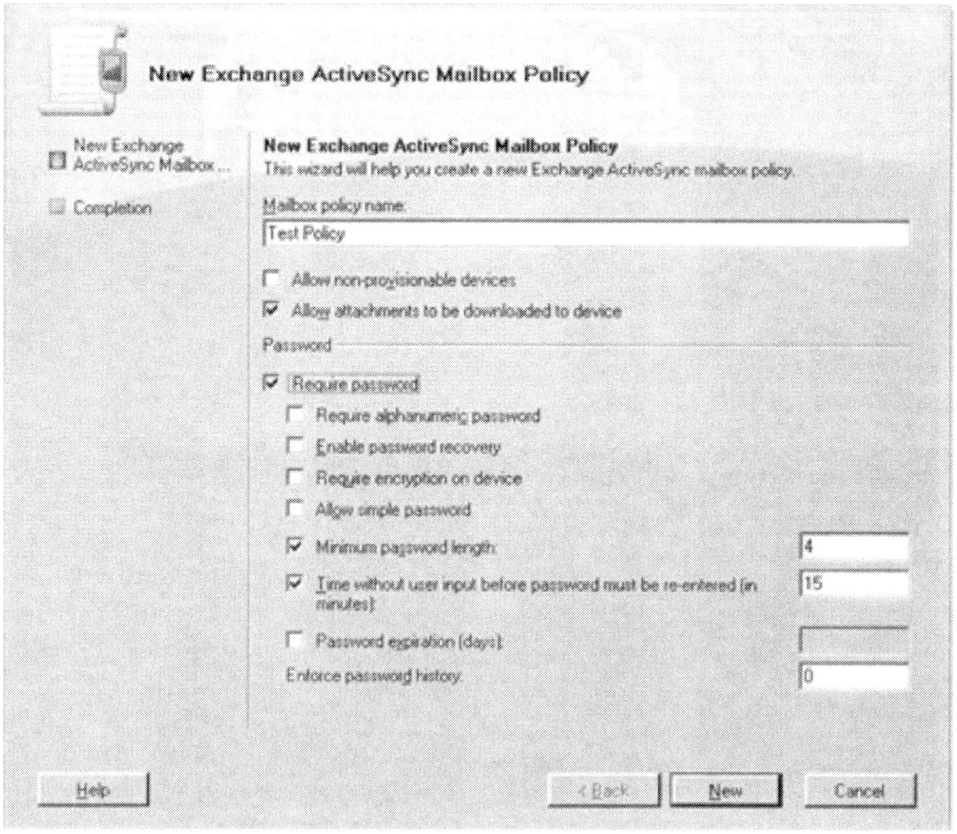

Figure 4–11. *Configuring Exchange mobile device policies*

These policies include whether to include numbers and letters in passwords, whether to allow users to perform password recovery if they lose their passwords, whether to require device-based encryption, and whether to have a minimum length for passwords. For more information on defining ActiveSync policies by using these options, see the TechNet article at http://technet.microsoft.com/en-us/library/bb123484.aspx.

Managing Policies from PowerShell

Some iOS-based devices can have a problem with some Exchange servers because they are not fully manageable through ActiveSync policies. The New-ActiveSyncMailboxPolicy commandlet can be used with the -Name parameter to assign a name to the new ActiveSyncMailboxPolicy, which we'll call iPhone. To allow devices that are not fully manageable to use ActiveSync, an ActiveSyncMailboxPolicy needs to be created where -AllowNonProvisionableDevices is set to $true. For example, if we were to create such a policy and call it iPhone, we would use the following command:

```
New-ActiveSyncMailboxPolicy -Name iPhone -AllowNonProvisionableDevices $true
```

Using Remote Wipe

Remote wipe is a feature enabling you to remotely erase data from your mobile device—you send a message to the device from a server that tells the device to erase itself. A remote wipe is most commonly used when a device has fallen outside the ownership of an organization (for example, by being lost or stolen). Once an iOS-based device is known to Exchange, then Exchange will be able to perform a remote wipe on the device in an ad hoc fashion. However, the device must have a functioning antenna and be powered on (otherwise, it will be unable to get the instructions the server sends it).

You can wipe devices from the Exchange tools on the server and you can allow users to wipe their own devices from within the Outlook Web Access portal. When you are going to wipe a device from within Outlook Web Access, you will first log into the portal to bring up a screen similar to that shown in Figure 4–12.

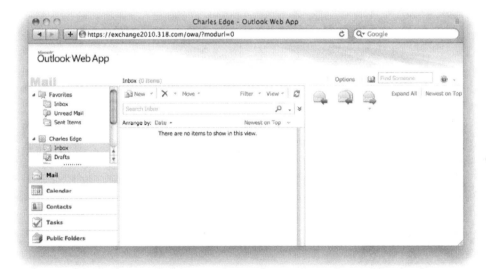

Figure 4–12. *The Outlook web app*

Remote wiping a device after you have authenticated into the web portal for Outlook Web access can then be done by clicking Options and then Mobile Devices, selecting the device, and then clicking Wipe All Data from Device, as shown in Figure 4–13.

Figure 4–13. *Wiping a device*

After you have chosen to wipe the data from the device, you will see a screen similar to that in Figure 4–14, with only an Apple logo and a status bar indicating how far into the remote wipe that the process has gone.

Figure 4–14. *Wiping an iOS-based device*

The Exchange ActiveSync capabilities for mobile device management are fairly substantial, but there are other solutions that you will look at in the next part of this chapter.

Using Alternative Groupware Solutions

Exchange is prevalent in many environments, but it is not the only groupware solution available. In fact, many other solutions come with more-desirable features, such as repositories for non-groupware data or built-in message hygiene. In Appendix B, you will look at building your own groupware solution running on Mac OS X Server. In this section, you will look at leveraging some common public-cloud-based solutions (with a focus on MobileMe).

MobileMe

The MobileMe service is a cloud-based messaging and groupware platform from Apple. By using MobileMe, you can leverage the same contacts, calendars, and mail across a number of computers. MobileMe also comes with storage, which is useful in situations where you cannot e-mail that large attachment because of limitations imposed on internal messaging solutions. MobileMe is often used to synchronize data over the air for personal accounts or extremely small deployment. The enterprise ramification of this is that if you have only a small number of users with iOS-based devices and cannot get Exchange synchronizing properly or find that it does not meet your needs, you have another option in MobileMe.

Setting up a MobileMe account is similar to Exchange. From the New Account screen, the second item in the list (Figure 4–15) is MobileMe.

Figure 4–15. *Adding another account*

After you have provided your username (in the form of your me.com e-mail address) and password, tap the Next button. As you can see in Figure 4–16, there are also Name and Description fields. These do not impact authentication. The Name field is what appears on outgoing mail, and the Description field is used only for a descriptor of the account configured on the mobile device.

Figure 4–16. *Providing MobileMe settings*

You will then see a screen listing the items that will be synchronized from the mobile device to the MobileMe cloud service. Choose the items that you would like to have synchronized (mail, contacts, calendars, and Safari bookmarks can all be seen in Figure 4–17) and then whether you would like the mobile device to register with the MobileMe Find My iPhone service (iPhone may be transposed with iPod Touch or iPad, according to the type of iOS-based device that you are using).

Figure 4–17. *Choosing which services to synchronize*

> **NOTE:** MobileMe does not allow for the use of a custom domain name, but is popular among Apple aficionados and integrates seamlessly with a number of other applications.

Next, click the Save button to commit the new account's changes to your mobile device. If you choose to use the find feature, you will need to tap the Allow button to accept that the device will be tracked by the MobileMe service, as shown in Figure 4–18.

Figure 4–18. *Enabling Find My iPod (or Find My iPad or Find My iPod Touch, according to which device you are using)*

The items that you have chosen to synchronize will then begin to copy to their respective applications. While this process is completing, it is a good time to look and see how the remote wipe (and Find My Device) features of MobileMe work. If you have another iOS-based device, obtain the Find My iPhone app from the App Store. After it is installed, open it and provide the MobileMe username and password (Figure 4–19).

Figure 4–19. *Authenticating to Find My iPhone*

After Find My iPhone authenticates, tap the device name that you would like to manage. Then you will be able to use the Remote Wipe, Remote Lock, or Display Message or Play Sound options on the device (Figure 4–20). These options can help you to locate lost or stolen devices, or if the device is irretrievable, to wipe your organization's data from the device.

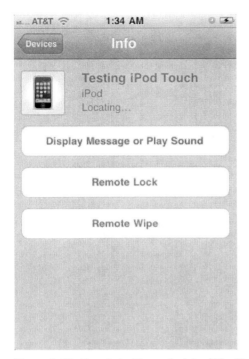

Figure 4–20. *Remote locking and wiping iOS with Find My iPod*

Finally, you can use a web browser to track the location of the device and wipe it. Simply log into the MobileMe portal at me.com and click the icon for the cloud in the upper-left corner of the screen. Then click the green Find My Device icon and click your device. You will see a map indicating the device's location, and when you click it, you will have the option to wipe it, lock the screen until the administrative code is entered, or display a message on the device (Figure 4–21).

Figure 4–21. *Remote locking and wiping iOS with the web by using MobileMe*

Leveraging the Cloud

Leveraging the cloud can mean hosting your Exchange environment. For the purposes of this section, we are going to focus on Gmail. Earlier in the chapter, you looked at using ActiveSync with Microsoft Exchange, but given that Google has licensed use of ActiveSync from Microsoft, you can use ActiveSync rather than a third-party client when you are using Google Apps instead of Gmail.

Configuring Gmail is very similar to configuring the MobileMe service. The reason for this is that the service runs on Google servers and so requires nothing more than a valid username and password for Gmail. To get started with Gmail, go to the Settings app and then tap Mail, Contacts, Calendars. Then tap the Add Account option on the Mail, Contacts, Calendars screen. From the Add Account screen (shown earlier in the chapter in Figure 4.5), tap Gmail and you will then see a Gmail screen, where you can provide a name (the name that will be displayed on messages that you send from the device), address (the e-mail address of the Gmail user, which is typically username@gmail.com), password (the password you would use when accessing Gmail from a web browser), and description (text that you can use as a reminder of what the account is for). These settings can be seen in Figure 4–22.

NOTE: Most enterprises will elect to use Google Apps instead of Gmail. Therefore, ActiveSync will be used rather than Gmail. ActiveSync would mean using your actual e-mail address instead of a Gmail address.

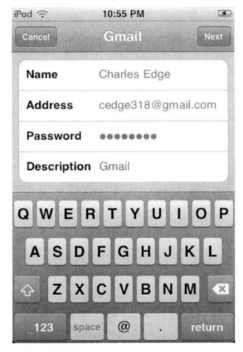

Figure 4–22. *Setting up Gmail*

When you are satisfied with your settings, tap the Next button in the upper-right corner of the screen. Provided that the username (Address) and password are valid for a Gmail account, the next screen will enable you to choose which information you would like to synchronize between Google and Gmail (Figure 4–23). Currently this includes Mail and Calendars. If you are using Google Apps instead of Gmail, you can instead choose to use ActiveSync.

Figure 4–23. *Gmail synchronization*

Tap the Save button with each setting toggled to the On position. Then, after they are configured, Gmail mail and calendar items will automatically appear in your device's Mail and Calendar applications.

After you have configured Gmail, there are a variety of third-party applications that you can use to extend the functionality of Google Apps, Google Docs, and of course Gmail. It is strongly recommended that you next search the App Store for any tools that work with your workflow and test those that are applicable to your specific situation.

Summary

Several vendors offer groupware solutions. The clients for messaging, calendaring, and contacts on iOS-based devices can work with many of them. Most are going to leverage ActiveSync. ActiveSync, from Microsoft, represents one of the more comprehensive solutions on the market today for accessing groupware and managing mobile devices remotely. The fact that a number of competitors license ActiveSync (Google, Apple, Kerio, and more) is a testament to the product's maturity and dominance in the marketplace.

The focus in this chapter may have seemed to have been on Microsoft Exchange Server integration. ActiveSync with Exchange is not the only game in town, but if the service being used (for example, Google Apps) provides an ActiveSync option, the same steps can be used as the ones outlined in this chapter. You have options, and some will work better than Exchange given very specific circumstances. Planning a large-scale deployment and then executing that deployment is often best left to a mature solution rather than attempting to cobble together a solution from disparate parts. Therefore, much of the chapter focused on Exchange integration.

Now that we have covered basic functionality of iOS and integration with enterprise messaging solutions, we'll move on to one of the most important aspects of using mobile devices, working with files, in Chapter 5.

Working with Documents and Files

As the iPad ekes its way into businesses, we're starting to hear a very common question: How do I access my files on the server? Apple does not yet have a standard file-sharing scenario that they expect users to use, but the closest thing it in the minds of Apple tends to be MobileMe, which we will cover later in this chapter. MobileMe is a good way to test moving data around and interacting with files in a lab or in a pilot. However, MobileMe will be cumbersome in an enterprise context given that it is a single-user environment. Therefore, we cover MobileMe with the assumption that most environments will outgrow the options available and move into something else very quickly.

There are two primary ways that you can access files on your Apple mobile device. The first is through a cloud-based solution, such as Box.net, Google Docs, or MobileMe. The second is through a traditional file server or a private portal, such as SharePoint. In this chapter, we will look at both strategies.

We will start off with the easiest way to put data on your iOS-based device: copying files via iTunes. Then, we will build a Mac OS X Server–based file server, just in case you don't have a server that will work with iOS-based devices. Finally, we will look at leveraging a server (whether it's an Mac server, a Windows file server or an existing network appliance) that is standards compliant to copy files to and from your iPhone, iPad, or iPod Touch.

Throughout this chapter, we will look at the third-party applications that make this file-sharing paradigm work (without them there are not many options). We will look at accessing servers using these third-party applications, and we will also look at many of the limitations you will encounter when doing so.

> **NOTE:** The landscape for sharing files to and from iOS-based devices is likely to take quantum leaps over the next few years (if not months). Before embarking on a deployment, make sure to test the applications we discuss here and look on the App Store for new applications that may have come out since the time of this writing, if only to see if there are better applications available than the ones we cover.

When designing your strategy to allow users to access files, consider the transaction to have two parts. The first is to get files accessible to the device, which includes deciding whether or they are cached to the device. The second is to determine what users can do with the files once those files are available to the device: can they edit the files or just view and share them? This is the journey that we take you on in this chapter.

Sharing Files Using iTunes

The Apple-supplied method of putting files on an iOS-based devices is to use iTunes. This isn't exactly the easiest method, and transferring files requires the device to be cradled or plugged into the computer. However, it works well and requires no server infrastructure or third-party services (in Apple environments) to be loaded onto computers.

To share files to your mobile device from iTunes, open iTunes, and click the name of the device while it is cradled. Next, click Apps along the device bar, and scroll to the bottom of the Apps screen. As Figure 5–1 shows, you will then see a list of applications that can be used to copy files to the device.

> **NOTE:** You will need to be running the latest version of iOS for file sharing to work.

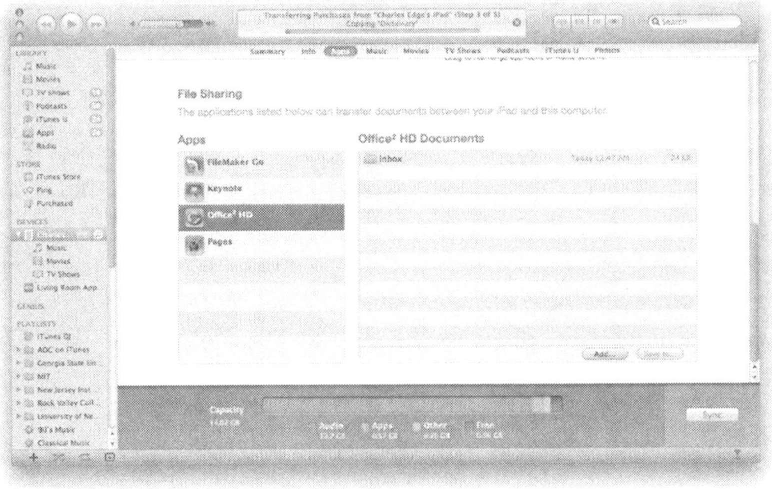

Figure 5–1. *Copying Files Through iTunes*

Click one of the applications, and a list of files available to that application that are currently on the device will appear. Here, you can click the Add button to copy files to the device. Doing so will bring up the Choose a File dialog box in Mac OS X, which can be used to browse to the file or folder and select it. Click the Choose button (see Figure 5–2) to add the file to those that will be synchronized at the next sync (you can click the Sync button in iTunes to synchronize files immediately).

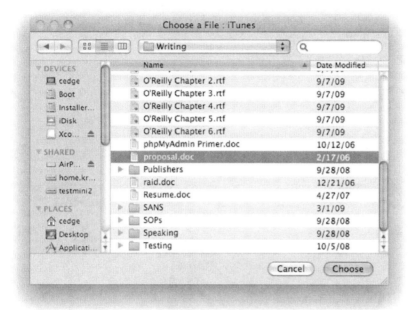

Figure 5–2. *Selecting a File to Copy*

Figure 5–2 shows that files that have been synchronized to the devices will appear among the documents for the specified application. Once a file has been synchronized to the device, you can then edit it from within the application that you specified when adding it to the device. Once you have finished editing the file, you can click it (with the device cradled) and click the Save To button to synchronize the file to the client computer.

Overall, the ability to synchronize files to and from iOS-based devices from iTunes allows you to have files offline and on the go with you; however, most users will want an option that allows for over-the-air access (and in most cases synchronization) of data, which we will spend the rest of this chapter covering.

> **NOTE:** Documents to Go has similar, if not more automated, functionality than iTunes. If cradled synchronization appeals to you, make sure to check it out on the App Store.

Building a File Sharing Environment

Many organizations will have comprehensive and complex environments already in use for file sharing. However, there may be reasons why you cannot use these with iOS-based devices, such as policies on the servers that prohibit connectivity from mobile devices. In some cases, these file sharing environments will also not be compatible with your iOS devices. Therefore, here, we will look at leveraging Mac OS X Server to provide access to files. In the examples provided, we will focus on the Apple Filing Protocol (AFP) service, because it is unique to Mac OS X Server. Suffice it to say that similar steps could be employed for SMB, NFS, and even FTP.

Selecting Your Service

The first step to setting up the NFS, SMB, or AFP services is to show the service in Server Admin. To do so, first open Server Admin from `/Applications/Server`. After authenticating, click the name of the server where you will be installing the service, and open the server's base settings. Here, click the Settings icon in the toolbar to open the service's selection screen, where you can configure which services will run on the server (although simply enabling them in this screen will not start them); see Figure 5–3.

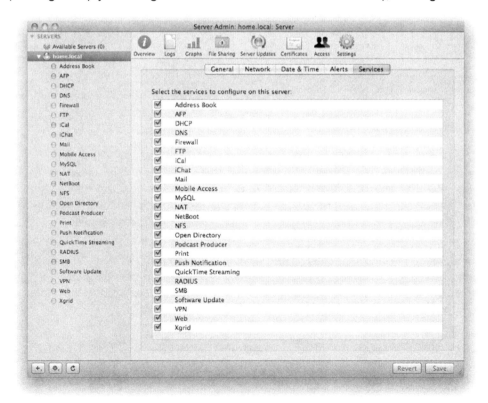

Figure 5–3. *Enabling the services*

Select the box for the appropriate service (AFP, SMB, NFS, or FTP), and click the Save button. You should see the service appear in the SERVERS list when you click the disclosure triangle to show the active services on the server. Here, click the Settings icon in the Server Admin toolbar to open the settings that Apple has provided for that service.

AFP

The AFP is loved and hated by Mac admins. On one level, it has a ton of features and services that you still can't find in something such as SMB (such as the way connections are tickled), but it also has some drawbacks (you can have only a single authenticated session per computer, so you can't connect to the same server as two different users at the same time). For the most part, it is one of the simplest protocols to work with when it comes to configuration, and it will just work as a logical extension of the local filesystem with Mac OS X applications. In Snow Leopard, Apple has revised AFP to version 3.3.

Configuring AFP

Once you have enabled AFP, select the AFP service from Server Admin, and click the Settings icon in the Server Admin toolbar. The first screen you will see on the Settings tab is the area for creating the login greeting. Here, you can put your company-appropriate usage policy, and by selecting "show this message only once per user," you will send it to users only the very first time they connect to this server. It is useful, but in many cases, we have never configured the welcome screen at all and just gone on to the next tab, Access. See Figure 5–4 for the AFP Access screen.

On the Access tab, you have a few more options. For authentication, you can pick Any Method, Standard, or Kerberos. Any Method will allow a user to authenticate with a Kerberos ticket if he or she has it. If the users' client is configured for Kerberos but does not have a Ticket Granting Ticket (TGT), they will be prompted to get one when they connect. If they don't, it will allow them to log in directly, using the less secure Standard method. By selecting Kerberos only, you are ensuring that only users who properly have a more secure Kerberos ticket are able to connect to the server; this will require more administrative oversight, because as discussed earlier, Kerberos is a complicated service, and some users may not understand why they can't log into their primary work server when their password is fine but maybe their clock is out of sync.

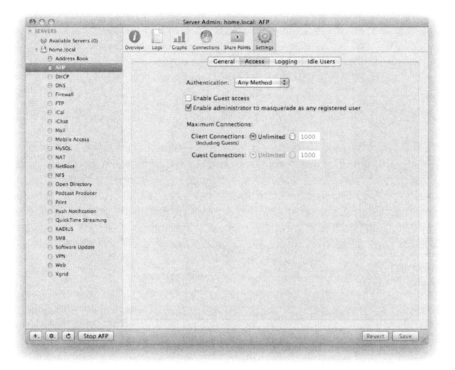

Figure 5–4. *The AFP Access tab*

Defining AFP Authentication

Standard authentication is just that; it uses a method that has no external verification, so it is technically not as secure as Kerberos (Kerberos also provides single sign-on access for workstations that are joined to your directory system). However, it is a fairly secure authentication method, and it's acceptable to configure if you want to have a fallback in cases when Kerberos is not an option (such as you have mobile users who have Kerberos access while in the office but not while remotely connecting over the VPN). Of those options, leaving it set to Any Method is adequate in most circumstances.

Enable Guest Access does exactly that. This does not allow guests to connect to your server specifically, but it does allow for you to enable shares with guest access on them, and then when a user connects to the server, they will be prompted to provide a password or select Guest. When they connect as a guest, it will show them those shares that have been enabled with guest access.

Allowing the administrator to masquerade can be a security risk, because there is no way to tell from the logs whether files were deleted from the server by the user or by someone masquerading as a user. This may not sound like an issue if you are a small business, but if you have requirements for auditing related to industry compliance, you would want to make sure this setting is off. It is useful if you need to troubleshoot users' network access permissions but do not know or want to reset their passwords. It also makes it possible for someone who has acquired the administrator's password to access other users' files, without having to change or alter their passwords. This creates a bigger problem, because the longer compromised administrator credentials go unnoticed, the greater damage can be done. By default the feature is enabled, but it should be disabled and turned on only for short times when trying to troubleshoot a specific issue.

NOTE: To use masquerading, simply log into the server via AFP using the user's name and any valid administrative password, and you will authenticate to the server as that user.

Setting Limits

The connection limits are there to help cap the services. Under Mac OS X 10.6 Server (Snow Leopard Server), the limits have shown that an eight-core Xserve with enough RAM and fast enough storage can handle a few hundred simultaneous users. Leaving the settings as unlimited is adequate, unless you start seeing enough users to push the performance limits of your machine, in which case you may want to consider capping the connections. However, in most cases, end users would rather be able to connect to a slow server than see an error message denying them access outright (and since OS X will cache connections for users whose machines are asleep, you can have more connections than actual active file transfers). If you do start pushing the limits of a single server sharing out your files, you will probably want to consider adding faster external storage such as a Promise RAID (Redundant Array of Inexpensive Disks or sometimes Redundant Array of Independent Disks), adding more RAM, or moving one or two of the shares to another dedicated server to speed up access to each share (which is another reason for directory services—you don't have to re-create user accounts on the second server if it is tied into the directory services).

Moving on to the Logging tab, you will see that it is fairly self-explanatory. The big thing to note is that in the AFP logging world, actions are logged by IP address, not by user. So although it is possible to correlate actions with a specific user (and this is one of the biggest reasons why you should always use individual user logins), you will have to do so by first finding the username of the person to last connect from that IP. A quick way of doing so is using the console application (in /Applications/Utilities), finding the entry you are looking for (such as the name of a file that was deleted), and then filtering the view by that correlated IP address. Figure 5–5 shows the logging configuration pane.

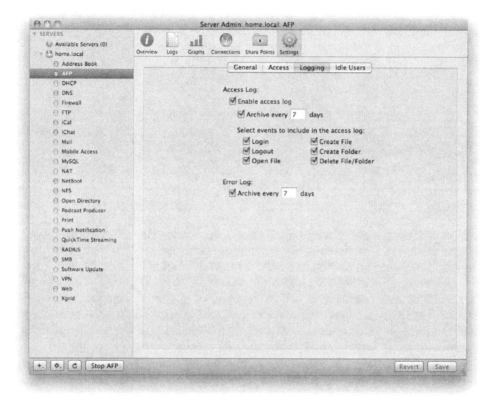

Figure 5–5. *Logging settings*

Managing Idle User Handling

On the Idle Users tab, shown in Figure 5–6, you can allow for them to keep their AFP session key cached, which means they will be able to reconnect automatically if their workstation goes to sleep and reawakens in the set time frame. Another option is to disconnect idle users; if you are in an environment where server performance is critical, you may want to minimize the amount of passive, idling connections. In most environments, it is common practice for users to mount all their network shares first thing in the morning and sometimes never access any files from them. This is, in theory, done because they would only have to log into those shares all at once, but if you are using Kerberos, which gives users a Ticket Granting Ticket when they log into their desktops in the morning, you may be able to get away with aliases and entries in the users' Docks that reference these shares and connect only when the users actually needs to retrieve their files. If that is the workflow you want to enforce, you will want to enable it so that users who have tried to log in during the morning to be disconnected if they truly aren't using the network share for anything. You don't have to worry about them losing open documents, because the server will allow you to toggle those options so the server can check to see whether they left documents open while they went to lunch before unmounting the share. Below the idle options, you can specify what message the user would see if they are automatically disconnected.

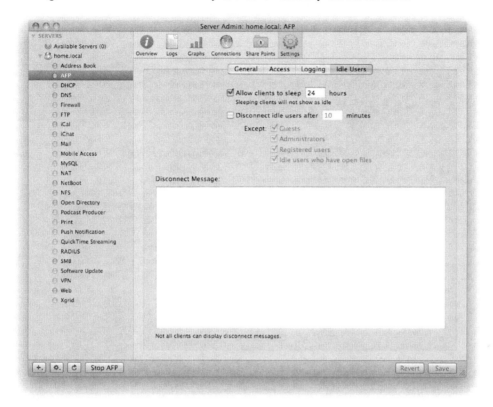

Figure 5–6. *Idle Users settings*

The first thing to ensure when working on a server is that you know where you want your share points to reside. Although OS X Server creates a Shared Items folder at the root of your boot drive, which contains a Public and Groups folder, you always remove the default shares as they may not be pertinent to your environment. Instead, set up a new folder containing all the share points on the disks set aside as dedicated storage space. Remember, you will want to create a folder such as Share Points or similar on the root of any disk, and do not try to share out that disk directly as you can introduce needless security risks doing so.

Setting up Share Points

To enable a folder as a share point, you will need to get to the File Sharing tab in the server settings view by selecting the server in Server Admin (or the Share Points tab if you are already in the AFP, SMB, NFS, or FTP services). By default, it will show you just the configured share points, but you will want to click Volumes and Browse so you can see the entire filesystem available to the server. Figure 5–7 shows the view of the default

Shared Items folder. From this interface, you can also create a new folder (in the upper-right corner of the panel) and enable that folder as a share. Once you have done that, you can click the Save button in the bottom-right corner and toggle back the view to Share Points to see your new share point with the default options enabled.

> **NOTE:** This book does not allow for a thorough explanation of setting up and configuring a Mac OS X Server. For more information on doing so, see *Beginning Mac OS X Snow Leopard Server* by Charles Edge, Ehren Schwiebert, and Chris Barker, also from Apress.

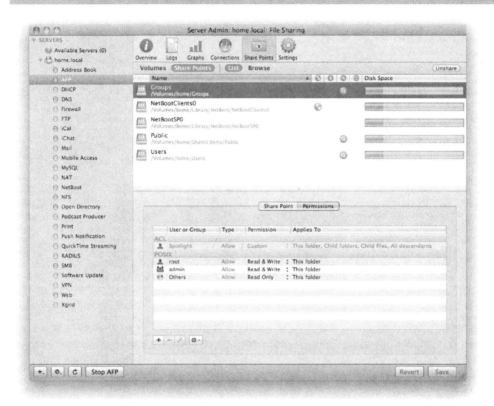

Figure 5–7. *File sharing view*

By default, a new share point is configured to be accessible by AFP and SMB, and you will have to manually enable FTP and NFS settings on your own. There are some extra options, such as to publish the share point in Open Directory (so clients in Open Directory can automatically mount it), enable Spotlight indexing, and allow users to use a specific share point as a Time Machine destination, as shown in Figure 5–8.

Figure 5–8. *Share-point–specific settings*

We could additionally enable SMB, the native file sharing protocol for Microsoft Windows, or NFS, the native file sharing protocol for Linux, on our Mac OS X Server. Given that in most enterprises, some form of a network attached storage (NAS) device will exist that provides these services already, we won't look at configuring them on Mac OS X Server, but their setup is fairly straightforward. You can read more about those other services in *Beginning Mac OS X Snow Leopard Server*.

Accessing Servers With Third-Party Software

Now that you've built out a server, let's take a look at a few ways of accessing that server from an iOS-based device. At the time of this writing, to access a file share, you are going to need some third-party software. Applications primarily allow users to write files into the application's saved space but do not make the files available to other applications, causing a workflow that isn't going to work for all environments. Therefore, it is best to test each application for your environment in order to develop a strategy for accessing files both onsite and remotely.

One aspect of accessing servers that can be difficult for users when they are remote is when the server is automatically discovered. Zero-configuration networking works by discovering servers that are on their network based on traditionally nonroutable protocols, or protocols that (at least by default) cannot function across subnets. One such protocol is Apple's Bonjour. Discoverable servers, or those installed using zero-configuration networking options are rarely enterprise class (although they are frequently used at enterprises for niche uses), and when users switch between onsite and remote statuses, the issues that can be encountered with flaky connections are only compounded. Therefore, we recommend that when you configure the servers in each of these sections that, while they may automatically discover servers, that you add each server manually. This will help keep support calls down to a minimum!

EZSharePro

EZShare Pro (http://antecea.com/products/ezshare-proezshare-pro.html) is another application that can be used to connect to various forms of file servers. EZShare Pro can connect to Amazon S3, SFTP, WebDAV, Google Docs, and TimeCapsule and to Windows computers. This means it supports NFS, SMB, AFP and WebDAV protocols.

> **NOTE:** EZShare Pro also supports accessing servers and computers over RDP (Remote Desktop Protocol), which allows you to control video, keyboard and mouse of Windows systems remotely.

EZShare Pro is used to access a wide variety of protocols, then EZShare may be a better option than using a number of different applications. In this section, we're going to look at accessing the server that we set up previously, which is at 192.168.210.2. We will access the server via AFP and using a cached user name and password.

Once you have downloaded and installed EZShare Pro, open it, and you will be placed in the initial File Servers screen. Click the plus sign in the upper right-hand corner of the screen to add a new server (see Figure 5–9).

Figure 5–9. *The EZShare splash page*

At the "Choose a server type screen," you will see the impressive list of server types supported, as shown in Figure 5–10. Tap Others for an even more comprehensive list of supported options.

Figure 5–10. *Choosing a Connection Type (or Discoverable Server)*

Using the Add Server screen, tap the Select a Protocol field, and choose AFP, as shown in Figure 5–11. Here, you could also use a number of other protocols, including SMB (SMB/CIFS) and NFS.

Figure 5–11. *Selecting a type of server*

At the next Add Server screen, tap the Hostname field, and provide the IP address or DNS name of the server to connect to, as shown in Figure 5–12.

Figure 5–12. *Setting up the server*

Tap the Next button to proceed to the next screen of the Add Server wizard, where you will provide your username and password in the corresponding fields (see Figure 5–13).

Figure 5–13. *Authenticating to the Server*

Tap Next, and at the final screen of the Add Server wizard, provide a name for EZShare Pro to use to associate the server you just set up with. As shown in Figure 5–14, we called ours OS X Test Server, but you can call yours anything you like.

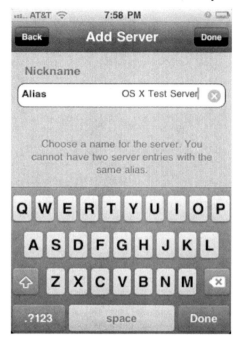

Figure 5–14. *Configuring Server Nicknames*

Tap the Done button when you are satisfied with the alias to give your connection. Then, tap the server at the main screen, and provided it authenticates correctly, you should see a listing of all of your file shares, or share points, as in Figure 5–15.

Figure 5–15. *Browsing shared volumes*

From here, tap a share, and browse to a directory to access specific files. Once you have located the files you want, you can tap on files to access them (see Figure 5–16).

Figure 5–16. *Browsing files*

EZShare Pro is a versatile application, and being able to interact with the clipboard gives it the ability to interact with data in a roundtrip fashion (saving data to and from servers). EZShare Pro also supports the widest range of protocols of any file-sharing application on the App Store, although at the time of this writing, it is built for iPhone only (it works on the iPad, but is formatted for the iPhone screen). You can see the clipboard integration in Figure 5–17.

Figure 5–17. *Creating a New File*

NetPortal and NetPortal Lite

Stratopherix (http://www.stratospherix.com) has released NetPortal and NetPortal Lite, which can mount a standard SMB file share from Windows, Linux, or Mac OS X and then provide access to the resources on the share. NetPortal will allow you to connect to servers and view files as you would from a regular desktop computer, wirelessly or over a network connection.

> **NOTE:** NetPortal will let you view files, but you will not be able to edit them.

As was the case in the "Accessing Servers" section of this chapter, connections to servers should be configured manually. When you first open NetPortal, you will be prompted to set up your first server connection, as shown in Figure 5–18.

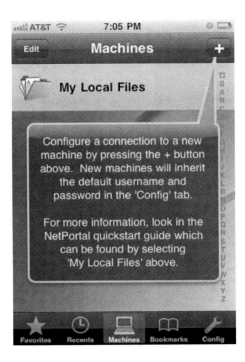

Figure 5–18. *Opening NetPortal for the first time*

Click the plus sign to add your first server. At the New Machine screen, provide a name for the server in the Display Name field and a DNS name or IP address in the Name / IP address field. As shown in Figure 5–19, for this example, we chose to use the IP address of the server; however, it is typically best to use a name where possible. The Auto Connect field can then be used to determine whether NetPortal will automatically open a connection to the server when the application is opened. If you only have one server, it will likely be best for users to enable this setting; however, if you have a number of servers leave it at the default OFF position.

Figure 5–19. *Configuring NetPortal*

Scroll down, and you will be able to provide a username and password in the Login As… section. Here, type the account name that you use to access the server in the Username field and the password in the Password field. Tap the Save button in the upper right-hand corner of the screen when you are ready to save your settings. Then, you will be placed back at the main NetPortal screen, and you can see whether the connection is functioning as intended. If you can connect to the server, you will see a connected message (see Figure 5–20), and if you could not, you will see a connection refused message.

> **TIP:** If you find that you cannot access Windows file shares once installed, look for policy issues on file servers (mostly those that do double duty as domain controllers). If you are remotely accessing files, you might need to either forward ports to the server or first establish a VPN connection into the environment.

Figure 5–20. *Accessing a Server in NetPortal*

If you are connected, you can then tap the Display Name of the server, and you will go to a screen with the Display Name in the title bar of the screen. Here, you will see a listing of each share, or share point, that NetPortal has access to. Browse to a file, and tap it to open it. Once the file is opened, you will be able to copy it to the device (Figure 5–21) so you can view it while offline or e-mail it as an attachment.

Figure 5–21. *Working with documents in NetPortal*

FileBrowser

Another tool from Stratopherix (http://www.stratospherix.com) is FileBrowser. FileBrowser more closely mimics the use of the Finder on Mac OS X or Windows Explorer on Windows by providing access to a share that you can browse and then allowing you to access data from the share using the Open In option that is starting to become prevalent in many applications (see the section on Dropbox later in this chapter for another example of leveraging Open In). FileBrowser is an application with a single purpose: to provide access to shares.

Once you install FileBrowser, configure your server as you would have for NetPortal. Then, browse to a file that you would like to work with. Once you see the file in your file browser, tap the blue circle to the right of the file name, and a contextual menu will appear. As shown in Figure 5–22, there will be options to preview, rename, delete, or cache files within FileBrowser (using "Copy file to local folder") as well as one of the most important options, Open In.

Figure 5–22. *Accessing documents in FileBrowser*

Tap Open In, and you will see a list of applications capable of opening the file. As shown in Figure 5–23, Office2 HD, Pages, and FileBrowser appear in the list. Office2 HD is a third-party application that lets users read and edit Microsoft Office documents. For the example shown here, we're going to choose Office2 HD.

Figure 5–23. *Choosing an application from FileBrowser*

As shown in Figure 5–24, the document will open in another application (note the different style of application). You can then edit the file using the various options built into the application.

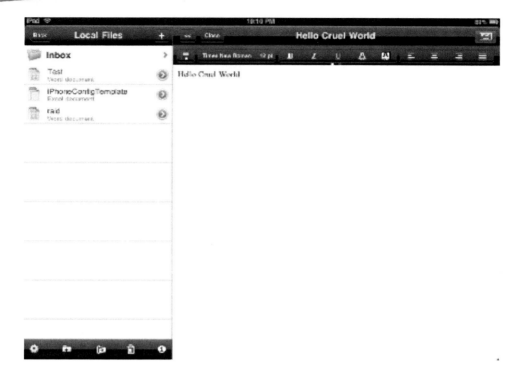

Figure 5-24. *Opening documents in another application*

The FileBrowser and Office2 HD or FileBrowser and Pages combination is, at this time, one of the most seamless interactions between applications for environments that have a desire to leverage existing Windows file servers and allow editing of files stored on those servers.

Using iWork

The easiest and most mature applications available for working with documents right now are from Apple. Apple's Pages, Numbers, and Keynote are used to build documents, spreadsheets, and presentations respectively. These applications are collectively known as iWork on the desktop computer, and files can be traded back and forth between a desktop running Mac OS X and the iPad seamlessly using iDisk or a file server, the use of which is shown earlier in this chapter.

You can also use the iWork.com Public beta version of Apple's cloud service for owners of iWork to trade files between applications; however, this strategy (as with an iDisk) has each user with a silo of documents of his or her own, rather than fostering the collaboration typically found with file servers. Pages (see Figure 5-25), Keynote, and Numbers were among the very first applications that showcased the new features of the iPad and the most recent updates to the iOS overall. Because the tools are developed by Apple themselves, they provide one of the most seamless applications to work with when you need to trade data back and forth between systems (with Google Docs and Dropbox using Office2 HD being equal in terms of workflow) and offer some insight into the strategy and architecture that Apple assumes users will work with moving forward. There are options to use the cloud (iDisk and the iWork.com Public beta) and you can share documents back and forth using iTunes.

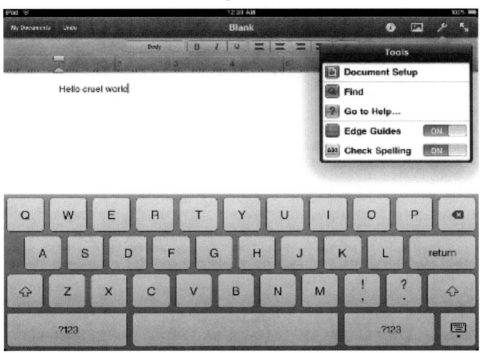

Figure 5–25. *Using Pages*

But something is missing from the predefined Apple scenario, which is the ability to access files and folders on traditional file servers. Because file servers are only part of the equation of working with files, for the remainder of the chapter, we will look at leveraging various cloud-based offerings.

Leveraging Public Clouds

The year leading up to the release of this book has been a period where the term "cloud" was simply overused. Therefore, if there were a better word to use in this section, we would have done so. However, the "cloud" does perfectly define the services we are about to cover. Here, we will look at leveraging public clouds from Apple (MobileMe), Google (Google Docs), Box.net, and Microsoft (SharePoint) to provide access to data over the wireless connection (3G or Wi-Fi) on an iOS-based device. A public cloud is a service, provided to many, typically from a vendor who is selling cloud services. Public cloud vendors typically provide access to data through a web site, such as mobileme.com, drobbox.com, or docs.google.com. Some offer the ability to use your own domain name, and some allow you to brand the portal that users will use to access data, but one of the tenants of a public cloud is that the data stored in that cloud resides offsite from your place of business.

MobileMe

MobileMe is the Apple service that can be used to interact with Apple's cloud-based storage. MobileMe also includes an e-mail address (e.g., krypted@me.com) and can be used to send links that can access files stored on the service. MobileMe is built for individuals. Users can share specific folders to other users, but the granularity of controls is not typically robust enough for large workgroups. However, for a small pilot, MobileMe will often be enough to allow users to trade files from their desktop systems to their mobile devices over the air, perform minimal file sharing between users, and extend some of the remote control over iOS-based devices.

MobileMe can do calendar, contact, and mail synchronization, but in this section, we will be focused solely on Apple's iDisk feature. In MobileMe, your iDisk is the space you can use to store files. These files can be any file type and can be used from a desktop computer, a mobile device, or a standard web browser. Configuring the iDisk is, for most, going to be a two-part process. The first part involves configuring a client computer to access the service. The second part is to configure the mobile device to also access that same repository of files.

NOTE: You can also connect to your iDisk from a web browser.

Configuring the Desktop

To get started with the desktop side of the iDisk configuration, open System Preferences from a Mac OS X computer, and click the MobileMe System Preference pane. Here, you will be prompted for a username and password, as shown in Figure 5–26. Provide a username and password for an active MobileMe account, and click the Sign In button, or click the Learn More button to get a trial account for the service.

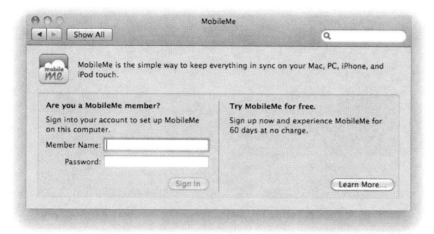

Figure 5–26. *Configuring MobileMe in Mac OS X*

Once authenticated, you will see your account details. Click the iDisk tab to see a screen showing how much space you have used, the path to connect to your iDisk from a web browser, and an option to enable synchronization from the computer to the service, which allows you to interact with your iDisk as though it were a local folder, whether online or offline. Click the Start button to start synchronizing your iDisk. As shown in Figure 5–27, once you have started to synchronize the iDisk, you can choose to update it automatically or manually. There will be times when a file is out of synchronization (e.g., the file was edited in two different locations at the same time or synchronizations did not occur properly). Therefore, you can also predefine how conflict resolution will be handled by enabling the "Always keep the most recent version of the file" option.

> **NOTE:** Be careful if you choose to use "Always keep the most recent version of a file," because it can result in data loss. I personally prefer to resolve my conflicts manually, rather than have the iDisk synchronization agent do so for me.

Figure 5–27. *Synchronizing to iDisk*

Whether or not you have chosen to use iDisk synchronizing, you should see an iDisk icon in the sidebar of your Mac OS X computer at this point. This icon will show you your computers interpretation of what is on the iDisk, as you can see in Figure 5–28.

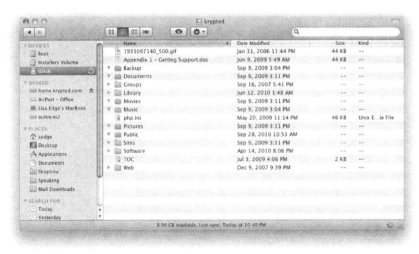

Figure 5–28. *Synchronizing the Desktop to iDisk*

Here, you will also see a synchronize button, just to the left of the iDisk entry in the sidebar. You can use this button and one that corresponds to it in the menu at the upper right-hand corner of Mac OS X to perform an immediate synchronization of data between the local cached version of the iDisk and the one stored on Apple's cloud. Go ahead and upload some files, if only for testing.

Connecting to the iDisk

Now that you have configured the desktop to synchronize your files to your iDisk, it is time to configure the iDisk to be accessible from an iOS-based device. To get started using MobileMe on your iOS-based devices, first search for an application called iDisk on the App Store. Once found, purchase and install it. When you first open the application, you will see a login screen, as shown in Figure 5–29.

Figure 5–29. *Logging into MobileMe*

At the login screen, provide your MobileMe username and password and tap Go when you are finished doing so. You will then be placed into the file browser screen by default (see Figure 5–30). Here, you can browse the folders that you have uploaded to your iDisk and open files that the iDisk application is able to read (i.e., .jpg, .png, .gif, .pdf, .doc, .xls, .ppt, .numbers, and .pages).

At this time, iDisk does not support editing documents, but you can use the Open In option to open your files in Pages or Office2 HD.

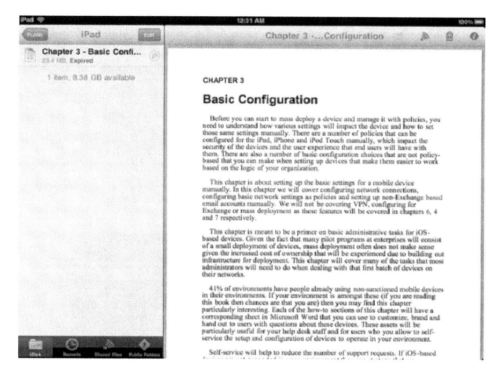

Figure 5–30. *Viewing a File From iDisk*

The file can then be opened from pages and accessed through file sharing when a device is cradled.

> **NOTE:** At this time, there is no way to put the file back on an iDisk over the air.

Google Docs

Google Docs is a popular cloud-based service that can be used to access and edit documents, spreadsheets, and presentations. At the time of this writing, the best option for interacting with Google Docs is to use mobile Safari to do so. This means that there will be no working with files while offline or using an application from the App Store to access files unless they have been cached to the device (e.g., through Office2 HD). There are applications available for doing so, but to say that the current crop of options is underwhelming would be doing the programmers of said applications a favor.

> **NOTE:** Google is one of the most innovative organizations in the IT industry. The Google Docs team is working to maximize what can be done using iOS but did not get there quickly enough for inclusion in this book. For more on what they are up to, see `http://googleblog.blogspot.com/2010/09/three-million-businesses-have-gone.html`.

Box.net

Box.net is similar to Google Apps but runs more fluidly on iOS. This fluidity is caused by the facts that Box.net has an application geared just for the platform and that it can be leveraged in conjunction with other applications to provide the ability to find, view, and edit files.

> **NOTE:** As with previous examples, you will need a Box.net account prior to working through these walkthroughs. You should also download and install the application from the App Store, which can be found by searching for Box.net.

Once you have downloaded and installed the Box.net application (called "box" on the screen of your iOS-based device), you will need to configure it to connect to the Box.net cloud. To do so, open the application. Once opened, you will be prompted to Register or Login. Assuming you already have an account, log in by tapping the Login tab and providing the user ID and password you use to access the Box.net web portal in the corresponding fields (see Figure 5–31).

Figure 5–31. *Initially setting up Box.net*

When you are satisfied with your entry, tap the Submit button. Provided that the credentials work, you will see a file browser that shows all of the directories and files you have access to. On this main screen, you will also see the total number of files you have on the Box.net site, along with the total capacity that those require. As shown in Figure 5–32, you will use the All Files option when you are connected to a network that has access to Box.net.

Figure 5–32. *Browsing Box.net*

If you tap the Manage button in the file browser list, you will notice that files have hollow circles just to the left of them. If you click these circles in Manage mode, you will cache the files to the local device. Once cached, the files will have a checkmark beside them to indicate they are accessible offline (see Figure 5–33). You can then access the files using the Saved tab of the file browser overlay screen.

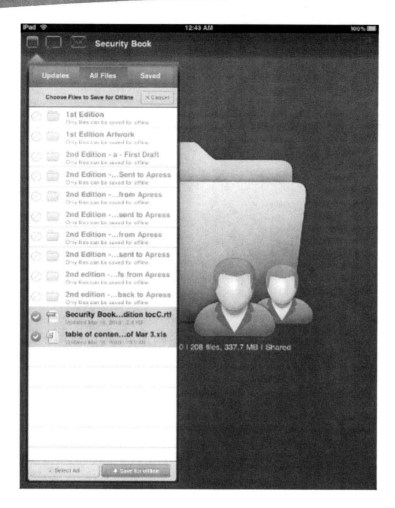

Figure 5–33. *Caching Files with Box.net*

As shown in Figure 5–34, tapping a file will bring the file up in a view mode, provided that the Box.net application can preview the file. Once the file is opened, you can e-mail it, annotate it, and use the Open In feature to open it using a variety of third-party applications.

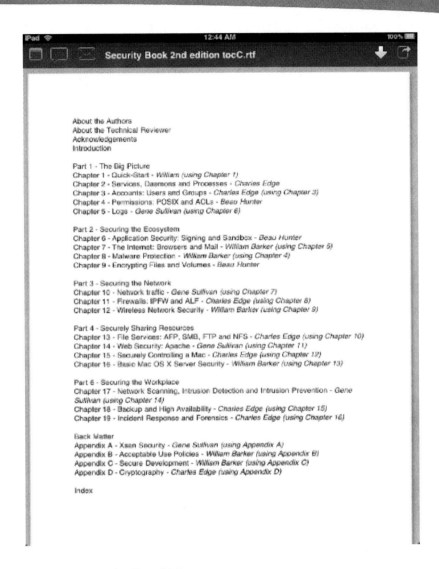

Figure 5–34. *Viewing files with Box.net*

Box.net is one of the easiest cloud-based solutions available to users of iOS-based devices. This is due to the mature application available and the ability to cache files locally for editing.

SharePoint

The most widely integrated private cloud is Microsoft SharePoint. A number of third-party applications can be installed on iOS-based devices that will provide access to a SharePoint portal. These include SharePlus Office Mobile Client, PocketPoint, Attache, and Moshare. Of these, SharePlus Office Mobile Client (see Figure 5–35) is the most full featured currently on the market.

Figure 5–35. *SharePlus Office Mobile Client*

Summary

In Chapter 4, we looked at leveraging a number of different strategies to access mail, contacts, and calendars, collectively known as groupware. Other than accessing the web and groupware options available in an organization, accessing files becomes one of the most critical conundrums facing organizations. Regrettably, it's also one of the least mature for iOS-based devices at this time.

The goal of this chapter was to assist you in formulating a strategy for accessing files. Doing so is one of the most common needs for enterprises. Throughout this chapter, we looked at two predominant aspects of working with files and regrettably pointed out a disconnected workflow to do so: you need to open files in one application and edit the files in the other. The weakness of this workflow becomes the round trip that data often needs to make: saving it back to the server when you are finished editing the files.

In order to achieve our goal, we looked at a number of options involving cloud-based services, traditional file servers, and cradled synchronization. While the options presented in this chapter aren't perfect, they do work. Using the clipboard options introduced in some of the latest versions of iOS will enable you to complete the circuit and send data in a roundtrip to servers once edited, a process that is far more seamless and mature in desktop systems but is made possible using one of a number of strategies discussed in this chapter.

In Chapter 6, we will move on to connecting iOS-based devices to your organization's network, so you can access the files you've made accessible from anywhere in the world (provided there is an available network connection).

Remote Access for iOS

In Chapter 3, you took a look at integrating iOS-based devices with your wireless network and some tasks you might perform when those devices are on your network. In this chapter, you're going to look at strategies for remotely accessing your network and then learn how to accomplish such a lofty goal while maintaining a maximum level of security.

The traditional way to access a corporate network is through a virtual private network (VPN). A VPN enables users to generate a secure tunnel to an organization's network over an insecure network. If your users are in a hotel, chances are that you will want to protect their communications with your office. You will want to give them access to resources that aren't otherwise (publicly) accessible. You may even secure assets with SSL certificates, a VPN, and multifactor authentication (authentication that requires more than one form of identification, such as a randomly generated passcode token, a fingerprint, or even a DNA sample—OK, so not so much on the DNA thing—yet!).

Because most organizations already have an infrastructure in place to provide VPN access for selective (or all) users, this chapter first covers using the default VPN client included with iOS for remotely accessing information. For many, the VPN explanation will suffice, because all you need to remotely provide is access to your environment. The chapter then looks at using the Cisco VPN client, used for connecting to a Cisco-based VPN appliance.

However, VPN doesn't work for every situation. Mac OS X Server, the server product developed by Apple, can act as a centralized server, enabling users to communicate with one another when away the office, even without a VPN connection. This process includes two services: Mobile Access Server and Push Notification, both of which are detailed later in the chapter.

> **NOTE:** Because Microsoft Exchange Server has its own mechanism(s) for providing remote access, please see Chapter 4 for more information on doing so.

Introducing Mac OS X Server Services

The first service of Mac OS X Server is Mobile Access, which enables the server acting as a proxy to be placed into a demilitarized zone in your network environment. A *demilitarized zone* is an area of a network that has a different level of protection than other areas of the network, making it attractive for the placement of services (or devices) that facilitate connectivity over presumably insecure networks. The Mobile Access Server device would then be exposed to potential threats from the outside world while also acting as a single point of contact for clients to access your collaborative servers when they are outside your network environment. The demilitarized zone is then the only point of contact with the outside world, and you can granularly configure controls between the hosts in your demilitarized zone and those on your internal network.

The final remote connectivity feature from Apple is Push Notification. Push Notification is new in the latest version of Mac OS X Server, 10.6, and comes with a lot of design requirements as of this writing, which are covered later in this chapter. Push Notification was specifically designed for iOS, although until the release of iOS 4.0, the service was not built into iOS and therefore was not that useful.

Configuring the VPN Client

Out of the box, the VPN client on iOS-based devices includes support for connecting to a VPN that leverages Internet Protocol Security (IPsec—Cisco-based VPN), Point-to-Point Tunneling Protocol (PPTP), and Layer 2 Tunneling Protocol (L2TP). For now, I will assume that you are already running one of them and just need to set up the iPhone, iPad, or iPod Touch as a client. If you do not have a VPN server, the setup and configuration is described later in this chapter, in the section titled "Providing VPN Services."

The protocol that you use will depend on what is supported by your VPN server. The differences between these protocols are as follows:

PPTP: The most widely supported and easiest to use VPN protocol, developed by Microsoft, has had a number of security flaws over the years.

L2TP: Developed together by Cisco and Microsoft, this protocol is widely supported and further secured by the use of digital certificates.

Cisco VPN Client: This proprietary client is for use with Cisco-based VPNs.

To access the VPN settings on an iOS device, tap Settings from the home screen. Tap General and then Network. You will see Wi-Fi and VPN options. Tap VPN and then tap the Add VPN Configuration button, shown in Figure 6–1. You can then configure your VPN client for one of the protocols.

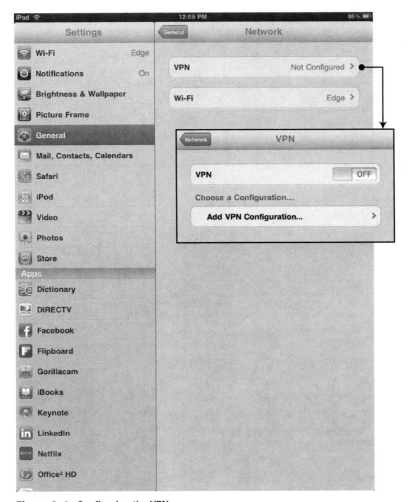

Figure 6–1. *Configuring the VPN*

L2TP

After you have tapped the Add VPN Configuration button, you will see the Add Configuration screen, which shows three tabs: L2TP, PPTP, and IPSec. If you are using any of these protocols, you more than likely already have a VPN server, and the configuration for iOS will closely resemble configuring the VPN settings for any other platform in use in your environment. Here, provide the appropriate information for your organization, which can be obtained from the administrator of the VPN server(s).

Where possible, you should strive to leverage L2TP rather than PPTP, as shown in Figure 6–2. The L2TP protocol is more secure and, although it has one additional configuration step, will leave data encrypted in a far superior manner, given either an RSA SecurID card, a shared secret, or both, to act as an additional layer of encryption.

Figure 6–2. *Configuring iPad for L2TP*

NOTE: VPN connections do not persist across different networks; changes between 3G access and Wi-Fi require the VPN tunnel to be reestablished.

The settings for L2TP include the following:

Description: Makes it easier to see what each VPN connection does if you have multiple instances (for example, multiple physical offices that you connect to).

Server: The IP address or hostname of the L2TP server.

Account: The username of the account that you will be authenticating to the VPN service.

RSA SecurID: When moved to the On position, this option provides integration with RSA tokens.

Password: The password for the account provided previously.

Secret: The shared secret used on the L2TP server (often the same value for all users of the VPN).

Send All Traffic: When moved to the On position, this option routes all traffic, not just the traffic destined for your organization's network through the VPN tunnel.

After you have assigned the appropriate settings, you can move on to setting up a proxy, if you have one.

PPTP

PPTP is a bit less secure than L2TP but still more secure than no VPN at all. In order to configure the PPTP-based VPN client, first obtain the address and which credentials you are supposed to use to access the VPN. Then open the Settings application and tap the General button in the sidebar. Tap in the VPN field to bring up the Add Configuration screen. Then click the PPTP tab, which brings up the screen shown in Figure 6–3.

Figure 6–3. *PPTP from the iPhone*

> **NOTE:** I am showing some options on the iPhone and some on the iPad to showcase how similar they are, not because there is any technical difference between them.

Here you can configure many of the same settings as with L2TP. Match these up with the settings from the VPN server and fill in the following:

Description: Describes the configuration profile being used (useful if you have multiple profiles).

Server: The hostname or IP address of the PPTP-based VPN server.

Account: The username used with the PPTP-based VPN server (often this will be the same as your username for other services hosted in your environment).

RSA SecurID: Enables the RSA SecurID two-factor authentication token. For more on RSA SecurID, see `www.rsa.com/node.aspx?id=1156`.

Password: The password used with the PPTP-based VPN server (often this too will be the same as your username for other services hosted in the environment).

Encryption Level: Enables you to set the encryption level to Auto (which automatically accepts the best possible algorithm offered by the server), Maximum (which requires the maximum level), or None (uses no encryption).In most cases, this option should be set to Auto, enabling the server to negotiate the encryption level as it sees fit.

Send All Traffic: When set to the On position, allows you to configure all traffic to traverse the VPN rather than just traffic destined for the subnet that hosts the VPN.

Although many of the settings are similar between protocols, you will notice the lack of a shared key, or secret. This shared object becomes a key focal point around the integration of an IPsec-based solution, covered in the next section.

Using the Cisco VPN Client

If you are using the standard Cisco VPN client included in iOS, the settings will appear similar to those from the other protocols. These include the following options (see Figure 6–4):

Description: Describes the configuration profile being used.

Server: IP address or DNS name of the Cisco firewall or VPN appliance.

Account: Username to be used to access the VPN.

Password: Password to be used to access the VPN. Can be entered, or if blank will be requested at each authentication event.

Use Certificate: When set to the On position, allows the use of an SSL certificate as the preshared key.

Group Name: Not required, allows grouping of objects.

Secret: Shared secret used by members of the group or globally.

Figure 6–4. *Standard Cisco VPN client settings*

Now that you've looked at the most commonly used VPN client protocols, let's turn our attention to leveraging the proxy configuration, a feature that is similar among the three VPN protocols.

NOTE: Non-Cisco, IPsec-based VPNs may or may not be supported by the Cisco VPN client. Check with your vendor or network administration team to determine whether support is available. If the Cisco-based appliance supports one of the aforementioned VPN protocols, you will most likely have minimal issues. Many vendors, such as Check Point, now have dedicated portals (in the form of applications or web sites) for their iPhone customers (www.checkpoint.com/iphone). If your company uses a nonstandard VPN technology, such as SSL, I have some bad news for you. Because of the sandboxed nature of the iPhone software stack, this type of device-wide network control is not possible. Do not hold your breath for third-party support of web/SSL-based VPN technologies, at least not until Apple announces some policy changes.

Assigning a Proxy to a VPN Connection

A proxy will help perform analytics on traffic, restrict access to only allowable content, and obscure end points so that they will provide less-meaningful data to the outside world. A proxy is also likely to make the user experience better, by transferring files faster when users are in your environment. However, when users are outside your environment, it can, at times, make connections appear slower than they otherwise might be.

To configure the VPN connection to leverage a proxy, you will need to be on the same screen that you used to configure the protocol initially. Toward the bottom of the screen, you will then see the options for Proxy, as shown in Figure 6–5. You will notice that the options also appear for other types of VPNs, which is why the Proxy configuration is in its own section. To configure the proxy, set the following items, based on information obtained by a network administrator of your environment. There are three ways to use the proxy, and each can have multiple options:

Off: Disables the use of proxy services.

Manual: Manually assigns the proxy server and information for using it.

- *Server*: IP address or DNS name of the proxy server.

- *Port*: TCP/IP port number that the proxy service runs on.

- *Authentication*: When toggled to the On position, allows you to use authentication when communicating with your proxy server. In many cases, this is forced in order to further secure the proxy server itself.

Auto: Automatically assigns the proxy server based on a proxy automatic configuration file, or PAC file. There is only one setting if you are using this option, which is the URL of the PAC file.

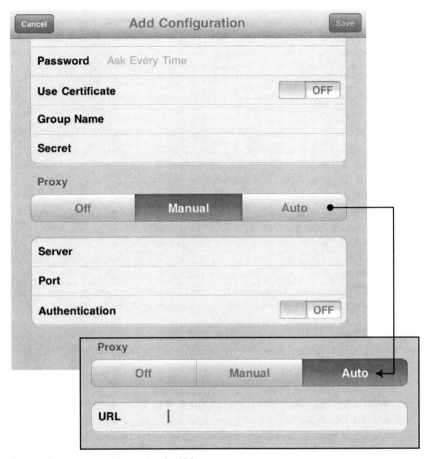

Figure 6–5. *Proxy configuration for iOS*

As with L2TP configuration, configuration of the proxy service will rely heavily on input from the administrator(s) of the proxy server. Regrettably, there is no silver bullet whereby the proxy service can be configured the same way for any environment and just work. Settings are specific to the server offering up the service. Having said this, if you have documentation for configuring Windows, Mac OS X, or Linux clients, the process should be similar no matter the platform. After all, a username is a username is a username. This is true with L2TP, proxy settings, and PPTP as well.

Providing VPN Services

There are two very different protocols to be used for serving and connecting to the VPN. The first is PPTP, and the second is L2TP. As stated before, it's best to use L2TP because it's plainly and simply a more secure protocol. If it's more secure, then why would you still offer PPTP? Well, PPTP is easier to set up and supports practically any operating system. There is a lot of legacy equipment still in use that requires PPTP. If this were the case, you should more than likely provide both protocols and have clients connect to the protocol that provides the maximum security available for that client.

> **NOTE:** This book does not cover configuring a Cisco VPN server to allow connectivity from iOS-based devices.

When you're setting up the services, the service setup will require a pool of IP addresses and a collection of other settings. The IP addresses are a dedicated Dynamic Host Configuration Protocol (DHCP) range for that service and should not in any way overlap the IP address space supplied by other DHCP scopes. For example, let's say you will be installing a server for about forty people. Of those forty, eight people will need to access the network from a remote location. In addition, the organization has six other servers, and there are six printers. If you have a pool of IP addresses from 192.168.210.1 to 192.168.210.254, you will want to carve out different parts of that range to use for different purposes. As an example, you can use 192.168.210.2 through 192.168.210.10 for servers, 192.168.210.11 through 192.168.210.20 for printers, 192.168.210.21 through 192.168.210.30 for IP addresses to be handed out by L2TP, and then use a pool of 192.168.210.100 through 192.168.210.200 for the standard DHCP pool.

> **NOTE:** You could also use an entirely different subnet if you have multiple subnets in use in your environment.

The more structured the approach, the less long-term hassle you will have. In this regard, it is wise to front-load a certain amount of future-proofing so that you don't have to go reconfiguring services after you've put them into production. In the preceding example, we have a couple of spare IP addresses to be handed off by the VPN service and about twice the size of the required IP addresses for the overall DHCP pool. We also have extra space for printers, and then there are a lot of IP addresses to still be provided to Voice over IP (VoIP) solutions and other devices that need IP addresses. You could double most of these and still not fully saturate the available IP addresses for a network environment sized as mentioned in this example.

After you have decided how large you want to make your DHCP pool, it's time to set up the server. Before setting up your VPN, first make sure that you have a functional Open Directory environment for VPN to use. Assuming that your Open Directory is fully functional, next open Server Admin from /Applications/Server and click the name or IP address of the server that you will be installing the VPN service onto, as indicated in Figure 6–6.

> **NOTE:** See *Beginning Mac OS X Snow Leopard Server* by Charles Edge, Chris Barker, and Ehren Schwiebert (Apress, 2010) for more information on Open Directory.

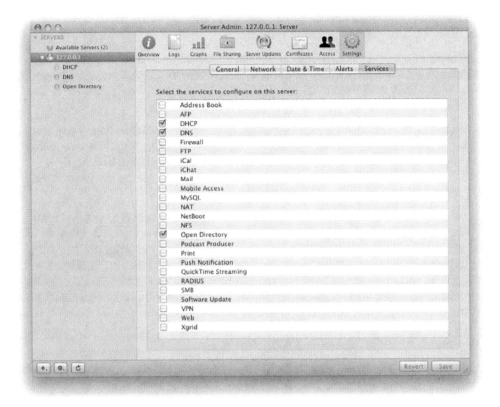

Figure 6–6. *Enabling the VPN service*

Next, select the VPN check box. Then click the Save button, which will result in the VPN service appearing in the list of services in the Servers panel of the screen. You can now configure the VPN server, which is different per protocol being used.

Setting Up a PPTP Server

Let's configure the PPTP server first, because that is the simpler of the two to manage.

Before you set up the server, first consider the topology and make the required changes to the network ports. PPTP uses port 1723 of User Datagram Protocol (UDP) and Transmission Control Protocol (TCP). With the exception of services that need to be public facing (such as authoritative DNS, public web servers, and mail servers), many environments will need no ports open other than 1723. If you, like many businesses, have your web site managed by a web host (let's call them Fabrihost), that host will more than likely also be happy to manage (if they're not already) your publicly facing DNS presence. Fabrihost, or another vendor, may even already host your mail as well. In that case, if there is nothing that the general public needs from within your network environment, you should be able to have VPN ports, and only VPN ports, open into your environment, leveraging those ports to gain access to other services rather than exposing all of those other services to the public.

After you've decided which IP addresses to use, open Server Admin and click the VPN service for the server you will be deploying the VPN service on. Click the Settings icon in the Server Admin toolbar and then click the PPTP tab. Next, click the Enable PPTP check box, as shown in Figure 6–7.

Next, fill in the IP address range that will be handed out by the PPTP server. Type the first IP address in the range of addresses to be provided in the Starting IP address field, and the last contiguous IP address in the range to be provided into the Ending IP address field. The server will then provide IP addresses in the range by providing DHCP services to computers that log into the service.

After you have configured the address range, you can choose which encryption levels to be provided to clients. If the client supports 128-bit encryption, the server and client will negotiate a 128-bit encrypted tunnel. However, if the client does not support 128-bit encryption, the server will negotiate a lower encryption algorithm (40-bit). You enable this option by selecting the Allow 40-Bit Encryption Keys in Addition to 128-Bit check box. You should enable the 40-bit option only when absolutely required because it greatly reduces the encryption levels supported for PPTP clients.

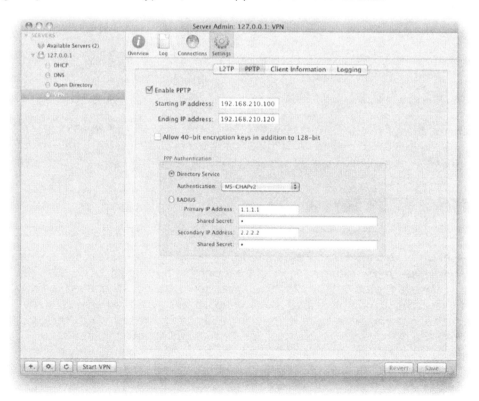

Figure 6–7. *Configuring PPTP settings*

Finally, it's time to configure the PPP authentication method to be used. The options are to use the Directory Service or to use Remote Authentication Dial In User Service (RADIUS). If your server is running as an Open Directory Master or is kerberized against a directory services domain that supports Kerberos, you can choose Directory Service from the PPP Authentication section and then choose Kerberos from the Authentication field. If the server has not joined a Kerberos realm, and you will be pulling directory services information from Open Directory or Active Directory, use MS-CHAPv2. You can also choose RADIUS if you have a RADIUS server(s) IP address and a shared secret, which would be entered into their corresponding fields.

Click Save when you are finished with the configuration and then click the Client Information tab. As you can see in Figure 6–8, you can choose the DNS servers that are provided to the client computers as part of their DHCP lease. You can also enter a search domain as you would in the Network System Preference pane for each adapter.

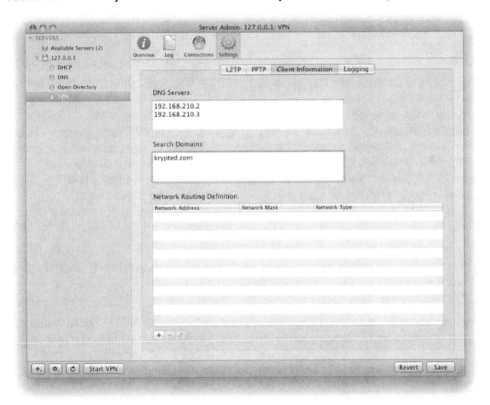

Figure 6–8. *VPN client information*

The final setting before you save your changes again and start the service is the Network Routing Definition. Here you can choose which traffic will be routed through the VPN and which will be routed through the default gateway for the default network interface of client systems. Use the plus sign (+) to provide an IP address, mask, and type for traffic. For example, if you wanted all traffic destined for 192.168.211.x IP addresses to be routed through the private network, and that were a class C, you would use 192.168.211.0 as the IP address and 255.255.255.0 as the mask. Then choose Private so traffic is routed over the tunnel and click the OK button.

When you are satisfied with all of your PPTP settings, click Save and then click the Start VPN button in the bottom toolbar of the screen.

Setting Up an L2TP Server

Configuring an L2TP server is similar to configuring PPTP except that there is an additional parameter of a key, used to establish trust with a host prior to sending a password over the connection to the server. This key can be a simple password, an SSL certificate, or even a physical hardware token, such as an RSA token.

> **NOTE:** When using both PPTP and L2TP, they should have unique addresses that do not overlap with one another.

Although many of the settings are the same as for PPTP, you also have the option to Enable Load Balancing and choose an authentication mechanism for IPsec. After the VPN service has been enabled, to configure it to serve L2TP, click the VPN service in Server Admin for the server you will be setting up and then click the Settings icon in the Server Admin toolbar. From here, select the Enable L2TP over IPsec check box, and provide a beginning and ending IP address for clients, as you did previously in the "Setting Up a PPTP Server" section of this chapter. For example, in Figure 6–9, I configured a starting IP address of 192.168.1.128 and an ending IP address of 192.168.1.254, which provides half of a class C of IP addresses for clients to use with the L2TP service.

Next, choose whether to configure two L2TP servers. If you use the Enable Load Balancing check box, you will be able to have a second server. Each server should reference the other in the Cluster IP Address field.

Now it's time to set up how authentication will work on your server. First, configure the PPP authentication settings as was described in the "Setting Up a PPTP Server" section of this chapter. In addition to the standard PPP authentication, you will need to set up IPsec authentication. In order to do so, you can use a shared secret, which is simply a password used as a preshared key. The server will need the client to submit its shared secret prior to accepting a username and password to authenticate into the VPN.

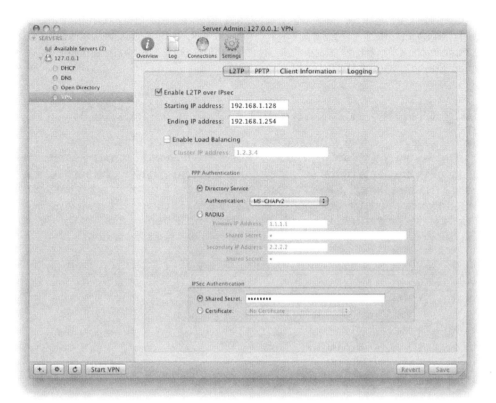

Figure 6–9. *Configuring L2TP*

> **NOTE:** If you are using a shared secret, all of the clients will need the same secret typed in that the server is using.

You can alternatively use a certificate, which leverages SSL. The SSL certificate should be installed on the server prior to enabling this feature, also described in *Beginning Mac OS X Snow Leopard Server*. Provided the SSL certificate is assigned, you will see it populated in the list of certificates, as shown in Figure 6–10.

Figure 6–10. *Choosing a certificate*

To choose the certificate, simply click the Certificate radio button, and then from the drop-down list of certificates, select the certificate you will be using. After a certificate has been chosen, click Save and then click Start VPN (unless it's already started, in which case go ahead and restart it).

Installing Mobile Access and Push Notification

The first step to setting up either Mobile Access or Push Notification is to show the service in Server Admin. To do so, open Server Admin from /Applications/Server. After authenticating, click the name of the server where you will be installing the service, and open the server's base settings. Click the Settings icon in the toolbar to open the service selection screen, where you can configure which services will run on the server, as shown in Figure 6–11. (In the image, we have enabled Mobile Access but not yet Push Notification.) Simply enabling the services on this screen will not start them.

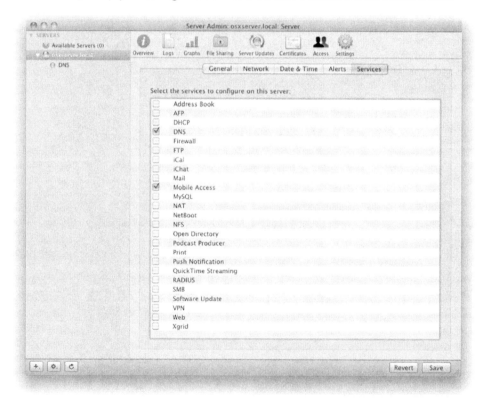

Figure 6–11. *Enabling the services*

Select the check box for the appropriate service (either Push Notification or Mobile Access—or both), and then click the Save button. You should then see the service appear in the Servers list when you click the disclosure triangle to the left of the server name. Click the Settings icon in the Server Admin toolbar to open the settings that Apple has provided for that service.

Setting Up Mobile Access

Now that you have enabled the services, you will want to start and configure the services that you need. The first service that we'll cover is Mobile Access. Mobile Access provides reverse proxy functionality for the Mac OS X collaborative services. This includes Mail, iCal, iChat, and web services (sadly, Mobile Access does not cover the built-in Mac OS X Wiki service).

By proxying connections, you have fewer hosts to secure. You also can place the server proxying those connections into a demilitarized zone and therefore allow as small a footprint of items exposed outside your network as possible. To properly leverage the Mobile Access server, though, you're going to need a demilitarized zone. Figure 6–12 shows the layout of this.

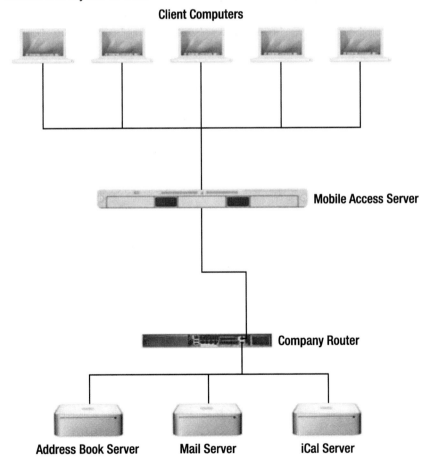

Figure 6–12. *Mobile Access network design*

You'll also need to plan for some technical design considerations when setting up DNS and SSL and deciding how to authenticate the services that are proxied.

Planning Design Considerations

You need to consider a number of factors with regard to how remote users will interface with your systems. These include DNS, SSL, authentication mechanisms, and the layout of the services in your network environment.

The DNS configuration for the environment is pretty straightforward. The clients on the internal network need to access the servers that run each service. The remote clients need to access the Mobile Access server by the same name. If you are using an external DNS service for your public-facing DNS service, you will be able to take the names and point them at your Mobile Access server while allowing your internal DNS to handle pointing those same names at your internal servers.

SSL is another consideration. Each server that hosts your services will need to use a certificate for providing that service. The easiest and least secure way to configure SSL is to simply use a wildcard SSL certificate. But if you cannot do so, you will need to import each of those certificates into the Mobile Access server.

The authentication mechanisms used by services can vary. But when you use Mobile Access to proxy mail services, you need to configure the mail server and clients to use plain-text passwords. The passwords and contents of messages are still secured by the SSL certificate, one of the main reasons that the service requires SSL in order to function properly. Additionally, Kerberos-based passwords will not traditionally be usable for any proxied service.

> **NOTE:** Many consider a proxy to be synonymous with a host that caches content. Mobile Access does not cache data but instead uses a reverse proxy that helps keep incoming traffic in a centralized location and helps keep it easy for users to access.

Configuring Mobile Access

By default, the Mobile Access service doesn't proxy any services. When you click Mobile Access in Server Admin and then click the Settings button in the Server Admin toolbar, you will see a list of the services that can be proxied. At this point, your Mobile Access server should be sitting in the demilitarized zone of your network. In the settings for the service, you will see each service that is supported, as shown in Figure 6–13.

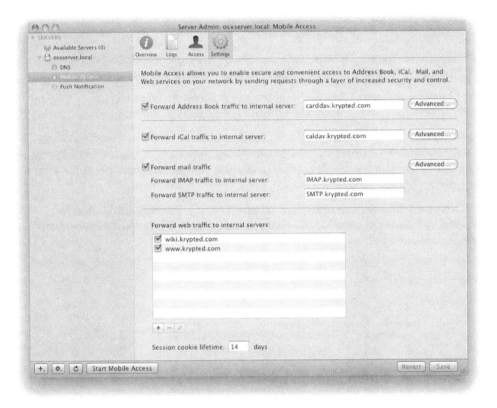

Figure 6–13. *Mobile Access service settings*

To enable the proxy for each service, select the check box for the service, and provide the name or IP address that traffic will be destined to in the supplied field. If you are using a wildcard certificate and it is the default certificate, then in many environments the default settings will suffice. However, if this is not the case, then after you have imported the certificate for a server, click the Advanced button for each service to select it.

Configuring the Address Book Proxy

On the Advanced screen for the Address Book service, you can define granular options for accessing the Address Book service remotely. Before you configure the service, first import the SSL certificate from your Address Book server by using Keychain Access. To do so, open Keychain Access from /Applications/Utilities on your Address Book server. Then locate the certificate for that server and drag it to the desktop. Next, copy the certificate to the Mobile Access server, and drag it into Keychain Access on the target.

After the SSL certificate is installed, in the Mobile Access service settings, click Advanced. You will notice a number of External Connections settings that you can use. These include the following, as shown in Figure 6–14:

Incoming Port: This is the port that the client computers outside your network will use to access the service (it defaults to 8843).

SSL Certificate: Provided that the certificate from the Address Book server was imported properly, you should see it listed in this drop-down menu.

Address Book Host Name: This is the name or IP address to forward communications to that are destined for the Address Book service.

Address Book Host Port: This is the port used to communicate between the Mobile Access server and the Address Book server (it defaults to 8843, but it should match whatever is used in the SSL Port setting under the Authentication option for your Address Book server).

Use SSL: This enables you to configure whether to use the SSL certificate for communications between the Mobile Access server and the Address Book server (over the Address Book host port).

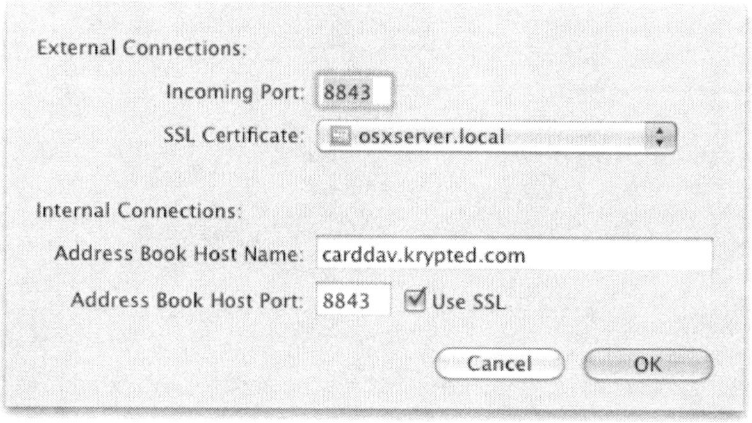

Figure 6–14. *Mobile Access Address Book advanced settings*

Configuring the iCal Proxy

Just as you configured an SSL certificate to proxy Address Book communications in the previous section, you will need to do so for iCal communications as well. The options for configuring an iCal proxy are similar to those used to configure an Address Book proxy; however, you will use the calendar server and the ports that are appropriate for these communications, as noted here and as shown in Figure 6–15:

Incoming Port: This is the port that the client computers outside your network will use to access the service (defaults to 8443).

SSL Certificate: Provided that the certificate from the iCal server was imported properly, you should see it listed in this drop-down menu.

iCal Host Name: This is the name or IP address to forward communications to that are destined for the iCal service.

iCal Host Port: This is the port used to communicate between the Mobile Access server and the iCal server (it defaults to 8443 but should be set to the same as the SSL port that is specified under Authentication in the Server Admin Settings for the iCal service on your iCal server).

Use SSL: This enables you to configure whether to use the SSL certificate for communications between the Mobile Access server and the iCal server (over the iCal host port).

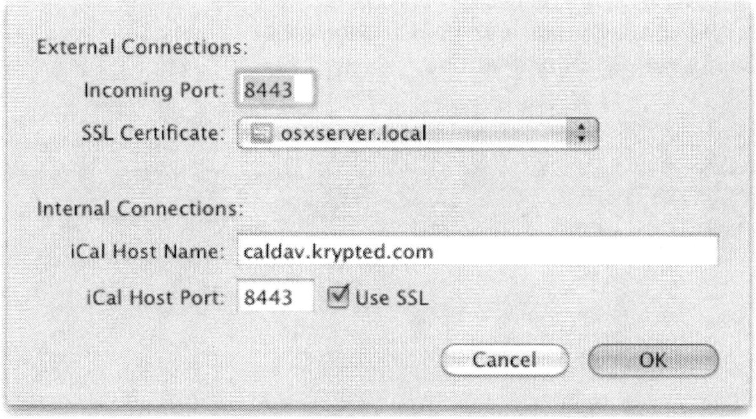

Figure 6–15. *Mobile Access iCal advanced settings*

Configuring the Mail Proxy

Prior to configuring the mail options in Mobile Access, make sure you have installed the SSL certificates for your mail service, as covered in the "Configuring the Address Book Proxy" section earlier in this chapter. On the Advanced screen for the mail proxy, you will see settings that are different from the previously configured iCal and Address Book proxies. Namely, this is because you are proxying two ports. Here, you will be able to configure ports and SSL options as you did previously. The settings include the following, as shown in Figure 6–16:

Incoming IMAP Port: This is the port that clients will use when accessing the IMAP service from outside your environment.

IMAP SSL Certificate: Select the certificate that you imported from your IMAP server.

Incoming SMTP Port: This is the port that clients will use when accessing the SMTP service from outside your environment.

SMTP SSL Certificate: Select the certificate that you previously imported for your SMTP server.

IMAP Host Name: This is the DNS name or IP address of the internal IMAP server on your local area network.

IMAP Host Port: This is the port that IMAP will be running on the mail server.

Use SSL: Enable SSL for communications between your internal IMAP server and the Mobile Access server.

SMTP Host Name: This is the name or IP address of the internal SMTP server.

SMTP Host Port: This is the port that will be used to communicate between the local SMTP service of the mail server and the Mobile Access server. The SSL option is used so that remote mail servers will be able to communicate with the Mobile Access server in order to exchange mail with your organization. While SSL is optional here, SSL use is strongly recommended.

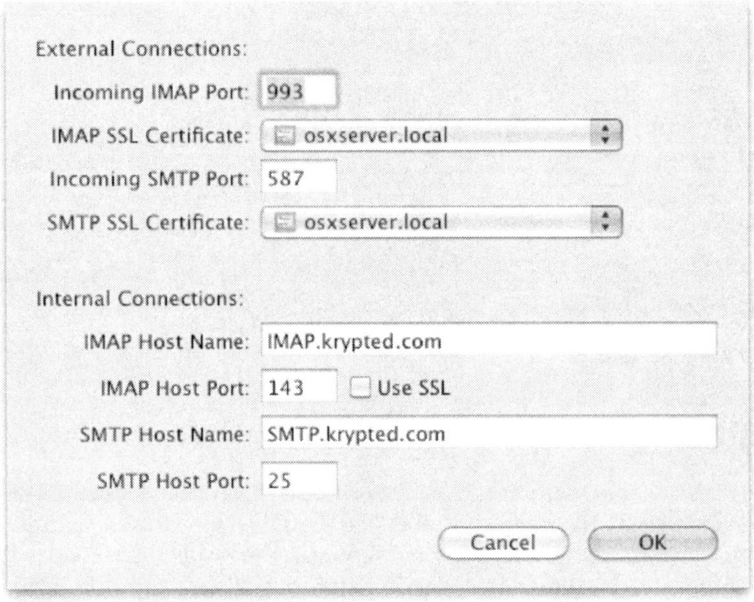

Figure 6–16. *Defining Mobile Access ports and hosts*

Configuring Web Proxy Entries

Many organizations will have a number of web servers. For example, you can host a web server for your environment's web site(s), another for the web mail functionality in Mac OS X Server's Mail service, another for accessing the iCal service over a web browser, and finally one for your blog and wiki. Mobile Access for web proxying is not supported with the Mac OS X Wiki service. However, it does function for a number of other services. Because you can have multiple servers, you can also define multiple entries in Mobile Access for web proxies, with each referred to as a *web proxy entry*. You can add the entries by clicking the plus sign in the Forward Web Traffic to Internal Servers field in the Mobile Access Settings pane of Server Admin.

On the Edit screen for each web proxy entry, you will be able to configure more-granular options for the entry. To do so, click the entry on the Server Admin Settings screen, and then click the pencil icon for that entry. The resultant screen will provide options for configuring the entry, as shown in Figure 6–17. These entries will allow you to configure the following:

Enable This Web Proxy Entry: This enables you to have unused proxies for testing purposes.

Incoming Port: This is the port that in-bound traffic from the Internet will use.

Web Host Name: This is the DNS name or IP address of the internal web server used for the web proxy entry.

Web Host Port: This is the port used to communicate between the internal web server and the Mobile Access service.

Use SSL: Not all web sites will use SSL. Select this option if you require an SSL certificate for the site in question.

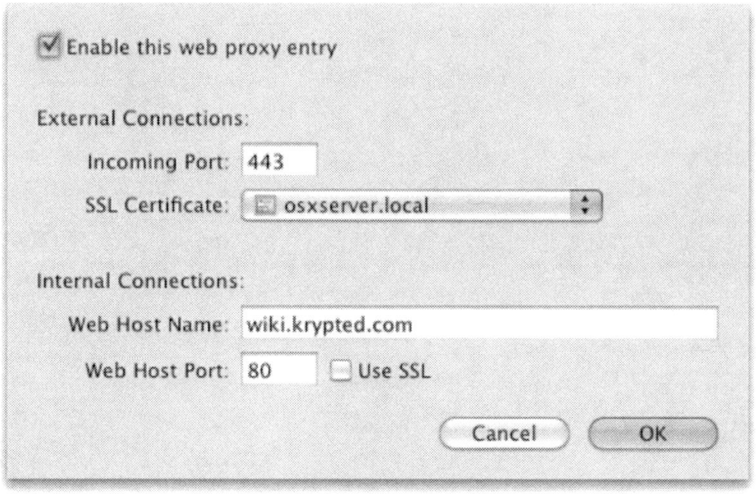

Figure 6–17. *Enabling the Mobile Access web proxy*

NOTE: SSL-enabled virtual hosts are not compatible (by default) with the Mobile Access service.

Starting the Service and Checking the Status

After you are satisfied with your settings, click the Start Mobile Access button toward the bottom of the Server Admin screen. The service will start, and you will be able to click the Overview button in the Server Admin toolbar. On the Overview screen, you will see which proxies are configured and to which hosts traffic is being forwarded for each proxied service, as shown in Figure 6–18.

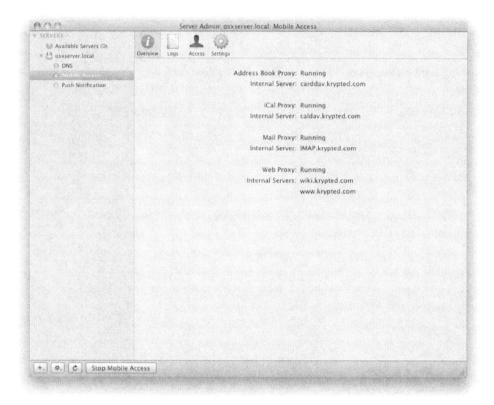

Figure 6–18. *Statuses for Mobile Access proxied services*

Controlling Access

When you enable the Mobile Access service, you will be enabling access for all users of the server. However, in many environments, not all users will be allowed to remotely access collaborative services. Therefore, you can use the Access option to limit who is able to log into the server over each service. This Access option is similar to a service access control list (SACL). However, rather than configure the SACL option for the server, you configure these access controls in the Mobile Access service so you can restrict specific features within the service if you desire to do so.

To configure access controls, open Server Admin, and click Mobile Access for your Mobile Access server. Then click the Access icon in the Server Admin toolbar. By default, the option labeled Allow Access to Address Book, iCal, Mail and Web Proxies for Everyone will be selected (Figure 6–19), meaning that all users with accounts on the server will be able to access all the services proxied using Mobile Access.

Click the Allow Access to the Selected Proxies for These Users and Groups option to limit which users will be able to authenticate to these services. At this point, no users will be able to access the services. Next, click the plus sign, and drag a user to whom you would like to grant access to the list of users and groups.

After you have dragged a user into the list, you will notice there is a check box for each of the services that Mobile Access can currently act as a proxy for. Select the box for each of the services (that is, Address, iCal, Mail, and Web) that the selected user should be able to access. Then click Save to commit your changes, and test that the authentication is allowed as intended.

NOTE: The user list that is provided will by default be empty unless the server is connected to a directory service, as shown in Figure 6–19. Therefore, you may need to provide access for users outside of your environment to the Mobile Access server that sits in the demilitarized zone.

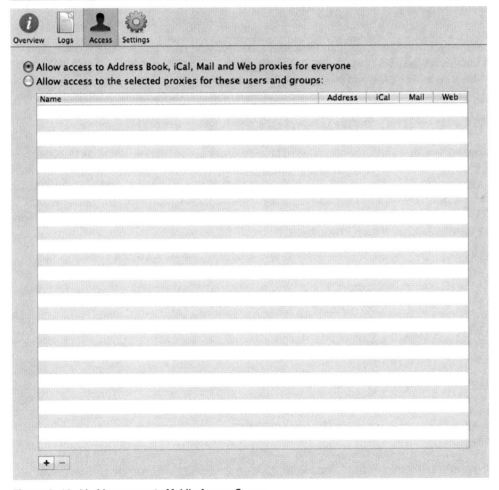

Figure 6–19. *Limiting access to Mobile Access Server*

Connecting Clients

After you have configured each service, you'll want to make sure your firewall is configured properly. To do so, make sure that incoming traffic for the Mobile Access server is allowed into your demilitarized zone. Provided that it is, check that the required ports (and ideally only the required ports) between your Mobile Access server and your proxied services inside your network are allowed as well.

> **NOTE:** Port scanning will not always be possible (or feasible) for one reason or another. See the following article for more on testing connectivity when using SSL: `http://krypted.com/mac-os-x/using-openssl-to-test-connectivity`.

After you have verified that data can flow as intended, you can test a mobile device. Provided that everything is configured properly, the client will be able to communicate with the services when located remotely as they would when they are in your office!

Setting Up Push Notification for the iPhone

In the Knowledge Base article located at `http://support.apple.com/kb/HT3947`, Apple indicates that "iPhone Mail and Calendar apps do not support Push Notifications from Mac OS X Server v10.6." Therefore, for the purposes of this chapter, I will be limiting the Push Notification coverage to configuring Push Notification to function for services as needed; you can return to that article or the Apple Knowledge Base for more information on using Push Notification as it matures.

We covered installing the Push Notification and Mobile Access services earlier in the chapter. After you enable Push Notification, you can use the service to push events from the server into a client application. For example, if you create an event in the web portal for the iCal service, you should see it appear "automagically" in the iCal application.

Before configuring Push Notification, first you'll need to configure the services for which you'll be sending events, namely Mail and iCal. To configure Mail to work with Push Notification, follow these steps:

1. Open Server Admin.

2. Click the Mail service of your mail server, keeping in mind that the mail server isn't necessarily the same as the Push Notification server if you have a multiserver environment.

3. From the Mail service, click the Settings icon in the Server Admin toolbar. Then click the Add button, shown in Figure 6–20.

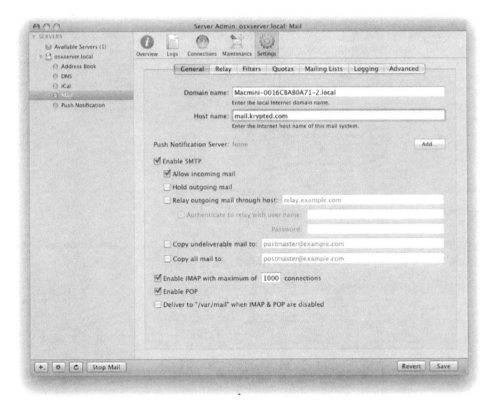

Figure 6–20. *Adding Push Notification*

4. Clicking the Add button opens a dialog box to provide a server that will handle
    notifications from the service. If you are using the same server for Push
    Notification that you are using for mail, you can enter **127.0.0.1**; otherwise, enter
    the IP address or hostname of the server that will be configured as the Push
    Notification server.

5. Provide an administrative username and password, and click the Connect button,
    as shown in Figure 6–21.

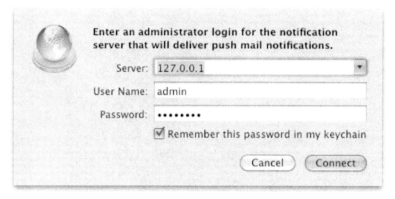

Figure 6–21. *Authenticating to the Push Notification server*

6.   Click the iCal service on your iCal server. On the General tab, you will see an entry for Push Notification, as shown in Figure 6–22.

7.   Click the Add button as you did for the Mail service.

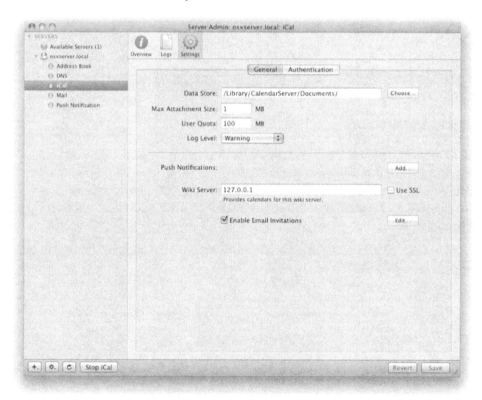

Figure 6–22. *Enabling Push Notification for iCal*

8. Clicking the Add button opens a dialog box to provide a server to handle notifications from the service. If you are using the same server for Push Notification that you are using for iCal, you can enter **127.0.0.1**; otherwise, enter the IP address or hostname of the server that will be configured as the Push Notification server.

9. Provide an administrative username and password, and click the Connect button.

After you have configured the services in your environment that require Push Notification, click the Push Notification service in the Servers list of Server Admin (configured earlier in this chapter). Then click the Start Push Notifications button, and the Push Notification service should change its status to Running, as shown in Figure 6–23.

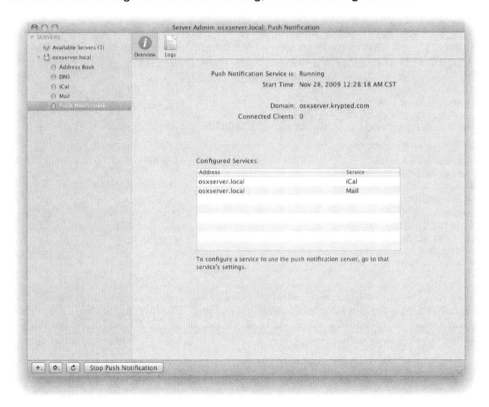

Figure 6–23. *Starting Push Notification*

You can then use the Overview button in Server Admin to view the status of the server, the number of clients, and the date that the service was started on an ongoing basis.

Using the Command Line to Manage Mobile Access and Push Notification

The command-line options for Mobile Access and Push Notification services are fairly rudimentary compared to some of the other services in Mac OS X Server. The serveradmin command is capable of starting and stopping the services and of more granularly configuring settings. When running the serveradmin command, you will use the proxy and notification options to specify the service that you are working with as Mobile Access and Push Notification, respectively. A basic version of this would be to use the following command, which uses the status verb to determine whether the service is running:

```
serveradmin status proxy
```

In addition, you can use serveradmin to look at the critical settings for the service by running it with the fullstatus option. For example, the following command shows that the server is running along with a number of critical settings:

```
serveradmin fullstatus proxy
```

This command would provide output similar to the following:

```
proxy:calDAV:state = "STARTED"
proxy:mail:state = "STARTED"
proxy:mail:internalHost = ""
proxy:cardDAV:state = "STARTED"
proxy:readWriteSettingsVersion = 1
proxy:web:state = "STARTED"
proxy:web:internalHost = _empty_array
proxy:servicePortsAreRestricted = no
proxy:setStateVersion = 1
proxy:state = "STARTED"
```

NOTE: You can also run serveradmin settings proxy for a full listing of all settings, but because the output includes information on each update, it is far too verbose to include here.

Each of the settings for the services can then be altered using the serveradmin command with the settings option, followed by the string with the new content. To see the settings of a service, you will use the serveradmin command, followed by the settings verb and then the name of the service. For the Push Notification service, the service name to be used is notification and for the Mobile Access service, it is proxy. For example, if you wanted to see the settings for the Mobile Access service, you would use the following command:

```
serveradmin settings proxy
```

For Push Notification, you can use serveradmin with the notification service. The notification service can supply some indication as to what is going on behind the scenes and can help you get started with Push Notification. You can access the Push Notification settings by using the following command:

```
serveradmin settings notification
```

One aspect of the mobile services that you can configure through the command line but that is not available through Server Admin is allowing authentication to the Wiki service. This is because the Wiki service does not leverage clear-text authentication by default. Provided you are using SSL, you can enable clear-text authentication by using the `serveradmin` command and configuring the `teams` service, as follows:

```
serveradmin settings teams:enableClearTextAuth = yes
```

Another aspect of the server that can be configured from the command line, but not the graphical interface, is the black-list and white-list functionality in the proxy service.

Summary

Many of the collaborative services included with Mac OS X, such as iChat, Mail, and iCal, need to be interfaced with securely. VPN is the traditional way to do so. But Apple has integrated Push Notification and Mobile Access to give administrators even more options when using Mac OS X Server. These allow for a secure push to mobile devices and proxying services, respectively.

With Push Notification, you can interact with the server in a more immediate fashion, using the steps outlined in this chapter. You can also substantially increase the security of your environment by leveraging Mobile Access to integrate a proxy for secure remote connectivity with your server.

But the most burning question on the mind of most network administrators and platform stewards for iOS-based devices is going to be, "Can it work with my existing infrastructure?" In most cases, you will look to the VPN services to remotely access data as though you were on the local network. Given the dominance of Cisco and L2TP-based VPN appliances, most environments will already have this infrastructure in place today. If so, then the answer to whether iOS-based devices can function in your environment is a resounding yes!

## Chapter 7

Developing In-House Applications

Developing iPhone applications is a very large topic, much larger than we can cover in one chapter of a book, given that Apress has a number of books dedicated to this topic (a list is provided at the end of this chapter). However, we can look at creating some very simple applications based on templates and therefore lay the groundwork for more complicated development in the future.

There are a number of aspects to understand before you try to develop an application for iOS. First, consider whether you should be writing an application in the first place, or whether it would be wiser to leverage standardized web technologies. If you should be writing an application, that process begins with the software development kit (SDK), a tool from Apple that is used to write applications for the iPhone, iPad, and iPod Touch. The iPhone SDK is made available by Apple for free as part of the Xcode suite of tools. However, to install an application developed with the SDK, you will need an iPhone Developer Program account, which you'll see in the first part of this chapter.

> **NOTE:** There are other development environments for iOS, but this chapter will focus on the official Apple iPhone SDK.

Once we have explained the developer program and outfitted you with the necessary tools for development, we will move on to working with the SDK using Xcode.

Because sample code will only take you so far, we will then move to providing some concepts for building a custom application from the ground up. We will discuss tools to be used in planning and some ways to move your project to the next steps. We will also take a look at using the iPhone Simulator to build applications and test them in a sandbox before you purchase any of the developer programs, therefore giving you the chance to write a proof-of-concept application before spending any money and going through the process of obtaining an account with one of the developer programs.

Finally, a lot of information has been written about developing software for iOS. It would be unwise to reinvent that wheel, so at the end of this chapter, we will provide access to some resources for designing and programming a full-scale application for your organization.

Don't Develop If You Don't Have To

Are your users always online? Do you have a web portal that they can leverage that does what you already need to do? Well then, chances are that you might not need to develop anything. Do your users go offline and still need access to data? Do you need to extend the functionality of your Internet offerings to allow users to accomplish specific tasks? If so, you probably do. But, provided that the scalability that is required can be achieved without having developers learn a new language, it is worth trying to leverage skills with PHP and content management system (CMS) solutions to accomplish tasks without the need to do much, if any, lower level software development.

One example of foregoing a development project is leveraging WordPress, a CMS that many organizations already use, to provide a portal that is specifically formatted for the screens of iOS-based devices. In addition to being one of the world's most popular blogging engines, WordPress has a number of plug-ins that are pretty useful when it comes to aggregating data via RSS feeds (from Microsoft SharePoint and other typical tools) and displaying content to end users. This content can be restricted to only users with specific passwords and can even be extended to be a social network, using BuddyPress, which is a social networking plug-in that can be used with a standard WordPress 3.x installation.

WordPress is great for the mobile platforms that you may serve content for because it is supported by nearly every mobile device that has a web browser, and it can display content to different devices with the simple installation of a plug-in. If you have a basic WordPress installation up and running, navigate to your administrative pane to the Plugins page. Here, click on the Add New button, to search for and install a new WordPress Plugin (see Figure 7–1).

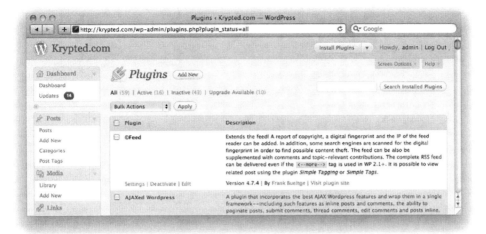

Figure 7–1. *Finding plug-ins*

At the Install Plugins screen, type **WPtouch iPhone Theme** into the search field and click the Search Installed Plugins button, shown in Figure 7–2.

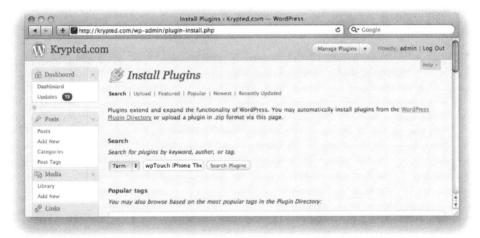

Figure 7–2. *Finding the WPtouch iPhone Theme*

You will then see a list of plug-ins that match your search. Click the Install Now link for WPtouch iPhone Theme (Figure 7–3).

Figure 7–3. *Installing the plug-in*

Once the plug-in is installed, you should activate it, which can be done using the Activate Plugin button (see Figure 7–4).

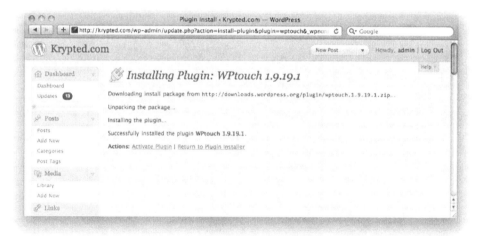

Figure 7–4. *Activating the plug-in*

Once the plug-in is activated, you should be able to browse to the site using an iPhone and see the content that you have on that site. As Figure 7–5 shows, the site will appear using a custom theme just for mobile devices. The site will load very quickly, because it will, by default, have minimal graphics to render on the iPhone screen. You can then customize the graphics as needed using standard CSS (or just replace the image).

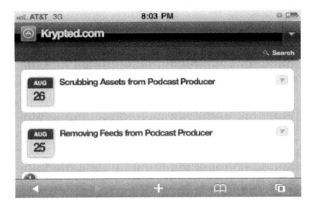

Figure 7–5. *Browsing content using the theme*

> **NOTE:** There is also a WPtouch Pro theme; it has more features and, most importantly for an enterprise, comes with commercial support. WP Touch Pro is available at `http://www.bravenewcode.com/products/wptouch-pro`.

Additional Plug-ins

There are other plug-ins for WordPress, including iPhone Theme Switcher, WordPress PDA and iPhone, and iPhone-WebApp-Redirection. You can also extend many other web portal solutions with little to no effort. In many portals, extending is just a matter of building out a new page formatted to the correct size and pointing a new DNS name to that site. For example, the ESPN site for mobile devices is `m.espn.com`. You can give your users the prefix to use, and no further action is necessary. However, if the portal should be accessible from desktop and mobile clients and you want those clients to each see the page tailored to them then you can take an additional step to unify your DNS namespace.

This involves what is known as *browser detection*. Browser detection works by reading the UserAgent of the browser, which is how a browser announces what version it is to the web server. There are a number of sites dedicated to programming around browser detection, with the following being a nice introduction: `http://www.webcredible.co.uk/user-friendly-resources/css/hacks-browser-detection.shtml`.

> **NOTE:** One portal that seems to be gaining traction is the Molly Open Source Project, which tends to be more attractive to higher education institutions given its academic licensing (see Figure 7–6.). Read more on the Molly Open Source Project at `http://mollyproject.org`.

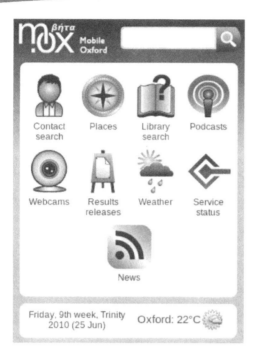

Figure 7–6. *Molly being used for Mobile Oxford*

Understanding iPhone Developer Programs

Apple has three options for those who wish to develop applications for iOS (access to all flavors of the iPhone Developer Program is available at http://developer.apple.com/iphone/index.action). The first is the iPhone Developer Program, meant for smaller organizations who have very basic distribution needs or who wish to distribute software exclusively through the application store (App Store), which acts as a clearing house for all purchased applications, including those your organization may develop. The second is the iPhone Enterprise Developer Program, which is tailored to larger organizations. The final option is for higher education institutions; it's called the iPhone Developer University Program and is meant to enable the next generation of programmers to be trained in the art of software development for iOS.

> **NOTE:** Development for iOS-based applications requires membership in one of the three programs.

While some of the iPhone Developer Programs offer additional features, which we will indicate later in this section, each comes with a copy of the iPhone SDK and Xcode, as well as access to resources to enable development. One such aspect is the iPhone Dev Center, a place where training materials, sample code, and other useful data can be obtained directly from Apple. All accounts also have access to Apple Developer forums.

Finally, all programs allow registered users within that program to deploy their software onto an iPad, iPhone, and/or iPod Touch for testing.

All development programs also come with a unique certificate that can be used to sign applications created through that program. These certificates are required, as iOS will only open signed applications.

The iPhone Developer Program

The iPhone Developer Program is tailored for the developer who wishes to sell applications on the App Store. If your organization is smaller than 500 people (and not a higher education institution), you will more than likely end up obtaining an account, or a few accounts, with the standard iPhone Developer Program. The iPhone Developer Program is the minimum required for developers who want to move from running software in the simulator to installing, testing, and distributing applications on mobile devices.

For individuals, membership in the iPhone Developer Program is required to publish software to actual mobile devices. This membership will also allow you to access the Dev Center and Developer forums. But you will be limited to how many copies of an application that you can distribute locally, meaning that most applications will need to be distributed through the App Store.

The iPhone Enterprise Developer Program

If your organization has more than 500 employees and you have a valid Dun and Bradstreet number, you can join the iPhone Enterprise Developer Program. An account costs $299 and provides you with all of the options available in the iPhone Developer Program, as well as those items deemed necessary for enterprise-level deployment. The Enterprise program will allow you to distribute applications in-house and provide technical support with code you are writing for the platform.

The iPhone Developer University Program

For qualified higher education environments, the iPhone Developer University Program is available. This program allows faculty, staff, and up to 200 students develop software alongside one another.

Getting a Developer Account

The first step to installing your applications on iOS-based devices is to get an account that will allow you to do so. To create an account, go to http://developer.apple.com/iphone, and click the Register button. To register, you will need an AppleID. If you do not yet have one, click the Create an Apple ID button. Otherwise, click the Use an Existing Apple ID button, and then click Continue (see Figure 7–7).

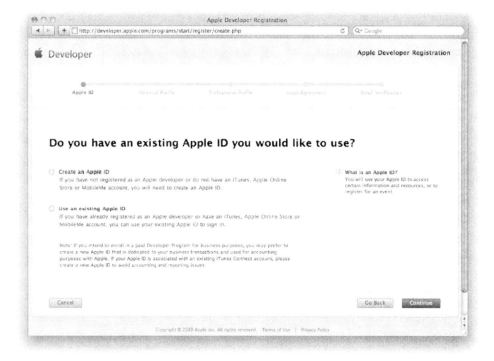

Figure 7–7. *Apple developer registration*

Next, complete the steps (surveys, licensing agreements, etc.) to create an account or add the iPhone developer tools to your existing account. Once you are a valid Apple developer, you will see the welcome screen shown in Figure 7–8.

Figure 7–8. *Registering as an Apple developer*

You can then click the Continue button to see the Member Center and choose the member program you would like to sign up for (see Figure 7–9). This should be the iPhone Developer Program, unless you qualify for one of the previously explained enterprise or higher education programs.

NOTE: The process is similar for all three versions, so we are covering the most common of the three.

Figure 7–9. *Choosing a Program*

Once you have made your selection, click the Continue button, agree to the licensing agreement, and pay for that program. You will then receive an e-mail from Apple and be able to activate your membership and obtain Xcode and the iPhone developer tools.

Xcode

Xcode is a collection of tools that you will use to develop software for Mac OS X, iPhone, iPod Touch and iPad. While Xcode is a development environment that supports more than just Objective-C, in this chapter, we're going to keep our blinders on a little and only look at developing in Objective-C.

The SDK is accessible in a program called Xcode. The SDK provides access to a kit of tools. These include libraries for accessing the built-in camera on devices, vide playback, Quartz (the graphics engine), multi-touch (the gesture oriented touch interface on devices), networking components, localization (for applications that will support multiple languages), and so on. Each application that you develop will be saved as a project within Xcode. One of the simplest and most meaningful ways to become accustomed to Xcode is to use sample code to build some simple applications.

Installing the Developer Tools

The next step is to install the Mac OS X Developer Tools, if they have not already been installed. The developer tools will include Xcode, along with a number of other tools useful in programming and debugging of applications. In order to use Xcode for developing applications for iOS, you will need to download the version of the developer tools directly from the iOS developer site, which includes the iOS SDK.

NOTE: The link to download the SDK is towards the bottom of the iOS developer site.

Once you download and extract Xcode with the iOS SDK (shown in Figure 7–10 as the iPhone SDK), you will see an installer for the Xcode and iPhone SDK for Snow Leopard. Double-click on that icon to start the installer.

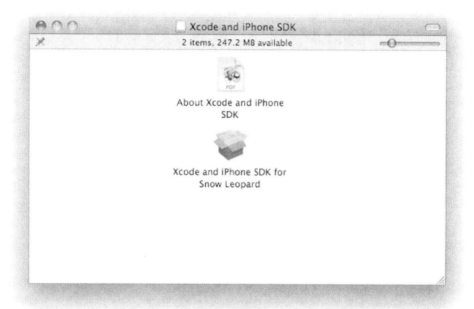

Figure 7–10. *Opening the Xcode and iPhone SDK .dmg*

When the installer opens you will be greeted by the Introduction screen. Here, click the Continue button to start the installer. You will then see the licensing screen, where (assuming you agree to the software license), you will click the Continue button and then the Agree button. You will then be asked to agree to a second license agreement, for the iPhone (iOS) SDK (see Figure 7–11).

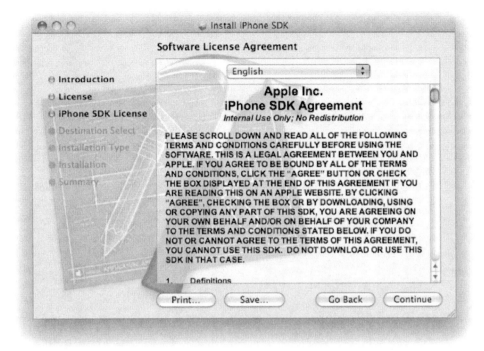

Figure 7–11. *iPhone SDK license agreement*

You will then progress to the Installation Type screen. Here, you will need to select which components you would like to install. If this is your first time here, simply leave the defaults selected and click the Continue button (see Figure 7–12).

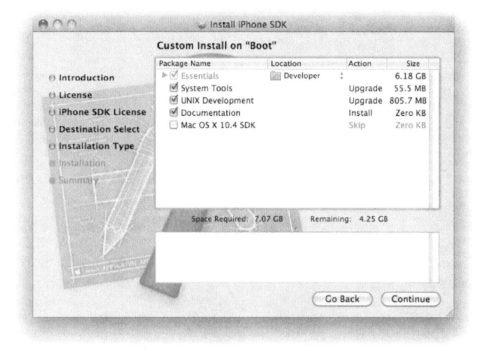

Figure 7–12. *The Installation Type screen*

The next screen will allow you to define on which drive to install the tools. Given that they take up more than 2GB of space, you may want to select a drive other than your boot partition; to do so, click the Change Install Location button (some components will still be installed onto your boot volume). Otherwise, you can simply select the boot drive on the Standard Install screen, which can be seen in Figure 7–13.

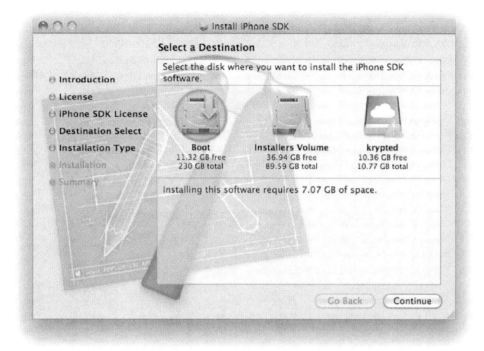

Figure 7–13. *Choosing Your Destination*

Finally, click Install, and the installer will ask for your administrative password (to authenticate you as an administrator) to complete the installation, showing a final Installation Complete screen. Once the installer has completed, run Software Update in Mac OS X to verify that you have the latest version of everything and then open Xcode, which by default is located in the /Developer/Applications directory on the drive you selected to install Xcode onto.

Using a Template

The most common application that people want to develop is an application that wraps an organization's web site or portal into a mobile application. While this is really more of a web viewer, if your organization has a site with a mobile skin (e.g., mobile.organization.com), this can allow you to appear to have developed an application even though you have really just wrapped your web site into a web view.

AppsAmuck has posted a number of templates at http://www.appsamuck.com. One of these, MyGoogle, is a simple web viewing application. We can use this as a template to build a custom application. To get started, download MyGoogle from the AppsAmuck site at http://appsamuck.com/day13.html.

Once you have downloaded the MyGoogle.zip file, extract it as is, and open the MyGoogle.xcodeproj file. Opening the file will open Xcode. Once you have opened the MyGoogle project in Xcode, locate the MainViewController.m in the list of file names and click it. Then, in the pane just below the files, locate the text that says http://www.google.com (see Figure 7–14), and change that to the URL that you would like to view with your application.

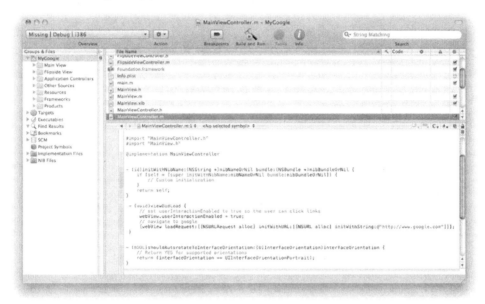

Figure 7–14. *Looking at MyGoogle*

This application has a second pane that shows the about.html file from the file list. Click it, and edit the HTML to display what you would like to show (we recommend at a minimum changing the e-mail address to contact for support), as shown in Figure 7–15.

Figure 7–15. *Customizing the MyGoogle URL*

Once you are satisfied with these edits, click the Build and Run button in the application toolbar. You will then see the application load in the iPhone Simulation Utility and look as it would to the end user.

Planning Custom Applications

Before you start creating custom applications, it is wise to do a little planning. The more complex the application, the more planning that should go into it. By mapping out what the application will look like and do, you will be able to stay on track during the development process. Furthermore, you can easily map progress as teams scale in size. If you do not have a clear idea of what you are trying to build, you should seriously consider whether the project has true enterprise merit.

Having said that, not everything needs to be planned out completely. During the development of software, it is very common to uncover application programming interfaces (APIs) that allow you to accomplish tasks far quicker than you may have thought, albeit sometimes with a different look and feel than originally planned. APIs and sample code can also allow for additional (and sometimes highly valuable) features that you hadn't thought of when planning your software. At regular intervals, meet with your team to review whether changes to the initial plan are warranted, and if so, update your schedule and the project stakeholders or individuals backing and/or involved in the project.

The planning often starts with a flow chart, or a diagram that shows how the software will operate visually. OmniGraffle provides a nice way to flow chart an application. OmniGraffle works by allowing you to drag visual elements from what are known as stencils, or graphics intended for use in a flow chart. OmniGraffle has a number of stencils built in, and it has the ability to save and share stencils. Graffletopia is a web site designed to allow for the sharing of such stencils, and it has a category dedicated to iPhone development available at http://graffletopia.com/categories/iphone. Some of the more mature stencils for use include the following:

- Ultimate iPhone Stencil: http://graffletopia.com/stencils/413

- iPhone and iPad Design: http://graffletopia.com/stencils/570

- Touch Gesture Reference: http://graffletopia.com/stencils/587

> **NOTE:** Another popular tool for flow charting development efforts is Microsoft Visio. However, we've chosen to focus on OmniGraffle here, because it's native to Mac OS X, and the iPhone SDK is only made available on the Mac OS X platform.

If you plan each element and how it will interact with actual data, you will end up with a diagram (or a number of diagrams in many cases) resembling the one shown in Figure 7–16. These diagrams act as a jumping-off point and a way to keep developers on the same page.

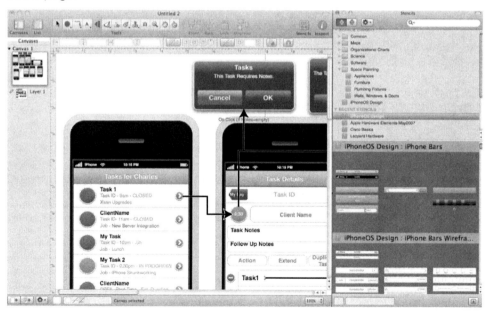

Figure 7–16. *Flow charting your application*

Training

Apple offers a number of training resources for developers looking to move into the development of software for the iOS platform (and Mac OS X, as the two go hand in hand). These are mostly available in the form of videos, sample code, and developer pages in the iOS Developer Center. But many will need more than self-paced training and will need to send potential developers to training.

Big Nerd Ranch is a training organization that specializes in the iPhone platform. There are some competitors out there that provide training, but Big Nerd Ranch offers training in Atlanta and Germany, and they wear really cool hats: `http://www.bignerdranch.com/ classes/beginning_ios_iphone/ipad`.

Outsourcing Application Development

Many an enterprise will train or hire talent at the outset of a development project. Simply tell the organization's headhunter to go find a bevy of hungry iPhone programmers, and then you are off to the races. But not all enterprises are going to want to hire a team of developers trained in Objective-C. There are a lot of companies out there doing application development for the iOS platform. Many have developed beautiful applications; many others have built applications with incredible functionality, and some have even developed an application with both. But few have built an application exactly like what you are looking for. Otherwise, you would likely be buying it on the App Store rather than writing it yourself.

Still, many other developers have never built even a working prototype of an application. The shared libraries of code that development houses build up over time when they develop a lot of applications allows an organization to build applications more efficiently, keeping costs in check and projects on track. But just because an organization has built a game doesn't mean it will understand how to query SQL, read an RSS feed, or publish data to your CRM. If your organization wants to build a game, hiring that company would be great, but if your organization wants to gain insight into the enterprise, look for an organization has a proven track record with developing code for similar tasks.

If you are outsourcing application development, in addition to finding a good organization to develop the software, you should have a clear understanding of what you want from that application. In my experience with insourcing, outsourcing, subcontracting, and managing developers, the more clearly defined your design requirements, the faster and more efficiently your application will be bid on and eventually designed.

Distributing Custom Applications

Once you have an application, it's time to push it out to actual devices. Before you can do so, you will need an SSL certificate from the iOS Developer Center, and this certificate will need to be installed on your computer and made available to Xcode. Apple has detailed instructions for this process in the Developer Center. Once you have signed the applications, you will be able to install them on physical devices.

A request we have seen from a number of customers is to host something similar to a custom App Store. A company named Apperian has released a tool called EASE (see

Figure 7–17), which makes this possible. Using EASE, you can provision applications and facilitate the ad-hoc or self-service deployment of custom applications without running your tools through Apple's App Store or deploying applications directly to the device, over the air.

Figure 7–17. *Apperian EASE*

Accessing Enterprise Databases with the iPhone

A number of tools are being released right now that provide iPhone users with access to data that is being warehoused in large corporate data farms. These include tools such as Sybase's Afaria, but also tools more familiar to traditional Mac OS X administrators, such as FileMaker Mobile, a common rapid application development tool.

Databases do not need to take years, or even months, to develop. Portals to databases that took years to develop do not have to take even more years to build before your organization can start to take value from them. There are a variety of rapid application tools that can be leveraged for

FileMaker Mobile provides access to databases created by FileMaker Pro and/or hosted by a web server or FileMaker Server. Using FileMaker, you can obtain data from a variety of sources, including those accessible via ODBC (Open Database Connectivity) and XMLT (Extensible Markup Language Translator) and even items located in documents, as shown in Figure 7–18.

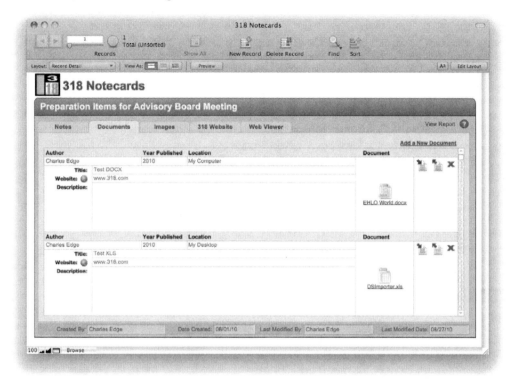

Figure 7–18. *FileMaker Mobile*

> **NOTE:** A number of other vendors are currently going to market with other solutions for rapid application development on the iOS platform, but currently, the most mature is FileMaker Mobile.

Additional Resources

A plethora of titles are available for development of iPhone applications. In fact, there are so many that we haven't been able to read them all. But from what we have read, those from Apress, our publisher, have been excellent. In the interest of full disclosure though, we have read more of theirs than others because they are provided to us for research. Therefore, if you have a style and type of book that you prefer, by all means, make a visit to your local retailer and check out theirs. But the currently available Apress books for iPhone development are worth listing here:

- *iPhone for Business* by Ryan Faas

- Objective-C for Absolute Beginners by Bennett, Fisher and Lees

- Learn Objective-C on the Mac by Mark Dalrymple and Scott Knaster

- *Pro Objective-C for Mac and iPhone* by Jim Dovey and Michael Ash

- *Beginning iPad Development for iPhone Developers: Mastering the iPad SDK* by Jack Nutting, David Mark, and Dave Wooldridge

- iPhone and iPad Apps for Absolute Beginners by Rory Lewis

- *Beginning iPhone Games Development* by PJ Cabrera, Peter Bakhirev, Eric Wing, Scott Penberthy, Ian Marsh, and Ben Britten Smith

- Building iPhone OS Accessories: Use the iPhone Accessories API to Control and Monitor Devices by Ken Maskrey

- *iPad Made Simple* by Gary Mazo and Martin Trautschold

- Pro iOS Application Architectures: for iPhone, iPad and iPod Touch by Ernie Svehla

- Beginning iPhone Web Apps: HTML5, CSS3, and JavaScript for WebKit by Estelle Weyl

Summary

In this chapter, we have taken a look at what is needed for your organization to undertake a project developing an application that will run on iOS. We didn't break out our magic wand and write that application that you put in front of your customers or organizational units to truly innovate your business model, and for that, we are truly sorry. We wish we could, but the beauty and power of the Objective-C language, the SDK, and the Xcode tools provided by Apple is that you have a lot of options. Options typically correlate to complexity. Therefore, we have instead looked at getting started.

Getting started includes installing the developer tools, learning to navigate in them, and testing a template application. We also discussed custom code, which included many of the tasks that should be performed before writing that first line of code as well as what to do if you can't yet write that first line of code, or even if you don't want to hire someone that can do so.

Now it's your turn. Go forth and innovate! And if you find success, please, feel free to let us know all about it, and we'll include it as a success story in the second edition of this book!

Now that we have finished looking at developing software, we'll shift our focus to getting that software, and the other settings we've looked at in the previous chapters, deployed to devices by creating configuration profiles in Chapter 8. In Chapter 9, we'll expand on that concept and look at deploying these applications and profiles created en masse.

Building Configuration Profiles

In earlier chapters, we looked into how to set up the iPhone to connect to common services that your organization may already have. However, if you've got a project where you need to deploy 100, 1,000, or 10,000 of these little buggers, then you're going to want the setup for each iOS device to be as automated as possible. In order to streamline deployment, Apple has developed the iPhone Configuration Utility, accessible at www.apple.com/support/iphone/enterprise/. Once this utility is installed, you can begin to build your configuration profiles.

Setting Up the Tool

Once you have downloaded the iPhone Configuration Utility, you will have a package that can be used to install the tool. When you open it, you will then see a brief description of what the application does, as can be seen in Figure 8–1. Click Continue at the Introduction dialog screen.

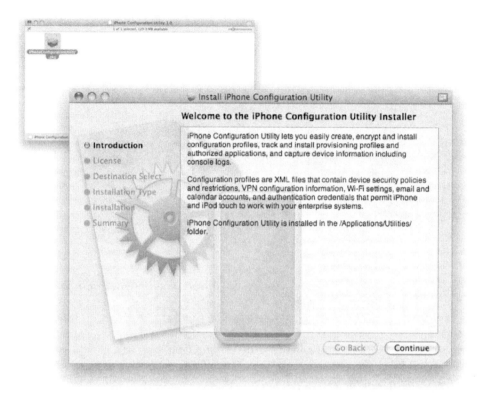

Figure 8–1. *Opening the installer package*

At the License screen, review the software license agreement and, provided you accept it, click the Continue button. You will then be prompted with a screen verifying that you agree to the licensing, as you can see in Figure 8–2. Here, click the Agree button.

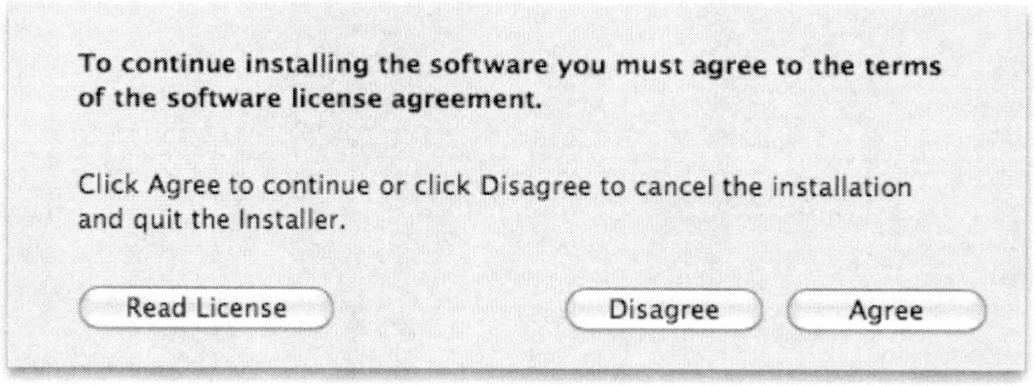

To continue installing the software you must agree to the terms of the software license agreement.

Click Agree to continue or click Disagree to cancel the installation and quit the Installer.

Read License   Disagree   Agree

Figure 8–2. *Agreeing to the licensing agreement*

You will then be placed into the Installation Type screen of the installer package. Here, click the Change Install Location button (Figure 8–3) if you would like to install the tool in a location other than the /Application/Utilities directory of your boot volume.

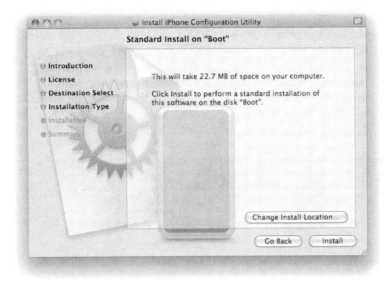

Figure 8–3. *Performing a standard install*

Once you are satisfied with your installation location, click the Install button. You will then be prompted to provide an administrative username and password to install the software. Do so, and click the OK button to complete the installation process. Then, click the Close button when the process is complete.

Building Configurations

The iPhone Configuration Utility can be used to develop configurations that can then be pushed out to iPhones and iPod touches. To begin, look in /Applications/Utilities on Mac OS X or by default in C:\Program Files\iPhone Configuration Utility, where you will find the application bundle. Go ahead and open it up, and you will see the initial configuration utility screen. Click Configuration Profiles, and then click the New icon in the iPhone Configuration Utility toolbar. You will now see a screen that allows you to configure a number of settings for the iPhone. In the following sections, we discuss the various tabs that appear on this page.

NOTE: The language in the utility refers to iPhone; however, the profiles created can be used with any iOS based device, including iPhone, iPad, and iPod Touch.

General Tab

The General tab is used to describe the profile you are creating. Here, you can enter a name, unique identifier (using reverse domain notation), an organization name, and finally a description of the profile you are creating. Here, we recommend a good naming convention. If you are going to build profiles per-user, then consider placing the user name, followed by the time frame or version of the profile in the name field. If you are going to use a generic profile, then consider entering a miniature description and/or a version number/date. In our example, we are creating a profile for our executive's phones. We specify a configuration name, MyCo Executives, our configuration identifier using reverse domain notation, com.myco.executives.profile, and then we enter relevant information for the Organization and Description, as shown in Figure 8–4.

Figure 8–4. *iPhone Configuration Utility: General tab*

Passcode Tab

The next section is the Passcode tab (Figure 8–5), where you can configure password policies, (which the iPhone and iPod touch refer to as passcodes). Various settings exist to affect password requirements for sleeping and device power-on. These include pretty standard options: the ability to set a lock timer and specify password minimum length enforcement and alphanumeric requirements. There are even internal routines to test for weak passwords. You also have the ability to prevent up to 50 previous passwords for re-use, as well as enforce periodic password changes. It's important to note that you do not configure an actual passcode at this time (that's done from the device itself after the configuration has loaded). If you wish to configure a passcode policy to be enforced on your company devices, start by checking the box for "Require passcode on device."

Next, select the appropriate options that fall within the boundaries of your organization's security policy:

- *Allow simple value*: Indicates that insecure character sequences can be used as a password. For example, if you insist on using a palindrome, you can use radar as your password using this option.

- *Require alphanumeric value*: Requires that at least one alphabetic (A–Z,a–z) character exist in the password.

- *Minimum passcode length*: Sets the minimum number of characters that a passcode must contain.

- Minimum number of complex characters: Sets the minimum number of characters allowable in a passcode.

- *Maximum passcode age (in days)*: Sets the number of days before a passcode will need to be changed.

- *Auto-Lock (in minutes)*: Configures the device to automatically lock and require a passcode to wake from the locked status.

- *Maximum number of failed attempts*: Number of times an incorrect password will be used before erasing all of the data on the device. (Not shown in Figure 8–5, but you'll see it when you scroll down.)

Figure 8–5. *iPhone Configuration Utility: Configuring passcode settings*

TIP: If you find that your passcode policies applied in the iPhone Configuration Utility are getting overridden, look into your Exchange Server for potential policy conflicts.

Restrictions Tab

The Restrictions tab shown in Figure 8–6 allows you to restrict certain activities on the iPhone. These restrictions include disabling built-in features such as the device camera, Safari, YouTube, and the iTunes Music Store. You can also configure restrictions to prevent only explicit content from being watched or heard in the iPod app, and you can prevent additional applications from being installed.

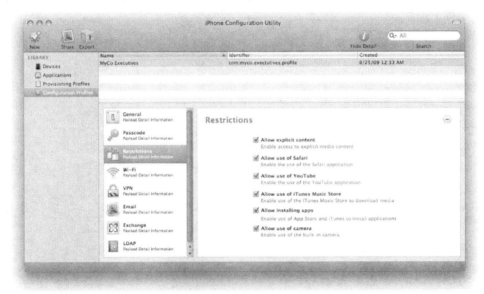

Figure 8–6. *iPhone Configuration Utility: Restricting Content*

Wi-Fi Tab

The Wi-Fi tab allows you to configure an iPhone and/or an iPod touch to connect to a variety of standards-compliant VPN appliances and servers. Wi-Fi supports WEP, WPA, and WPA2 Enterprise, which allow support for most modern wireless environments, including those that depend on 802.1x for authentication and authorization. At the Wi-Fi section, click Configure to be presented with configuration options. In the resulting screen, shown in Figure 8–7 enter the name of the SSID, the Wireless network's broadcast name. There is not a drop-down menu to select discovered Wireless networks, so you must type the network name by hand. Bear in mind that SSID's are case-sensitive. Cycle through all the settings, matching each one in the iPhone Configuration Utility with those you were able to discover while testing the handhelds.

Figure 8–7. *iPhone Configuration Utility: Wi-Fi*

Hidden Network

The Hidden Network field will allow you to connect to hidden networks and must be checked if the network does not publicly announce its SSID. Next, check the Security Type field and find the type of Wireless network encryption that your organization is using, shown in Figure 8–8. At its most basic, WEP and WPA/WPA2 Personal will not require further configuration. If you select WEP, or WPA/WPA2 options, then the user will need to enter the wireless network password; it cannot be embedded into the configuration file. However, if you select WEP Enterprise or WPA/WPA2 Enterprise, then you will need to configure your encryption protocol settings to match the configuration on your network appliances. The most important aspect of these settings is to maintain parity between computers running other operating systems in your environment.

Figure 8–8. *iPhone Configuration Utility: WPA Enterprise*

Protocols

Under the Protocols tab (shown earlier in Figure 8–7) for your enterprise Wi-Fi connection, you will configure the protocol stack for your wireless network. First, use the check boxes to select the authentication protocols that are supported. Options include TLS, LEAP, TTLS, PEAP, and EAP-FAST. If you are going to be using EAP-FAST, then also select the PAC (Protected Access Credential) by first choosing whether to use PAC, and if so, whether to provision PAC, and if you are, whether to do so anonymously.

> **NOTE:** The settings for the protocols and authentication methods are dictated by the settings on your wireless network. For example, if the wireless environment supports PEAP, then it will need to be checked. If you are unsure as to what protocols to select, check with the support for your wireless network appliances.

Authentication

Finally, select the authentication protocol to be used to access the inner ring (e.g., MSCHAPv2), and then click the Authentication tab of the Wi-Fi screen. Shown in Figure 8–9, use the Authentication tab within the Wi-Fi screen to provide the username to be used to authenticate to networks and whether you want to send an authentication password along with the configuration. Then select a certificate to use for authentication if you have one, and provide an outer identity (if required for your organization).

> **NOTE:** For more information on network settings configurations, see Chapter 3.

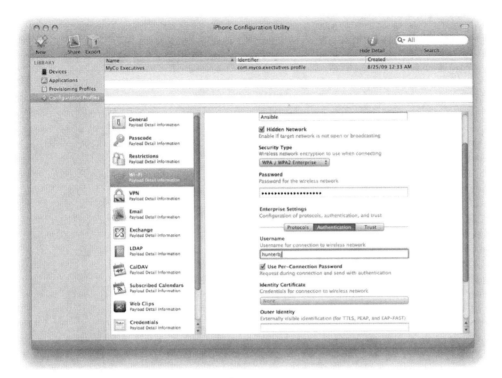

Figure 8–9. *iPhone Configuration Utility: WPA Enterprise user authentication*

Trust

Next, click the Trust tab of the Wi-Fi screen. Here, you will see the option to provide a certificate that can be used to satisfy the requirement that a client utilizes an SSL certificate to authenticate into the environment (Figure 8–10). The certificates that were added under Credentials tab are listed here. Once added, you would check the box for each certificate to trust and present at the time of authentication to the wireless network. To do so, click the check box for each certificate to be sent as part of the configuration. Here you will also want to trust specific Trusted Certificates (SSL certificates that you are granting access to). To do so, use the plus (+) icon below the Trusted Server Certificate Names and then type the name of each certificate to be trusted.

You can also provide multiple preconfigured networks that the mobile device can log into. Using the + and – buttons in the upper right-hand corner of the Wi-Fi screen, you can add and remove more networks.

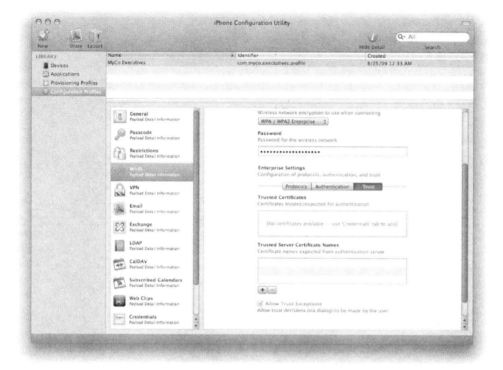

Figure 8–10. *iPhone Configuration Utility: WPA Enterprise trusts*

VPN Tab

Once you are satisfied with your wireless configuration settings, proceed to the VPN tab of your configuration profile, which is shown in Figure 8–11 on the left. If desired, click the Configure button in order to deploy a VPN payload to the device. First provide a friendly name for your end users that describes the connection. Next, select a protocol. You can use PPTP, L2TP, and IPSec (which Apple calls IPSec (Cisco)), much in the same way that you can use the same options in the VPN when configured on a single mobile device in Chapter 6.

Figure 8–11. *iPhone Configuration Utility: VPN configuration*

E-mail Tab

The next section, E-mail, allows for the configuration of non-ActiveSync-based e-mail accounts. Skip to the Exchange section if you have no IMAP/POP–based e-mail accounts to configure. Otherwise, click Configure to configure the e-mail section, and enter the appropriate information into the following fields:

- *Account Description*: A friendly identifier, you will typically want this to be similar to aid those in your remote support team who will likely end up providing phone support.

- *Account Type*: Choose POP if your account uses POP or IMAP if your account uses IMAP.

- *Account Name*: The name that will show on sent e-mail.

- *E-mail Address*: The e-mail address that will be used with the POP or IMAP account.

Once you have entered the global configuration information, use the Incoming Mail sub-tab from Figure 8–12 to configure the following:

- *Mail Server and Port*: The host name or IP address of the server that the POP or IMAP account is hosted from.

■ *User Name*: The userID for the server entered previously.

■ *Password*: Enables password authentication for the account.

■ *Use SSL*: Configures mail to leverage SSL (if you use this setting, then it does not hurt to also add and trust the certificate in the Credentials tab if said ticket was self-assigned rather than originating from a trusted CA).

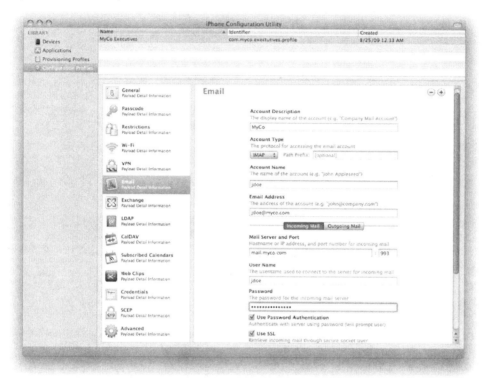

Figure 8–12. *iPhone Configuration Utility: IMAP/POP e-mail*

Once you are satisfied with your entries, click the Outgoing Mail sub-tab and you will be presented with a screen similar to that in Figure 8–13. Assuming your server requires (or at least allows) authenticated SMTP, enter the appropriate SMTP information supplied by your mail host.

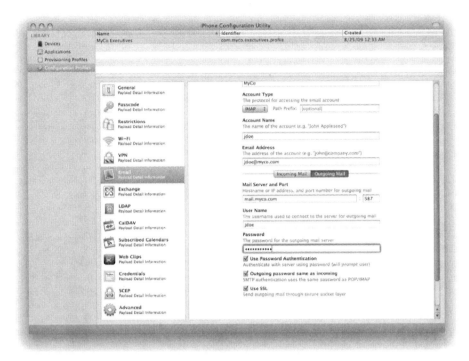

Figure 8–13. *iPhone Configuration Utility: SMTP e-mail settings*

Exchange Tab

If you wish to deploy Exchange configurations in this profile, you can configure the account settings appropriate for your Microsoft Exchange Server environment under the Exchange section (Figure 8–14). Only a single Exchange account can be configured on a device at any given time. These settings should match those in the Settings screen. To recap, you will need to enter the following settings:

- *Account Name*: The friendly name for the account.

- *Exchange ActiveSync Host*: The server that houses the Outlook Web Access role for your organization (i.e., your CAS server).

- *Use SSL*: Enable ActiveSync over SSL (again, enter the SSL certificate using the Credentials tab if you will be using this option).

- *Domain*: The name of your e-mail domain.

- *User*: The userID for the user in Active Directory/Exchange.

- *E-mail Address*: The e-mail address you will use.

- *Password*: The password for the e-mail account.

- *Authentication Credential*: Allows for the specification of a certificate used for authentication.

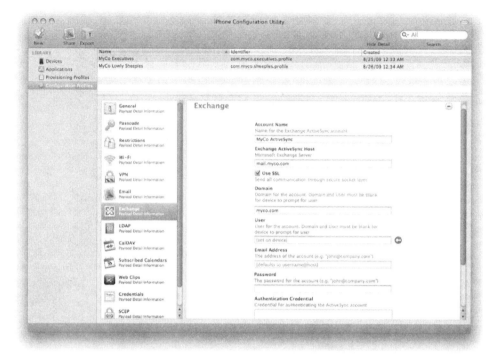

Figure 8–14. *iPhone Configuration Utility: Configuring exchange accounts*

LDAP Tab

With iPhone 3.0, we also saw the introduction of address lookup via the LDAP protocol. The iPhone configuration utility provides the ability to deploy these settings en masse to users. If you previously provided settings to configure an Exchange account, it is worth noting that the Global Address List (GAL) will be available for searching via the Contacts app as well as in the Mail app when specifying e-mail addresses. However, if your environment does not host Exchange, then configuring iPhones to utilize LDAP services can be very handy indeed. You can deploy multiple LDAP configurations. When deploying a configuration, it is necessary to provide the following information, as shown in Figure 8–15:

- Account Description: The friendly name for the account.

- *Account Username:* Allows for the specification of an LDAP user for authentication. If your LDAP server does not support anonymous connections, you may want to create a user specific for this cause, such as ldap_iphone.

- *Password*: Password for use with the account defined in the Account Username field.

- Account Hostname: The server that houses the LDAP service.

- *Port*: The TCP/IP port the device will use to connect to the LDAP server. By default this is TCP 389, or TCP 636 when using SSL. If those do not work then confirm the correct port number for your environment with your network administrator.

- *Use SSL*: Enable LDAP over SSL—make sure to specify the appropriate port.

- *Search Settings*: In this field, you can supply multiple search paths that will be searched, as well as the standard LDAP scope options: Base, One Level, Subtree. If a scope of Base is selected, searches will match only against the object specified by the distinguished name provided via the search path. Using "One Level" will search for objects residing directly in the container or organizational unit specified via the search path. In an OS X Open Directory environment, the default search path is "cn=Users,dc=myco,dc=com", but can also be "cn=People,dc=myco,dc=com". The subtree scope is the most forgiving, allowing one to search across all leaves of the provided search path. While forgiving, the subtree scope is quite taxing on LDAP servers and so should be used with caution according to the capabilities of your LDAP environment. A search path of "dc=myco,dc=com" would find entries in both cn=Users and cn=People. Subtree is also the slowest search pattern; search paths should be refined as much as possible.

Figure 8–15. *iPhone Configuration Utility: Configuring LDAP accounts*

CalDAV Tab

With iPhone 3.0, we also saw the introduction of CalDAV support, allowing the iPhone's built-in calendar app to integrate with CalDAV-based calendaring services, with full read/write privileges. Multiple accounts can be configured, and configuration itself of the CalDAV service is pretty basic, requiring only a few fields, illustrated here and shown in Figure 8–16:

- Account Description: The friendly name for the account.

- *Account Hostname and Port*: Specify server hostname or IP address that houses the CalDAV service, as well as the port over which the service is available. By default this is TCP 8008, TCP 8443 when using SSL.

- *Principal URL*: Specify the URL to the user's calendar.

- *Account Username*: Specify the username to authenticate as.

- *Password*: Specify the password to authenticate as. You will likely want to leave the Account Username and Password fields blank, which will require the user to enter them upon configuration.

- *Use SSL*: Enable CalDAV over SSL—make sure to specify the appropriate port.

Figure 8–16. *iPhone Configuration Utility: Configuring CalDAV settings*

Subscribed Calendars Tab

You can also deploy read-only web-based calendar subscriptions based upon the .ics format. These can be useful for publishing information such as staff meetings, holidays, and special events. The payload information for a subscribe calendar is fairly basic, and multiple subscriptions can be deployed. The following field information must be provided, as illustrated in Figure 8–17.

- *Description*: The friendly name for the calendar.

- *URL*: Specify the HTTP URL where the calendar can be accessed.

- *Account Username*: Allows for the specification of an LDAP user for authentication. If your LDAP server does not support anonymous connections, you may want to create a user specific for this cause, such as webcal_iphone.

- *Password*: Password for the foregoing account.

- *Use SSL*: Utilize SSL via the https protocol.

Figure 8–17. *iPhone Configuration Utility: Configuring WebCal subscriptions*

Web Clips Tab

The next section, Web Clips, allows you to create an iconified link to a web page, which is very useful for ensuring employees have quick, easy access to things like the company intranet or help desk system. Deploying Web Clips is as simple as specifying a name, a URL, and an icon. You can also specify whether the user can delete the Web Clip (Figure 8–18).

Figure 8–18. *Creating New Web Clips*

Credentials Tab

The next section allows you to deploy custom SSL certificates to your iPhone. If your establishment uses an internal certificate authority, you will need to deploy your CA's certificate to prevent users from receiving SSL errors when using encrypted services. Alternatively, if you are using certificate-based authentication for any of the supported services, you deploy them here. Your users will be thankful given that they will need to click fewer items to get set up, and your support desk will thank you as well, considering they will more than likely get fewer phone calls with users who need help isolating various SSL issues.

To install certificates, click the Configure button in the Credentials section, which is shown in Figure 8–19. You will be presented with an open dialog box; use it to navigate to the folder containing your certificates in .cer or .p12 format. With the certificate highlighted, click Open. Assuming your certificate is in a supported format, the certificate will then be displayed and added to the payload. You can use the plus (+) and minus (-) buttons to add more certificates or remove certificates respectively.

Figure 8–19. *iPhone Configuration Utility: Deploying certificates*

> **Tip** If you browse to an SSL-protected web site from your desktop using Safari or Firefox and accept the certificate, then it will be located in your Login.keychain, accessed via the Keychain Access application. From Keychain Access, you can drag it to the desktop to generate a CER file for the certificate. Alternatively, you can convert a standard PEM style cert (as used by OS X's certificate system) to the DER format used in .cer files using the following command:
>
> ```
> openssl x509 -in /etc/certificates/Default.crt -inform PEM -out
> /etc/certificates/Default.cer -outform DER
> ```

The SCEP Tab

Finally, SCEP allows you to utilize the Simple Certificate Enrollment Protocol for deploying configuration settings and certificates via SCEP, should you have such facilities in place. SCEP allows you to deploy highly customized, user- or device-specific configurations to iPhones. Unfortunately, setting up the system will require custom development. For more information on SCEP and Over-the-Air enrollment, see Apple's iPhone Enterprise Deployment Guide.

The Advanced section contains settings for the device Access Point Name and cellular proxy settings. They should not be altered unless specified by your carrier.

Deploying Configurations Using the iPhone Configuration Utility

There isn't much of a reason to build a configuration if you aren't then going to apply it to a device. The iPhone Configuration Utility can be used to deploy configurations to iPhone and iPod touch devices directly, or you can export a signed configuration for deployment via e-mail or web. The process is very similar to that of manually deploying certificates. To start, we're assuming that you are batch processing a large number of iPhones, and as such, you will be doing the deployment from a central location. The process involves first connecting the device to an admin station running the iPhone configuration utility with the appropriate mobile profile for deployment. Once connected, the iPhone Configuration Utility will discover and catalog the device, including the device serial number, unique identifier, and the device's public key. Figure 8–20 illustrates an iPhone discovered via the iPhone Configuration Utility.

Figure 8–20. *iPhone Configuration Utility: Devices*

From here, you can assign a user to the device, using the Address Book framework, and you can specify an e-mail address, though unfortunately this information isn't used during the deployment. At this point, you can deploy the configuration file to the device.

To do so, click the specific iPhone listed under the "Devices" section, and then select the Configuration Profiles tab (see Figure 8–21).

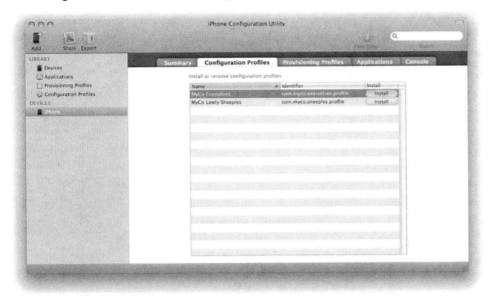

Figure 8–21. *iPhone Configuration Utility: Installing configuration profiles*

With the Configuration Profiles tab selected, you can click Install to install a specific profile onto the iOS-based device. Doing so will invoke the standard profile installation GUI, which is familiar to the process for importing certificates, explained in the Trust section of this chapter.

When loading a mobile configuration, the first screen that you will see is an overview screen, which displays the profile's intended configuration and trust settings, as shown in Figure 8–22.

Figure 8–22. *iPhone profile installation*

Tap the Install button on the iPhone to install the profile. At this point, you will be queried for any information missing from the mobile configuration. For instance, if you configured a VPN, Mail, or CalDAV payload, but did not specify a username, you will be prompted to provide that information at this point (see Figure 8–23). Likewise if your configuration contains passcode enforcement, you will need to enter the passcode at the tail end of this process. Thus, if you wish to batch process your iPhones prior to giving them to your users, your administrators will need your user's passwords, or the account creation process will need to be performed by users. In such a case, you will likely want to provide the configuration via a secured web service. This can be a two-step process as well. For instance, the batch process might include SSL certs, generic LDAP connections, and perhaps a Web Clip toward the web-hosted service-centric mobile profile. Users then need only click the custom icon that you provide, which sends them to the remote mobile configuration file, and thereby directly into the installation screen. While not completely automated, it provides a fairly user-friendly deployment method.

Unfortunately, there is no authentication sharing between the various services, so you will have to enter credentials for each individual service.

Figure 8–23. *iPhone Profile Installation: Setting a Passcode*

There are a number of reasons that importing a configuration profile can fail. If, for example, the profile tells the device to configure an ActiveSync account and one is already present, then the user will receive an error when attempting to install the profile. If the user fails to enter a passcode with the appropriate passcode strength and gives up, then the entire configuration process will fail. Alternatively, if you are deploying Mail accounts that are configured to use SSL that is either self-signed, or signed by a CA that is not included in the iPhone's base trust, then the profile installation will fail, even if it contains the CA root certificate in the profile. For instances such as this, you may need to build out and deploy two configurations, one with the SSL certificates, and the other with the Account configuration payloads.

> **TIP:** For a list of certificates trusted by default on iPhone 3.0, see Apple Knowledge Base article HT3580: `http://support.apple.com/kb/HT3580`.

Importing and Exporting Profiles

The iPhone Configuration Utility allows for importing and exporting configuration profiles for distribution via e-mail or web browser. To perform this task, first ensure that you have a configuration polished up and ready to go. Once this is done, highlight the profile, and then select either Share or Export from the toolbar, shown in Figure 8–24. The former option will e-mail the mobile configuration file, and the latter will present a standard save dialog box and allow you to specify the name and location for exporting.

Figure 8–24. *iPhone Profile Installation: Providing authentication credentials*

After selecting either option, you will be presented with a dialog asking whether you want to sign the configuration, shown in Figure 8–25. If you are exporting this for deployment, it is highly recommended that you do so. There are a few options here. First and foremost, you can opt not to sign the profile at all. This provides no security on the file, and leaves it open for alteration without any detection capabilities. When you sign the configuration, devices that seek to deploy its payload can verify that it is tamper-free. Obviously, this is always desirable.

Next, it is possible to simply sign the configuration, or we can encrypt it for each registered device. The former option is much more forgiving, and is desirable if you wish to deploy this to an unknown amount of iPhones, and want the task to be as hassle-free as possible. Alternatively, if you have all of your iPhones catalogued in the iPhone Configuration Utility, then you can create an encrypted profile for each phone.

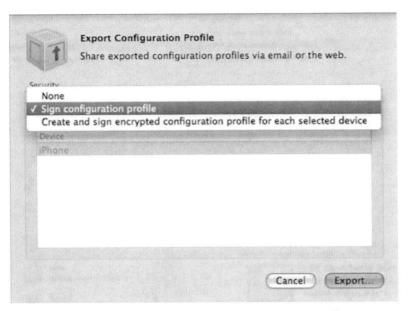

Figure 8–25. *iPhone Configuration Utility: Signing a configuration profile*

Summary

In this chapter, we have shown the various options available with the iPhone Configuration Utility for building a configuration profile. Currently, every strategy involving mass deployment or mass management of an iOS-based device involves using the configuration files that we have shown how to create in this chapter.

Because a number of settings can be managed on the fly via Microsoft Exchange or one of the third-party tools mentioned in the next chapter, you need not get every single setting configured in your configuration file. This is because your patch management solution or your Exchange server can set and even override the settings that you place into your configuration profile. These files are meant to push settings to the device, but in most cases, not to actually enforce the fact that they are there.

Once you are complete with building a profile, there are a number of things you can do with them. You can deploy them to computers using iTunes, as shown in this chapter. But you can also write a script that will personalize the profiles for each user, duplicating the profile in the process or creating them on the fly. You can also deploy them with third-party software such as AirWatch, the KACE appliance, the Casper Suite, or TARMAC (third-party solutions covered in depth in Chapter 9). In the next chapter, we will take a look at deploying that profile to mobile devices over the air, en masse, with a focus on leveraging third-party tools to do so.

Chapter **9**

Mass-Deploying Devices

At this point, you have spent a large part of the book learning how to perform tasks on iOS-based devices, interconnect those devices to other systems, and even perform a little light software development. In Chapter 8, you created a profile by using the iPhone Configuration Utility. In this chapter, you will take those profiles and deploy them to actual mobile devices, allowing for your initial pilot and/or deployment to occur.

As shown in Chapter 8, you can deploy profiles to mobile devices in smaller environments by using the iPhone Configuration Utility. However, that strategy can be somewhat difficult for larger environments. In mass deployments, you want to keep the number of times you need to "touch" a device to a minimum. But given that each device needs to be plugged into a machine running iTunes, deploying profiles over a cabled connection represents a second "touch," and a lengthy one at that.

In this chapter, you will look at products that ease the deployment and management of iOS on a large scale. This starts with understanding the terms that will be a recurring theme throughout the chapter. We then turn our attention to some options for organizations that would like to build their own solution. But we then switch our focus to AirWatch, JAMF's Casper Suite, Dell's KACE appliance, MobileIron, and TARMAC. These products provide the most seamless and labor-free deployment that can be had, along with the best long-term management strategies.

After you've looked at each of the products, you'll then look at how to remove them. After all, I hope you will test each of them before you purchase one!

NOTE: The products in this chapter are listed alphabetically, so the author does not play favorites with any. All products have their merits and specialties, which are showcased throughout this chapter.

Deployment Terminology

iOS 4 adds Mobile Device Management (MDM) to the picture, which provides additional resources for developers to build tools that seamlessly integrate into the enterprise. However, Apple does not currently sell an end-to-end solution that can be used to deploy iOS-based devices over the air. Being able to generate management profiles dynamically and then to composite profiles based on group membership becomes, for the most part, something that most organizations will rely on a third-party product to do. Each of the products included in this chapter can leverage MDM for this task.

One of the most important aspects of MDM is that it does not require an application to be installed. When a device needs to be enrolled with the server, the server will send a message (e-mail or text, according to which product you are using) to the device. The server can also be accessed via a web portal that is supplied to users. The end user will then provide a username and password (profiles are specific to users) and choose to accept the profile or not. If accepted, the profile will be installed. You can then look at the profile and see what kind of control the profile's server can exert over your device.

> **NOTE:** Technically, the profiles must be accepted on the device. This can happen prior to the device being supplied to an end user, or the profile can be accepted by the end user.

MDM works hand in hand with Simple Certificate Enrollment Protocol (SCEP). Apple has supported the ability to allow mobile devices to enroll into an existing SCEP server for some time. SCEP is a protocol that was developed by Cisco and is most commonly used to provide certificate services for routers, VPNs, and other devices. In Chapter 8, we discussed the importance of certificates as they relate to building and managing profiles for iOS-based devices. Therefore, it will be no surprise that Apple has chosen a protocol in such alignment with their own methodologies to automate the management of certificates.

Building Profiles from Scripts

The iPhone Configuration Utility is used to "image" iPhone, iPad, and iPod Touch. You aren't laying bits down as you would in a traditional imaging scenario. Instead, you are sending a profile and possibly some applications to the device. This is done through a configuration profile, which is a property list, prefixed with a .mobileconfig extension.

The iPhone Configuration Utility stores its data in the ~/Library/MobileDevice directory. Here you will find two subdirectories:

- Devices contains the device data for each device that has been docked to the iPhone Configuration Utility.

- Configuration Profiles contains the profiles that you will assign to devices in the form of .mobileconfig plists.

Both of these can be managed from the command line and therefore generated en masse. First, let's look at creating devices and then configuration profiles.

Creating Devices

If you go into the `Devices` directory, you will see a `.deviceinfo` file for each device that you have interacted with through the iPhone Configuration Utility. Each file is prefixed by the unique device identifier (UDID) of the device. You can view each `.deviceinfo` file as a standard property list, which appears in a very simplistic fashion, as shown in Listing 9–1.

Listing 9–1. *A Sample `.deviceinfo` File*

```
<?xml version="1.0" encoding="UTF-8"?>
<!DOCTYPE plist PUBLIC "-//Apple//DTD PLIST 1.0//EN" "http://www.apple.com/DTDs\
/PropertyList-1.0.dtd">
<plist version="1.0">
<dict>
<key>UniqueChipID</key>
<integer>0</integer>
<key>applicationDictionaries</key>
<array/>
<key>configurationProfiles</key>
<array/>
<key>deviceActivationState</key>
<string>WildcardActivated</string>
<key>deviceBuildVersion</key>
<string>7E18</string>
<key>deviceCapacityKey</key>
<integer>15333203968</integer>
<key>deviceIdentifier</key>
<string>12a0b688649cfe0ce5df2ab8b4f9eaaee0d000fc</string>
<key>deviceLastConnected</key>
<date>2010-05-27T00:17:17Z</date>
<key>deviceName</key>
<string>Charles Edge's iPhone</string>
<key>devicePhoneNumber</key>
<string>1 (310) 555-1212</string>
<key>deviceProductVersion</key>
<string>3.1.3</string>
<key>deviceSerialNumber</key>
<string>12345678901</string>
<key>deviceType</key>
<string>iPhone</string>
<key>provisioningProfiles</key>
<array/>
</dict>
</plist>
```

To find a UDID, you can plug a device into iTunes, select the device from the Devices list, and then click the Summary tab. You can then click the bold Software Version to see the build version. You can click the bold Phone Number to see the international mobile equipment identity (IMEI), or double-click to see the integrated circuit card identifier (ICCID) of the SIM card. Click the bold Serial Number to see the identifier (or UDID). This is shown in Figure 9–1.

> **NOTE:** ICCID, IMEI, and UDID are unique to the device, and each has a different purpose. The ICCID is attached to the SIM card of a device. The IMEI is for GSM (Global System for Mobile Communications) connectivity. The UDID is a unique number used exclusively for iOS-based devices, most commonly used for provisioning software.

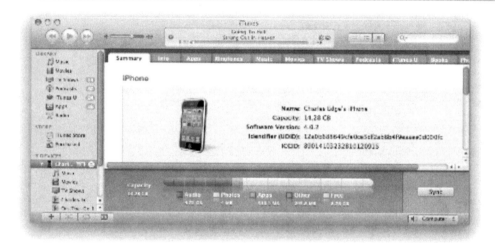

Figure 9–1. *Obtaining the UDID of a device*

The serial number can also be obtained from a bar code on the box that came with the device, although the UDID cannot at this time. The serial number, though, can then be brought into a database that has both, to correlate them (assuming you are programmatically going to wrangle this data at a later time) and assign profiles based on, for example, Open Directory or Active Directory group membership of the primary user.

You can copy a template file without unique identifiers and then use defaults to put the unique data into the file. Or you can use PlistBuddy to create a file from scratch. The data can then be viewed in somewhat of a 2D fashion up to this point, as shown with a sample CSV file (comma separated value file) in Figure 9–2. The problem then comes in the arrays, because in addition to referencing data from the .mobileconfig files we'll look at in a moment, these arrays are using localized plists to form a relational context to data.

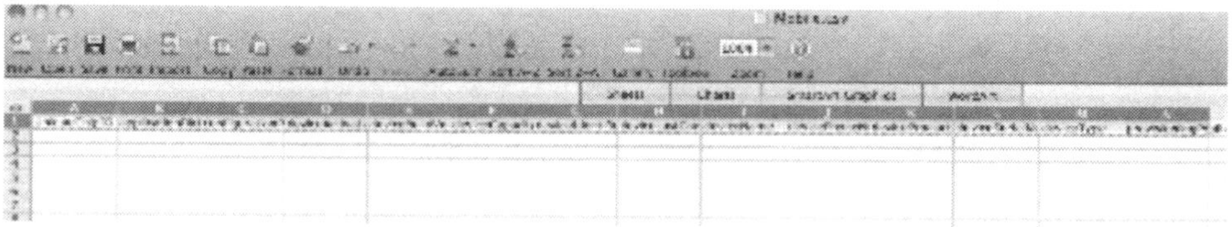

Figure 9–2. *Required fields*

Creating Configuration Profiles

You can then look at a `.mobileconfig` file, which appears in a very simplistic form, as shown in Listing 9.2.

Listing 9–2. *A Sample* `.mobileconfig` *Profile*

```
<?xml version="1.0" encoding="UTF-8"?>
<!DOCTYPE plist PUBLIC "-//Apple//DTD PLIST 1.0//EN" "http://www.apple.com/DTDs\
/PropertyList-1.0.dtd">
<plist version="1.0">
<dict>
 <key>PayloadContent</key>
 <array>
 <dict>
 <key>FullScreen</key>
 <false/>
 <key>IsRemovable</key>
 <true/>
 <key>Label</key>
 <string></string>
 <key>PayloadDescription</key>
 <string>Configures Web Clip</string>
 <key>PayloadDisplayName</key>
 <string>Web Clip</string>
 <key>PayloadIdentifier</key>
 <string></string>
 <key>PayloadOrganization</key>
 <string></string>
 <key>PayloadType</key>
 <string>com.apple.webClip.managed</string>
 <key>PayloadUUID</key>
 <string>80222944-B43C-4A43-AB93-2998CDCBE808</string>
 <key>PayloadVersion</key>
 <integer>1</integer>
 <key>Precomposed</key>
 <false/>
 <key>URL</key>
 <string></string>
 </dict>
 </array>
 <key>PayloadDescription</key>
 <string>Profile description.</string>
 <key>PayloadDisplayName</key>
 <string>Profile Name</string>
 <key>PayloadOrganization</key>
 <string></string>
 <key>PayloadRemovalDisallowed</key>
 <false/>
 <key>PayloadType</key>
 <string>Configuration</string>
 <key>PayloadUUID</key>
 <string>5B0879F3-9BA9-41E7-AC8F-F4703D4400DB</string>
 <key>PayloadVersion</key>
 <integer>1</integer>
</dict>
</plist>
```

You can then create a single .mobileconfig file, make it a template, and match the settings for your template user, per group. Those .mobileconfig files then get applied to each device, which you could do in batches. You can also dynamically copy the files to a web server and send an SMS (Short Message Service)/e-mail to the user, who could then click on the files to apply them or to dock the device.

You can also add applications by using a preexisting array and copying it, although if there are licensing concerns regarding the application you are distributing, it would be wise to investigate the ramifications of doing so first. Keys and such are defined in the *iPhone OS Enterprise Deployment Guide* (Apple, 2010) along with sample AppleScript for creation of files.

You can also copy the database by copying the property list files between machines. When the iPhone Configuration Utility is opened, it will automatically read in the new property lists and display the information. Overall, this process is going to be as much work as dynamically generating provisioning on the fly via the Ruby sample code provided by Apple, while netting you less of a result (unless of course, your shell scripting powers are demigod-like).

Apple's Sample Code

Although Apple doesn't provide an end-to-end solution, the makers of iOS do provide a fair amount of sample code for developers. This means Apple gives you the APIs, but that you will need developers to complete the solution.

It seems as though each year at Apple's Worldwide Developers Conference (WWDC) there is a lot of talk about new sample code, or about APIs released by Apple. Among these is the Ruby sample code referenced briefly in Chapter 1. Using this code as a starting point, an in-house development staff can build a tool that can be used to enroll mobile devices into your environment, creating a configuration profile as you go. Again, to leverage the sample code, you will need to develop the tool.

The sample code uses Ruby for auto-enrollment. This code is available at http://developer.apple.com/library/ios/#documentation/NetworkingInternet/Concep tual/iPhoneOTAConfiguration/Introduction/Introduction.html. Apple documents the mail, network, and policy settings here, and then goes on to cover certificate management, including certificate revocation information.

MDM manages iOS-based devices after they have initially been deployed. Similar to policy management, the goal of most MDM environments is to apply configuration files that in turn apply policies. This means that each tool will need an agent that can then communicate back to a centralized server and exchange configuration profiles as a part of the client-server relationship.

As with most other things in the IT industry, you can do practically anything you want, including developing your own MDM-based enrollment solution. However, many organizations have specific strategies indicating when to build a custom solution from the ground up and when to buy software that is officially supported by a vendor. All strategies have merits. We will not go into each here, but whatever strategy your organization employs for other solutions is applicable here as well.

For more information on the structure, strategy, and other big-picture concepts, regard the sample code provided by Apple at `http://images.apple.com/iphone/business/docs/iPhone_OTA_Enrollment_Configuration.pdf`.

Given that this book is not a title on Ruby or any other programming language, at this point we will look at third-party packages that can aid you in your mass deployment.

AirWatch

AirWatch is a tool that can be used to deploy profiles over the air, en masse. AirWatch runs on Windows servers in a .NET environment, currently leveraging Silverlight to provide a stellar experience with the management console and using the latest in Apple's MDM APIs to provide an even more stellar result to end users. AirWatch is mature, robust, and comes with several unique options, such as the capability to import devices from a CSV file and then automate sending SMS alerts to devices to enroll.

AirWatch can be acquired either as a software as a service (SaaS) solution or with an on-premises server. Questions about how to license or host a product are typically best left to the vendor, but suffice it to say that the choice between the two is a typical quandary for many environments and many types of technologies, ranging from messaging to files. Complexity of network environments, decision on pricing models, exposure of data to an outside vendor, and other factors can help play a role in the decision-making process.

Whether you choose to host the server at your location or outsource it to AirWatch, the configuration is likely not a "customer installable" process. This means that you will more than likely engage AirWatch to set up the solution for you (which is pretty similar to every other product mentioned throughout this chapter). Therefore, this section focuses on the use and management of the devices through the web portal after the solution is configured.

Managing Objects in the Portal

The first time you log into the AirWatch portal as an administrator, you will want to perform several tasks. These include creating users, creating location groups, creating a default device profile (or one per location group in some cases), connecting AirWatch to some of your back-end systems, and of course when you're finally ready, enrolling a device to be managed by the AirWatch agent.

Setting Up Administrative Users

We will get started with the global settings. If you require additional administrative accounts, you should create them. You can do so by using the Configure option in the AirWatch portal. Hovering over Configure brings up the User Setup option (Figure 9–3).

Clicking the User Setup option then brings up a screen enabling you to Search Users, check Login History, define Roles, and Add Users.

Figure 9–3. *Setting up administrators in AirWatch*

You will then see a screen asking for information about the user (Figure 9–4). Pay particular attention to the Role field, which sets the user as either an administrator or a reviewer over a given location group (and its children). Setting a user as an administrator provides that user full control over the location group that the setting was created for. After you have filled out the fields to generate the new user, click the Save button.

As with most other aspects of technology, it is recommended that administrative users have permission to access only items they need. Creating location groups and delegating permissions through them will enable you to maintain granular controls over your delegated administrative access much in the same way that an organization unit will enable you to do so in Active Directory.

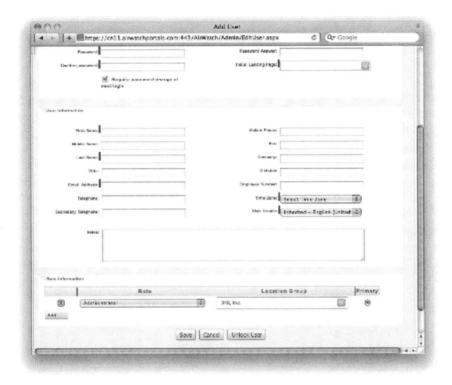

Figure 9–4. *User options and roles in AirWatch*

Configuring LDAP and SCEP

Next, you will want to configure what AirWatch refers to as *location groups*. Each location group can have its own Lightweight Directory Access Protocol (LDAP) and SCEP implementation. If you have an SCEP server (introduced earlier in this chapter), you will want to configure AirWatch to communicate with your server for certificate management. The SCEP server would then need to be accessible from the Internet provided that you will have devices managed when they are not on your network. LDAP is used to perform enrollment authentication requests; therefore, the LDAP server for your environment does not necessarily need to be exposed in the same fashion.

Configuring LDAP and SCEP are done on the same screen. Click Location in the top menu bar and then click the option for Location Groups. You will then see a list of all of the location groups that the user you are authenticated as can administer. Click the location group to manage and then click the Enrollment Configuration button. Next you will see the User Authentication configuration screen, where you can set up an LDAP connection, as you can see in Figure 9–5.

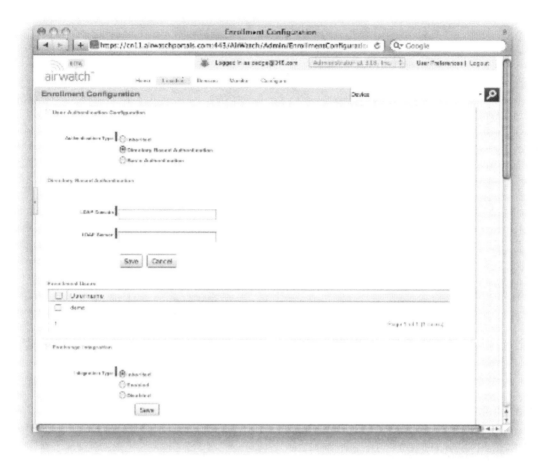

Figure 9–5. *Linking AirWatch to your LDAP environment*

Selecting the Directory Based Authentication option will allow you to enter an LDAP Domain and an LDAP Server. These will need to be supplied by the network administrator for the LDAP environment. The LDAP Server can be a name or an IP address, with a prefix (URI specification) of LDAP. For example, if you have a domain controller or an Open Directory server sitting at 192.168.55.2, you could use LDAP://192.168.55.2. The domain can be used in Active Directory environments to signify the Active Directory domain name.

NOTE: If you have an Exchange environment, you will want to enable Exchange Integration for AirWatch at this screen as well (which is not the default setting).

Next, scroll down to the SCEP Configuration section of the page. You will see the options that should correspond to your SCEP implementation (Figure 9–6). Match Key

Sizes, Key Types, SCEP Subject, SCEP Password, and SCEP Username with the address that you fill into the SCEP Server portion of the screen. For most environments, the remainder of the settings on this page will suffice.

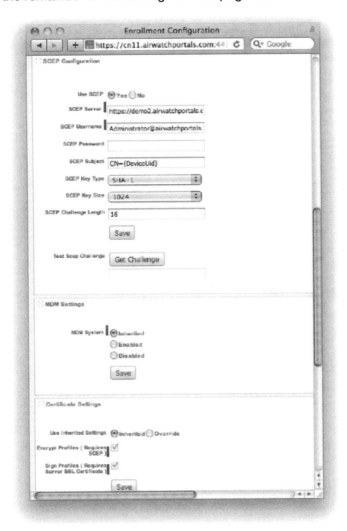

Figure 9–6. *Configuring SCEP settings in AirWatch*

After you click Save, we will move on to creating the profiles that can then be pushed out to clients.

Creating a Profile

Right now you are probably thinking that you were told that all of the 3rd party products for iOS mass deployment use the iPhone Configuration Utility. Well, close. AirWatch has done something pretty intelligent with their configuration profiles: duplicating what Apple did, but giving more options customized for AirWatch (and more important, automatic enrollment and configuration of applications).

Each location group should have a profile (or they can all inherit the profile from the parent location group). To create the profiles, click the Devices option and then click Device Profile Management, which brings up a screen similar to that in Figure 9–7.

Figure 9–7. *Managing profiles in AirWatch*

Click the New button and then select Managed Profile from the options, which brings up a screen with an option to set the platform (Figure 9–8).

Figure 9–8. *Setting the Platform field for AirWatch device profiles*

Set the Platform field to Apple and then you will see a screen that will look familiar, as it is based on the options available in the iPhone Configuration Utility. Configure the options as you would like (based on the walk-throughs available in Chapter 8) and then click Save when you are finished (Figure 9–9).

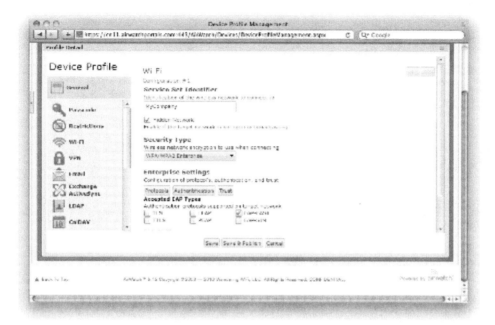

Figure 9–9. *iPhone Configuration Utility-like profile options*

Profiles can be assigned to a location group, and systems newly enrolled into that location group will take on the profile (Figure 9–10).

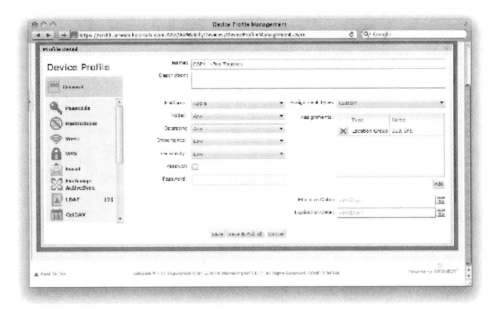

Figure 9–10. *Configuring the devices a profile will be assigned to*

NOTE: You can also create a location within a location group and assign a profile to just the location.

In order to see the assignment of these profiles via MDM in action, let's enroll the first client system to the server. You are now ready to enroll a device so it can be associated with the appropriate profile.

Enrolling a Device

The auto-enrollment process for AirWatch is straightforward to end users. They are sent a link (typically through SMS) and they then click that link. At the login prompt, the user will log in as himself or herself, thus allowing the profile to be personalized to that user account.

Figure 9–11. *Enrolling for Airwatch-based MDM*

After the user is enrolled, you will then see the device listed in the portal (Figure 9–12).

Figure 9-12. *Showing enrolled devices*

During the enrollment, you will be prompted to install the configuration profile. The user of the device must choose to accept the installation, or the process will end at this point. As a part of the enrollment process, AirWatch will then be able to manage the device remotely via MDM. You can use the icons along the top of the screen (Figure 9-13) to manage the device.

Figure 9-13. *Device management options*

Here you also find one of the most popular options: to remotely wipe a device. You have a few options for doing so, including using the web portal for Microsoft Exchange, as was shown in Chapter 4. The ability to do so through AirWatch (Figure 9–14), as well as unlock the passphrase to wake up a sleeping phone and lock the device, is a welcome addition to many environments.

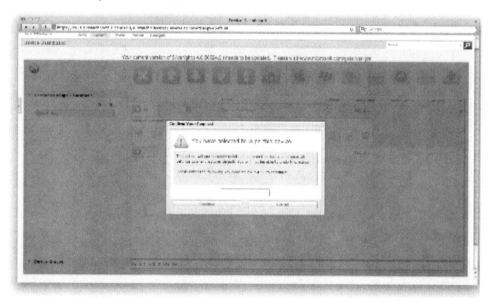

Figure 9–14. *Wiping devices by using AirWatch*

JAMF's Casper Suite

JAMF Software has a number of tools for imaging the Mac OS X platform. Among these are the Recon Suite, for obtaining an inventory of hardware and software assets, and the Casper Suite, a full-featured client management solution for Mac OS X that has been extended to include the management of iOS-based devices. The Casper Suite uses a server, referred to as the JAMF Software Server (JSS), for managing the database of devices, packages, automations, provisioning profiles, applications, and other information that is tracked and leveraged for management and imaging. JAMF also has a tool called the Imaging Suite, which is used for imaging computers, and another called Composer, used to build packages for deployment to the Mac OS X platform. However, neither of these is required for iOS-based devices and so they are not further covered in this chapter.

If you are already using the Casper Suite, the learning curve to start deploying iOS-based devices into your environment will be negligible. Provided you have a Casper Suite installation for a pilot, or have purchased the software and are currently using it on the Mac OS X platform, you can extend the use of your Casper Suite deployment. If you do not have a JSS for a pilot, you can use the MDM-based services on a cloud-based pilot provided from JAMF.

The main tasks to prepare your environment for mass management and deployment of iOS devices if you will be leveraging Casper for enrolling, configuring, managing, and tracking devices includes the following:

- Setting up the JSS to interact with SCEP, LDAP, and other aspects of your environment

- Logically grouping devices

- Creating configuration profiles to associate with devices or groups of devices

- Enrolling devices into Casper

- Adding applications to the catalog

- Managing devices

NOTE: We will look at these main tasks, but as with AirWatch in the previous section of this chapter, the Casper Suite can do much more than the common tasks covered in this section.

If you log into your JAMF Software Server and click the Management tab, you will see a screen similar to that in Figure 9–15.

Figure 9–15. *Using the JSS*

NOTE: Throughout the remainder of this section on the Casper Suite, I will simply refer to this location as *the Management tab*, given that it will be the starting navigation point for several tasks.

The options available for iOS-based systems (deployment and MDM) are listed in the right column, whereas the options available for the Mac OS X platform are listed on the left side of the screen. The Mobile Device Management options include the following:

Mobile Device Profiles: Enables you to create and edit configuration and provisioning profiles

Remote Commands: Enables you to lock screens, remotely wipe devices, and reset passcodes for iOS-based devices

Mobile Device App Catalog: Enables you to define internal applications and applications from the App Store that are then deployed over the air

Over-the-Air Enrollment: Sends invitations for computers to enroll with the server via SMS or e-mail

Smart Mobile Device Groups: Creates dynamic groups based on the contents of fields used in the JSS (for example, version of iOS, user, groups, locations, and so forth)

Static Mobile Device Groups: Creates groups by adding devices into the groups manually

Configuring Global Settings

It is usually best to start with configuring the global settings for the server itself so that you can perform meaningful tests on the devices that you are deploying. This is going to include configuring the JSS to communicate or leverage other services in your network environment. To get started, click the Settings tab at the top of the screen. Then click Mobile Device Management Framework Settings, which provides access to global settings specific to iOS-based device management. You will see options to configure the interval with which devices report to the JSS, the SCEP server, the SSL certificates that are used, how enrollment is handled, global options for self-service, and the URL to be used by devices to access the server.

The Inventory Collection Frequency defines how often the mobile device checks back in with the server. During the check-ins, the device will look to see whether new management profiles need to be applied and whether any settings are out of sync with those on the server. By default, devices will check back in with the JSS every day. To alter this, use the drop-down list in the Request an Inventory Report field (Figure 9–16) to provide a new frequency. At the next interval that the iOS-based devices have cached to check into the JSS, they will then all obtain the new interval and start checking in based on the defined time.

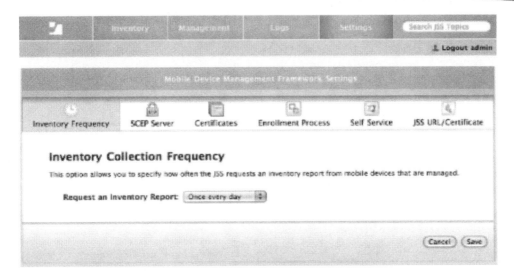

Figure 9–16. *Defining your inventory collection frequency*

As with the other products, you are going to need an instance of an SCEP server. The JSS can look to (and tell mobile devices to look to) any acceptable SCEP server that you have available in your environment. Using the options seen in Figure 9–17, you will define the URL of the SCEP server, the CA, the Subject, the Subject Type, the Challenge, the Key Size, and the Fingerprint string. You will also indicate whether the SCEP-provided certificates are used in digital signatures and whether to encrypt mobile devices. Each of these settings is provided in their corresponding fields and each is going to need to match the values available on your SCEP server.

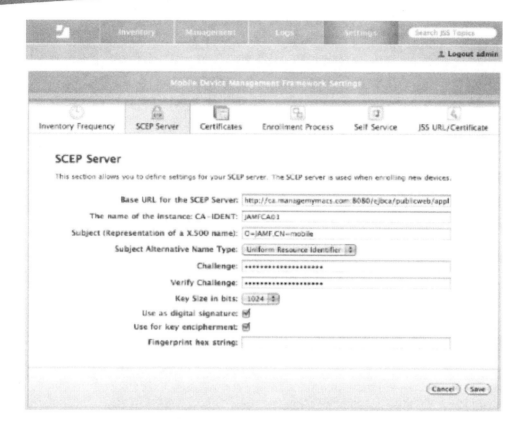

Figure 9–17. *Configuring SCEP on the JSS*

Next, click Certificates and then configure a signing certificate and a Push Notification certificate. You can use an intermediary CA or most other forms of certificate signing. Click the Generate New link (Figure 9–18) to create a new signing certificate and/or the Change button to select a new certificate for Push Notification.

> **NOTE:** Much of the MDM framework from Apple for iOS-based devices is heavily dependent upon certificates, so pay extra attention to the configuration of these.

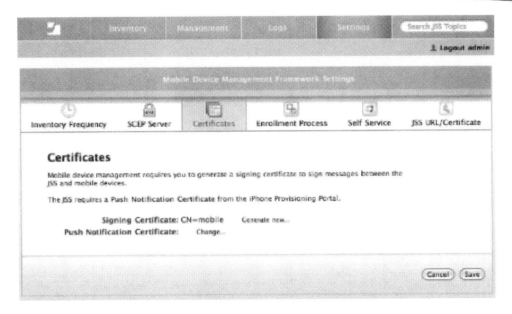

Figure 9–18. *Installing certificates for the JSS*

After you have configured your certificates, click Enrollment Process to configure the settings that apply to the end-user experience of enrolling devices into the server environment. Here, you will first decide whether devices (or accounts on devices) will need to have an invitation to join. If you have a large deployment of currently unmanaged devices and do not have the settings (UDID, and so forth) for them documented, this option is probably going to save you a lot of time while you are remediating the deployment into a managed environment. However, if you are starting off by pushing profiles to all new devices, you likely will not want to use this option. Strategically, you can use the option and then disable it after you have gotten all of the unknown devices input into the server.

The following fields, shown in Figure 9–19, control the look and feel of the enrollment page that the end user is shown:

Login Page Title: Defaults to OTA Enrollment (Over The Air), but you can replace that with the name of your organization.

Login Page Description: Text to instruct the user as to what to do at this page.

Profile Display Name: Text to indicate what the profile is used for (or in many cases from where it came).

Profile Description: Text to display more details, shown in conjunction with the profile description (more on where these appear to users in the upcoming "Enrolling Devices" section).

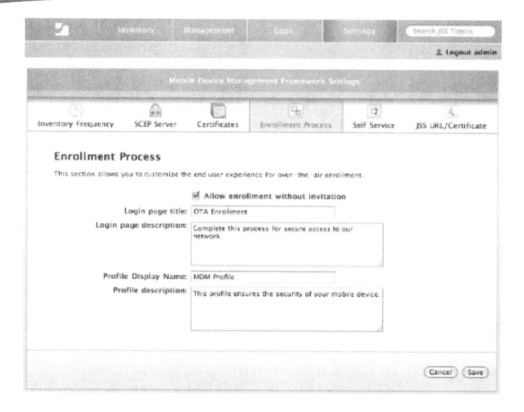

Figure 9–19. *Customizing the enrollment screen and process*

After you have customized how users will see this information, click the Self Service button. Here, as shown in Figure 9–20, you can control whether the self-service portal will be shown on each user's device and whether the Install All button (shown later in Figure 9–41) will be shown to users, thus allowing them to install all recommended software with one click, rather than installing each application separately (definitely recommended if you are pushing out a lot of applications).

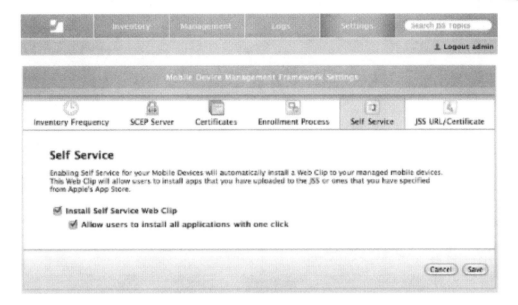

Figure 9–20. *Choosing whether to use self-service*

Finally, click JSS URL/Certificate. Here you specify the URL that the device will use to check back into the JSS (the interval for checking in having been defined previously in the Inventory Frequency section of the Mobile Device Management Framework Settings). You can specify any URL you wish (as you can see in Figure 9–21, the default is the local host name of the system running the JSS), provided that the port and the host name actually point to the JSS. You can also indicate whether the JSS server has been outfitted with a certificate trusted by one of the root certificate authorities included with all new iOS-based devices. This allows you to verify that the communications for JSS-specific traffic are secured while in transit between the JSS and the iOS-based device.

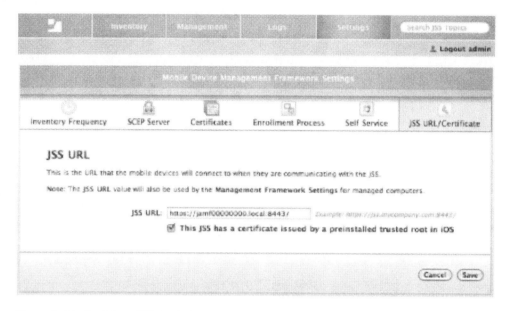

Figure 9–21. *Providing a URL for devices to access the JSS*

Click Save to commit your changes (for each screen) to the Mobile Device Management Framework. After you have configured the global settings for the JSS, you can then move on to starting to configure the more granular options, such as creating smart groups, building profiles, and ultimately enrolling devices.

Creating Configuration Profiles

You can use the iPhone Configuration Utility to build out a configuration profile (or provisioning profile) and then upload it to the JSS. If you use the Casper portal, there is no need to bounce between the iPhone Configuration Utility and the web browser. You can substitute variables and have the username that the user uses to authenticate against the directory service in order to populate fields. For example, in an Exchange server environment you might want to substitute a variable instead of actual usernames. We spent a considerable amount of time in Chapter 8 covering the iPhone Configuration Utility. That time was well spent because JAMF matched its settings to those of the iPhone Configuration Utility, meaning that the options are similar if not identical.

To create a new profile, click the Mobile Device Profiles option under the Management tab. You will see a list of all of the profiles that you have created (Figure 9–22). You can edit and delete those that you have already created. To add a new profile, click the Add Profile button.

Figure 9-22. *Listing mobile device profiles*

You will then see a screen allowing you to create a configuration profile or to upload a configuration or provisioning profile. Select the Create a Configuration Profile button and then click the Continue button, as shown in Figure 9-23.

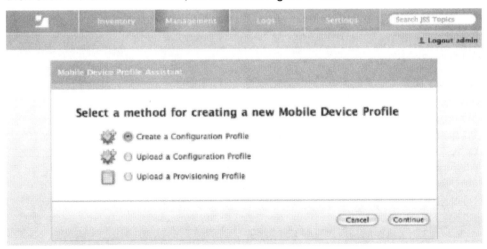

Figure 9-23. *Choosing the type of profile*

At the General tab, you will see a screen similar to the iPhone Configuration Utility. Provide a Display Name for the profile and optionally a description (Figure 9-24). The settings for most of these options are the same as those described in Chapter 8.

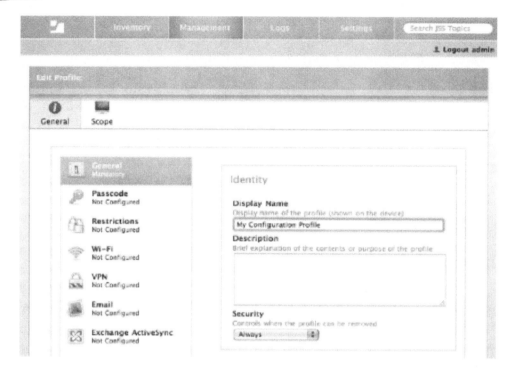

Figure 9–24. *Naming the Profile*

Next, click the Exchange ActiveSync option. You will then see the standard options, again similar to those covered in Chapter 8. But in this case, you have the option to provide a variable rather than the user's actual username. You can use the $USERNAME variable (as seen in Figure 9–25). You can also use the $EMAIL variable for the e-mail address of the user being configured. These options allow you to deploy fully functional settings (for example, fully configured mail accounts) to users over the air without touching devices.

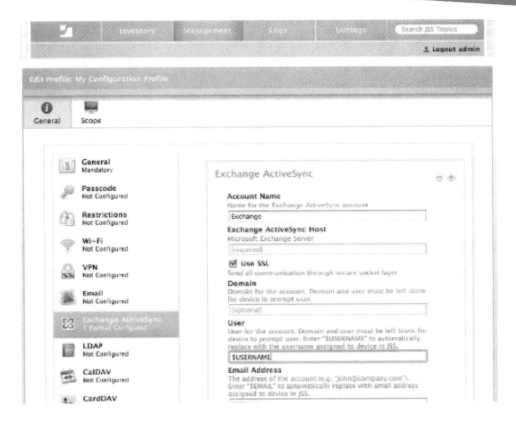

Figure 9–25. *Using variables in configuration profiles*

Enrolling Devices

You can't push anything to a device until you enroll it. Luckily, this is a process similar among all of the vendors who currently inhabit the market for iOS management. To send an invitation from the JSS, log in and click the Management tab. Then click the Mobile Over-the-Air Enrollment link. You will see the Recipients step in the Mobile Device Management Invitation Wizard. As indicated in Figure 9–26, you can choose to send invitations through mail or SMS. If you choose to send through mail, users will need a valid e-mail account already configured on the device in order to accept your invitation, or access to web mail to click the link. This option is usually best in environments where you have devices already deployed and do not have the UDID documented for the device. This option is also necessary for iPod Touch and iPads without a cell plan attached to them. Alternatively, you can use the SMS feature, which is best for large deployments of new devices, when you have the SMS information is accessible for each device.

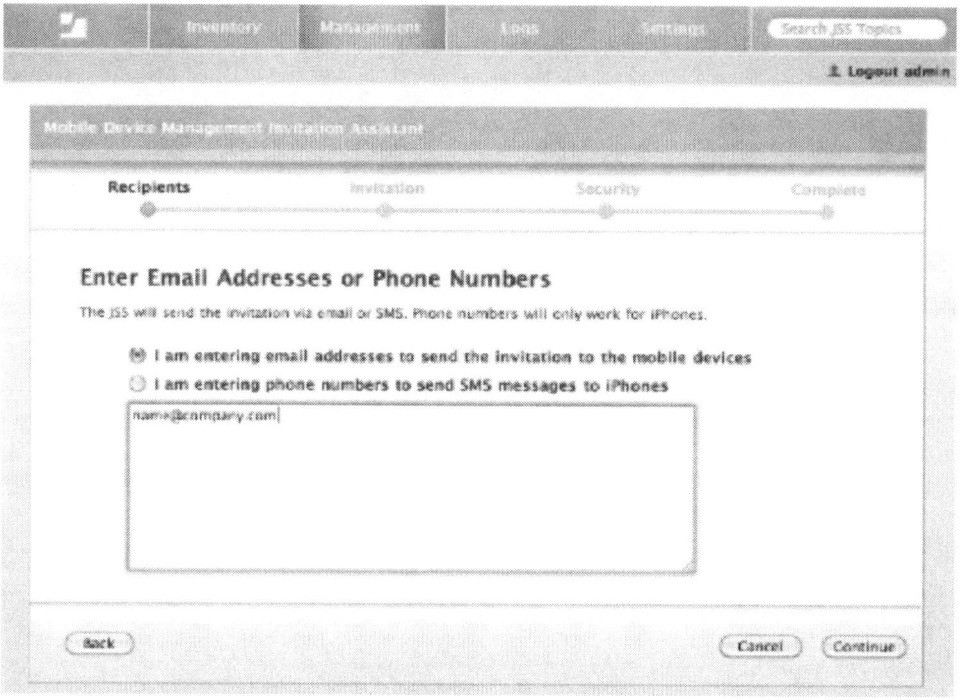

Figure 9–26. *Defining invitation recipients*

After you have provided the e-mail addresses or phone numbers to send SMS messages to, click the Continue button. You will see the Invitation step of the assistant (Figure 9–27). On this screen, you can configure two optional settings: the name the user will see as the message's sender and the Reply-To information, indicating the address two which a response will be sent. You can also indicate the Subject of the message and write the body of the message itself (note the inclusion of the %@ variable in the body that expands into the link to tap for enrollment). The body can be a useful place to store instructions, explain why you are sending the message, and indicate under whose authority the enrollment is being performed.

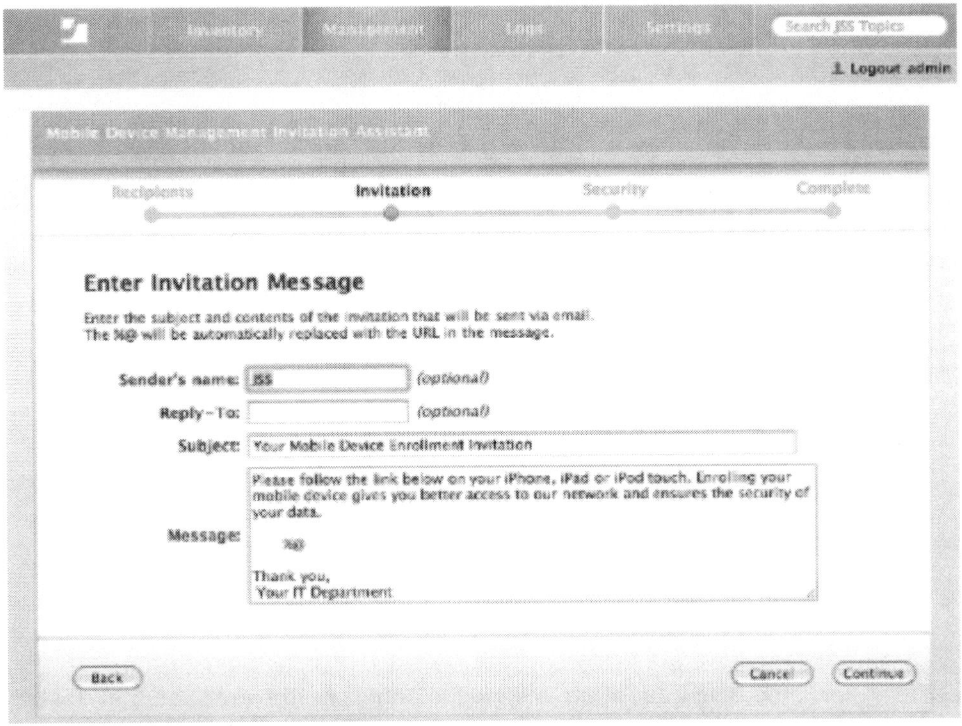

Figure 9–27. *Crafting the invitation communication*

When you are satisfied with your invitation customizations, click the Continue button. You will then set security options for the invitation you are about to send out. As Figure 9–28 shows, you can configure the expiration date and time, indicate whether the user must authenticate by using a known good password (that is, from Active Directory or Open Directory), and set whether a single invitation can be used on multiple devices. The Allow Multiple Uses of Invitations option allows an organization to provide users with iPad, iPod Touch, and iPhones with one e-mail that the users can then use on multiple devices. If your users do not have more than one device, then, for security purposes, it is recommended to disable this option.

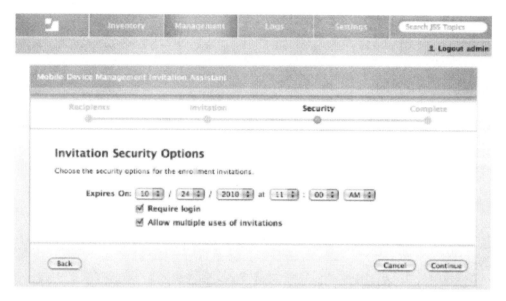

Figure 9–28. *Securing the option to enroll*

When you are finished customizing the security options for your invitation, click
Continue. At the final step of the assistant, review the details of the message that will be
sent out, which can be seen in Figure 9–29. Then click the Send button and select a
device to verify that the invitation was delivered.

Figure 9–29. *Sending the invitations to enroll*

On the iOS-based devices, you should then see an e-mail with the link. Tapping the link takes you to the OTA Enrollment page, where you provide the username and password for the LDAP environment, as indicated in Figure 9–30.

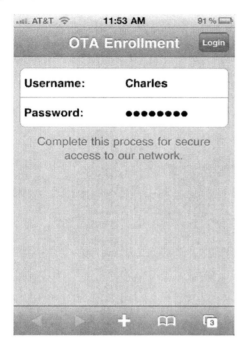

Figure 9–30. *Authenticating for enrollment*

Enter that information and then tap the Login button to be taken to the MDM profile installation page (Figure 9–31). You will see a customizable page that tells the user how to install the profile (which can be done by tapping the Install Profile button).

NOTE: This page can be customized by using the global settings, as explained in the "Configuring Global Settings" section earlier in this chapter.

Figure 9–31. *Enrolling devices*

The device is then enrolled into the server, having the MDM profile installed. That profile allows the MDM agent to communicate back to the server.

After you have enrolled a few devices, you will find that you need to manage them. The best way to do this en masse is through groups. At the Management tab, you can create what are known as *static groups* and *smart groups*. Smart groups are dynamically generated based on attributes (criteria) for the device, the location of the device, and the purchasing information pertaining to the device (for example, a warranty expiring within 30 days). Static groups require you to explicitly add a device to the group.

To create groups, from the Management tab click Smart Mobile Device Groups or Static Mobile Device Groups. Click the plus sign (+) to add new groups. If you are adding a smart group, you will see a screen similar to Figure 9–32, where you can specify more criteria for grouping devices that update dynamically.

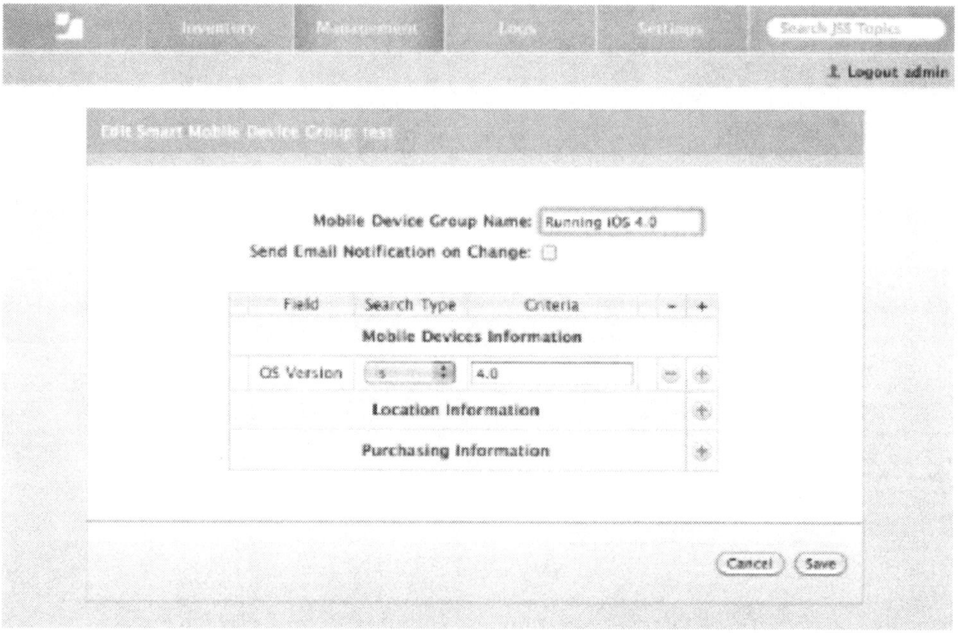

Figure 9–32. *Selection criteria for smart groups*

NOTE: You can import devices from a CSV file by using code available through the resource kit from JAMF.

Managing Devices

After your devices have been enrolled into the JSS, you can then send commands to them to perform specific tasks. At the time of this writing, three main commands are available: remote wipe, remote passcode reset, and remote lock (which locks a device until a specified passcode is entered). Because you are telling a device that is remote to do something immediately (run a command), these are referred to as *remote commands*.

To access the remote commands, start at the Management tab and then click Remote Commands. On the Remote Commands screen, you will see the option for each of the aforementioned commands that can be run (Figure 9–33).

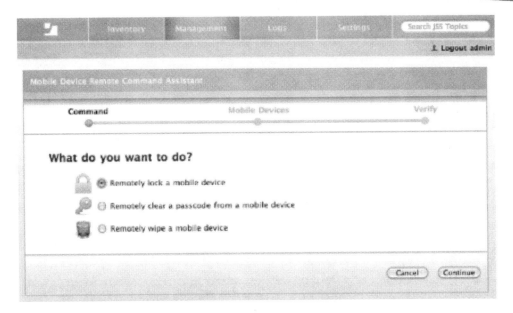

Figure 9–33. *Choosing a security command*

Click the option for the command you would like to run and then click the Continue button. You are then prompted to provide the device name, as shown in Figure 9–34. You can enter the name in one of three ways: begin typing the device name and then select from a list of devices that match what you are typing, type the full name, or click the Browse Mobile Devices button for a list of devices from which to select.

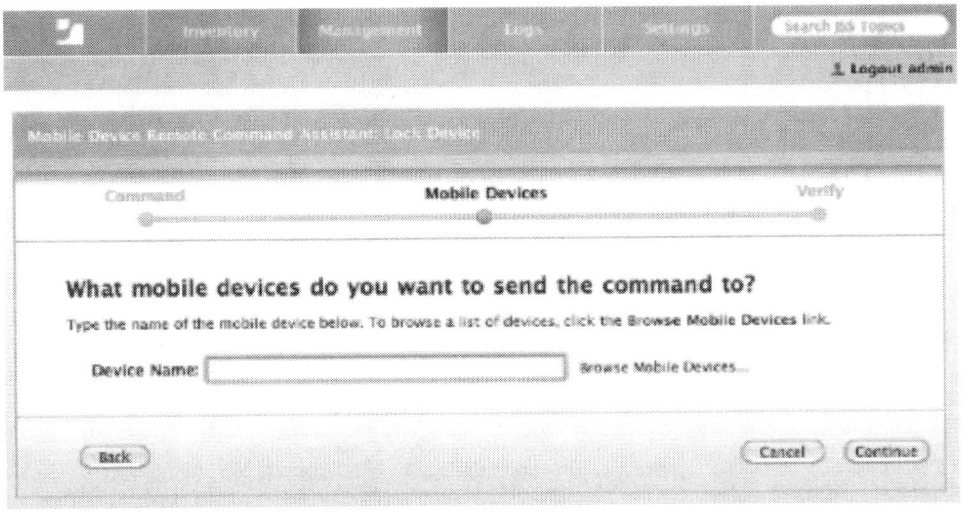

Figure 9–34. *Choosing a device to wipe (Choose carefully!)*

After you have selected the device to perform the action on, click the Continue button and verify that you would like to perform the remote command. These remote commands enable you to keep the devices secure and under your organization's control. As you saw in Chapter 4, your users can also remotely wipe a device by using Microsoft Exchange or Find My iPhone (for MobileMe users), but this provides a way for the administrator to perform these same tasks from a centralized location.

Adding Applications to the Catalog

The JAMF Software Server can also be used to deploy applications to the device. You cannot at this time push an application to the device by using the MDM APIs for iOS. However, you can provide what can be considered a private App Store. The Casper Suite does this through what is known as an App Catalog. To use the feature, you will add applications into the App Catalog on the JSS and then use the Self Service portal to install them from the device.

To add an application to the App Catalog, go to the Management tab and then click the link for Mobile Device App Catalog. The catalog is shown in Figure 9–35. From here, you will see a list of the applications in the App catalog, and you can Edit them (for example, change the icon or update the application to a new IPA file) or Delete them (that is, remove them from the Self Service portal).

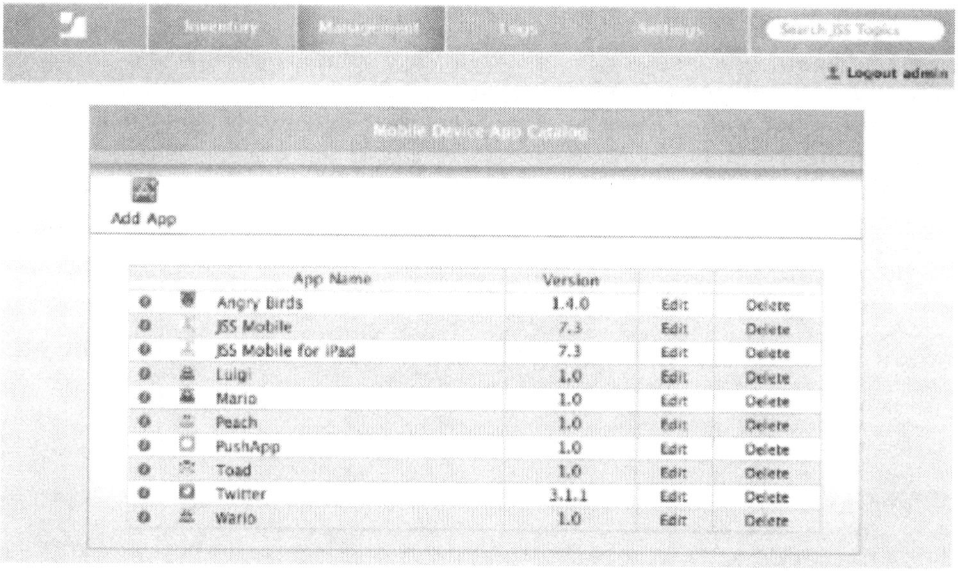

Figure 9–35. *The App Device Catalog*

Click the Add App icon to start the process of adding a New Mobile Device App (using the appropriately named New Mobile Device App screen shown in Figure 9–36). The Mobile Device App can be an application from the Apple App Store or a compiled application from Xcode in the form of an IPA file (using the Build and Archive option). For this example, we will use an internally built app (thus a compiled Xcode project).

Provided that you have a project (see Chapter 7 for more information on building projects), click Upload Internally Built App and then click Continue.

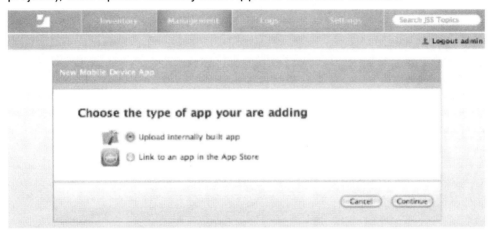

Figure 9–36. *Adding applications to the catalog*

You will then see options for the application being installed. The Edit Mobile Device App screen (Figure 9–37) has each of the options. Fill in the following fields:

App Name: The name that the application will have after it is installed on the device.

Bundle ID: Can match the bundle ID of the application from the Xcode project.

Version: This is a text field you provide that is not linked to the Xcode project.

Description: A text description to be shown to the user, explaining what the application is for.

Icon: The icon that will be used on the screen of the iOS device to access the application.

App Archive File: The IPA archive file from Xcode.

Provisioning Profile: The profile to which the application is attached.

Figure 9–37. *Providing application information for internally built apps*

After you are satisfied with your options, click the Save button. You can then click the Scope icon to assign which groups will be allowed to access, and therefore install, the application.

If you instead are providing an application from Apple's App Store, you will have the option to add that by choosing the Link to an App in the App Store option. This is akin to a list of recommended (and therefore, approved) applications. At the Add App from App Store screen, you provide a name for the application being added to the catalog and indicate the country where the application's App Store is located (Figure 9–38).

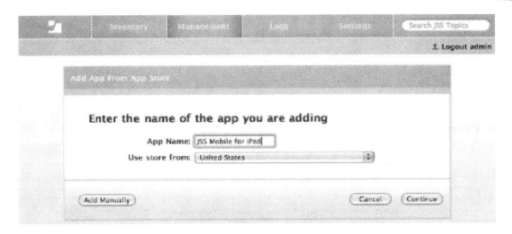

Figure 9–38. *Finding the app store application to add*

Click the Continue button to search for the application in question. You will see a Search Results page with each item that matched your search, as shown in Figure 9–39. You can then view the page of the application to make sure it is the one you are looking for, or simply click the Add button to add it.

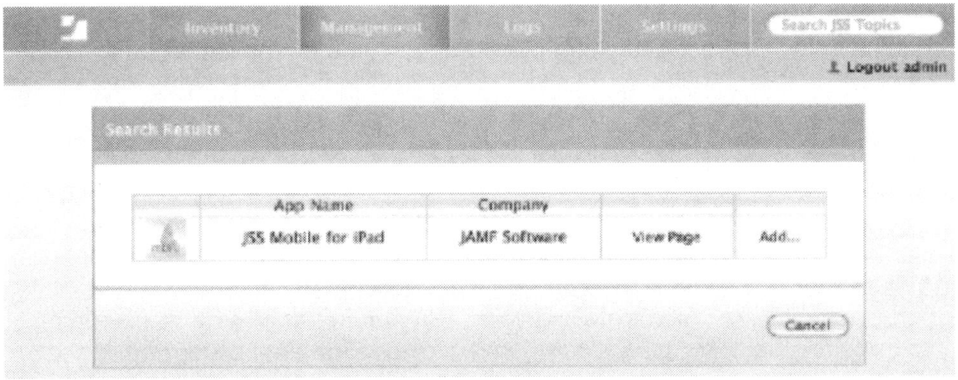

Figure 9–39. *Search results from Apple's App Store*

After you click on the Add button, you will see another rendition of the Edit Mobile Device App screen. However, as shown in Figure 9–40, this one shows only the URL used to access the application. (This URL can be obtained manually from iTunes by right-clicking or Control+clicking an application and then clicking Copy Link). The name the application shows on the iOS screen, the version number, and the icon can be changed here, and the scope options are similar to those from internally built applications. When you are satisfied with your options, click Save to publish the application to the groups defined in the Scope section for the application.

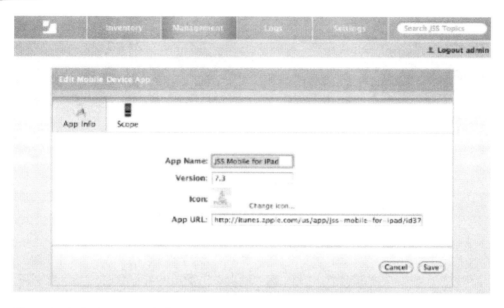

Figure 9–40. *Setting up the Mobile Device App for App Store URLs*

Applications can then be accessed by using the Self Service option (via the Self Service web clip enabled in the Global Settings) deployed at enrollment time (if that option was selected).

Providing Self-Service

One of the more complicated tasks facing systems administrators looking to mass deploy to iOS is how to push out applications. In the last major release of the Casper Suite, JAMF took the idea of the App Store and made a self-servicing portal for Mac OS X. Through this portal, users could install software without an administrative username and password on the user's Mac OS X computer, provided the application was in the organization's self-service portal, a repository of software that was approved by the organization. In Casper 8.0, JAMF has added this same feature for the iPhone, which addresses many of the challenges for deploying applications to iOS-based devices that have been discussed throughout this book.

When a device has been enrolled into the JAMF Software Server environment, you will see an application on the iOS-based device called Self Service. Tapping Self Service shows the users a list of software that is approved and/or recommended by the software administrator, as shown in Figure 9–41. The users can then tap each application and install the ones they wish to have, or they can tap the Install All button to install all of the software titles concurrently. The applications are divided into three categories along the bottom of the screen, with new Internal Apps, App Store Apps and Updates (from left to right). Internal Apps being applications distributed only within your organization, App Store Apps being links to applications hosted on Apple's App Store and Updates being applications that have updates available to them on either.

Figure 9–41. *Internal apps in Self Service*

The ability to install software through a portal is a great feature for any environment, but the ability to install all of the apps concurrently is a must for environments with multiple apps being distributed to all of your devices.

KACE Appliances

The KACE Deployment and Management appliances, from Dell, can be leveraged to provide centralized configuration management of the iPhone and iPod Touch. KACE appliances can be leveraged to provision, configure, and control policies with more granularity than can be found with the iPhone Configuration Utility. For example, you can leverage groups with your policies, monitor utilization and application installations, and track plans and renewals for wireless contracts for the iPhone (Figure 9–42). You can also use KACE appliances for the following:

- Performing iPhone configuration profile management
- Assigning profiles to user groups—for example, by function or geography
- Distributing profiles by e-mail
- Downloading profiles available from the K1000 or K2000 user portal
- Enabling iPhone user access to the K1000 or K2000 user portal

- Tracking and reporting iPhone asset information

- Tracking individual iPhone information

- Tracking the number of iPhone users

- Tracking iPhone equipment versions

- Tracking assigned serial numbers, including IMEI and ICCID identifiers

- Monitoring installed applications

- Allowing access to corresponding contracts

- Tracking individual plans and renewal dates

- Keeping asset data current via scheduled iPhone K-script refresh

- Delivering e-mail alerts based on changes in the asset fields

- Tracking related dependencies, that is, carrier contracts and associated renewal dates

More on KACE appliances and the ability to manage iPhone and iPod touch can be found at http://www.kace.com/products/systems-management-appliance/features/iphone-management.php

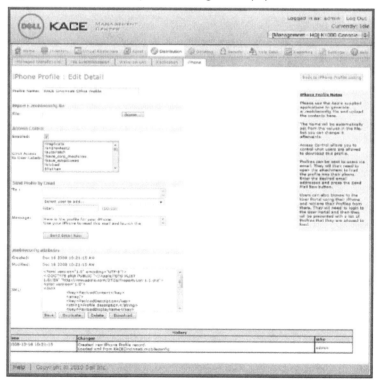

Figure 9–42. *The KACE Management Center*

NOTE: KACE was recently acquired by Dell Computers.

MobileIron

MobileIron provides another solution, similar to other deployment tools. MobileIron for iOS includes a corresponding iPhone application, available from the App Store. You can see how the MobileIron application appears to end users in Figure 9–43. With MobileIron, you can leverage a catalog of recommended applications that users are able to download through the App Store, similar to the Self Service tool from the Casper Suite. Because MobileIron uses an installed agent on the device (Figure 9–43), it is also able to track dropped calls and track locations of devices, which could be used for breadcrumb mapping, or tracking the devices movements based on GPS coordinates.

Figure 9–43. *MobileIron at work*

NOTE: MobileIron can also test the connection speed of an iOS-based device.

As one of the early developers of tools for the mass management of the iOS market, MobileIron has also released a tool called MobileIron Sentry for iPad. Sentry uses the iPad to provide IT with visibility and control over various aspects of ActiveSync in your Exchange environment. Using Sentry (Figure 9–44), you can see statistics about your mobile deployment via an easy-to-read dashboard, helpful when tracking the health of your environment.

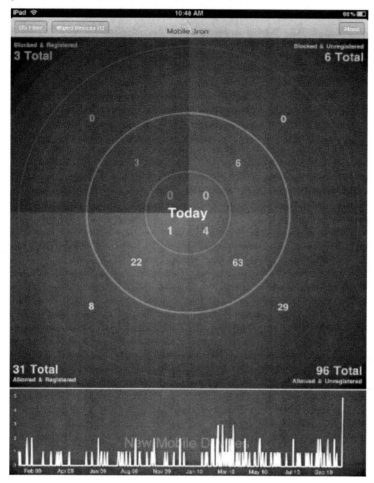

Figure 9–44. *MobileIron's Sentry*

Sybase Afaria

Many an enterprise has been using Sybase products for decades. That trust of the popular Sybase database engine seems to extend into the capabilities to manage numerous mobile devices by using a single, unified console in their product Afaria. Among the supported platforms that Afaria can manage is the iPhone.

As with many solutions that support numerous platforms, Afaria does not have a lot of specialty features for the iPhone. Instead it has a very legitimate presence in the market and a host of other products from Sybase, including Mobile Sales and iAnywhere Mobile Office for the iPhone, that provide a more comprehensive suite of products than just management en masse. Afaria includes support for most of the basic functions of MobileIron, TARMAC, and others with added support for features meant to specifically reduce support needs of mobile device users, such as resetting passwords (Figure 9–45), enrolling new previously unknown devices, and so forth.

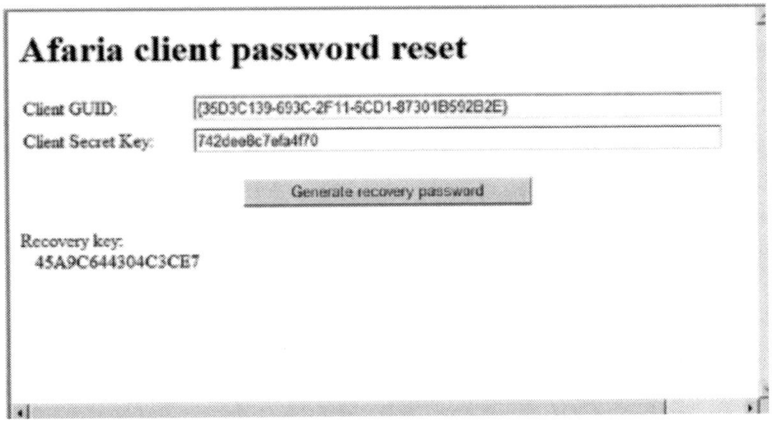

Figure 9–45. *Resetting a password with Afaria*

TARMAC

The final tool that I will reference for deployment of iOS-based devices is TARMAC. TARMAC configuration is done within the TARMAC web portal (Figure 9–46). Here you can import profiles, associate profiles with devices, integrate with your organization's directory services, and push out patch management policies.

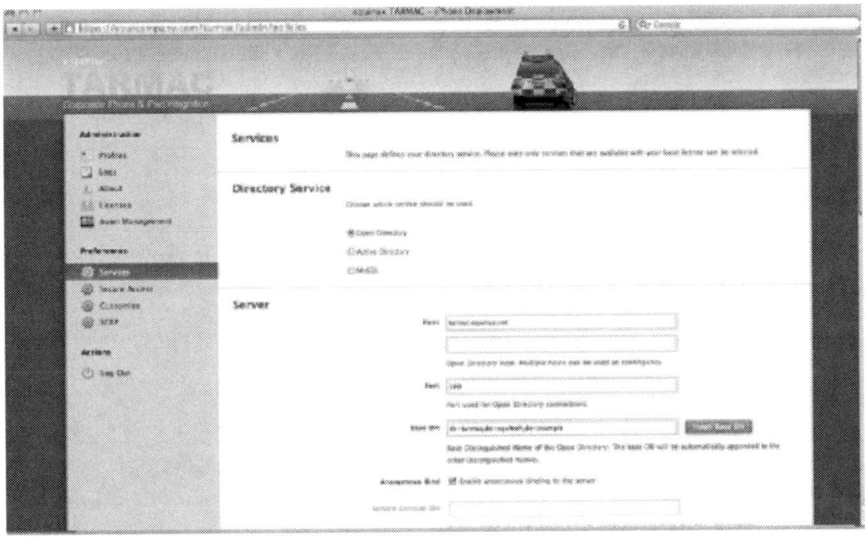

Figure 9–46. *Configuring TARMAC*

After the server has been properly configured, TARMAC then allows a device to authenticate to a web portal, which generates the configuration for the specified user at the time of login. TARMAC is one of the easier solutions available, following very closely along Apple's example code that was referenced in the beginning of this chapter.

Removing the Profiles

During all of this testing, there's a good chance that you may have installed a whole slew of profiles on your device that you will want to get rid of. Or if a device is leaving the management environment of your organization, you may want to remove the MDM, configuration, or provisioning profiles you deployed to the devices. Therefore, you will eventually want to remove a profile.

Profiles can be removed quickly and easily on your device in most cases without a reset. To delete a profile, first open the Settings application on the iOS-based device. Then tap General Settings and then Profiles. You will see a list of all of the profiles that have been installed on the device (Figure 9–47).

Figure 9–47. *Installed profiles*

Tap on a profile to see the Details, which will show the rights that the profile has when managing the device (Figure 9–48).

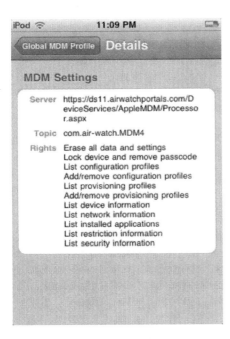

Figure 9–48. *Showing profile permissions*

To remove the profile, tap the Remove button on the Profile screen. You will then see a screen requiring you to confirm the removal of the profile, as shown in Figure 9–49. Click Remove to complete the process.

Figure 9–49. *Removing the Profile*

After the profile is removed, the device can no longer be managed with MDM policies deployed from the server. Practically any third-party product that can push a profile to a device can also revoke it, so you can also centrally remove these MDM policies.

Summary

One of the most critical aspects of mass integration of iOS in my organizations is the act of actually deploying profiles. Starting with the profiles created in Chapter 8, and using the tools and techniques in this chapter, we have laid out a framework that can be used to deploy hundreds or even tens of thousands of devices.

Most organizations that are going to deploy iOS-based devices en masse will need a strategy for automated deployment. To aid you in your endeavor, there are several competing products, many of which are fairly new to the market. Whether you think that AirWatch, the Casper Suite, KACE, MobileIron, or TARMAC are for you after reading this chapter, you should make sure to test each, reviewing their impact to the budget of your project and the features that you get as a return for that investment. Once you have found a product that meets your criteria for deployment, the rest of the pieces will start to fall in place.

Now that you've looked at many of the technical hurdles that you are likely to face in the first nine chapters of this book, we're going to move on to something a little more fun. In a look at many of the more enterprise-oriented applications available today for the iOS-based devices (Chapter 10), we will look at the true goal of any device in most environments: productivity.

Leveraging Third-Party Solutions for Productivity

The modern operating system comes with a lot of features that often go unnoticed. These range from calculators to text editing tools, to clients for logging onto file servers, to games to help while away the time, while you're waiting for that flight. But iOS is meant to be simple. As such, it doesn't come with a lot of applications, by default.

Thus far, we have looked at using the iPhone or iPad from an infrastructure standpoint. This has included how to plan for, use, mass deploy, and integrate iOS-based devices into existing infrastructure. In Chapter 7, we even looked at custom application development. In this chapter, we will turn our attention to applications geared for enhancing productivity using the devices.

Need to find a place to crash for the night? There's an app for that (couchsurfer, from David van Dugteren). Need to find a parking spot? There's an app for that (Find Parking, from Edward Tsang). In fact, to be more specific, want to find a WalMart to park in overnight? Well, there's an app for that, too (iExit Walmart Overnight Parking). But these applications don't do much for your organization, do they (we hope you don't tell your mobile workforce to crash on couches while they travel the globe)? Instead, many of the applications you find out there are games, for personal use, or involve off-color humor of one sort or another.

If your enterprise has a specific need and a strategy around that need, though, there are likely a number of resources at your disposal. If an application already exists, then there is no reason to build a custom application in many cases (unless, of course, it turns out to be dysfunctional with your workflow). For example, if you need an application to help keep mobile workers apprised of what is in your warehouses, then there's an app for that. Look at Inventory for iPad, from WahSoft LLC. If you need mobile workers to be able to manage the whole warehouse, then look to Warehouse Management, from Allessandro Busso. In both of these cases, there is little to no reason for most to write an application, especially during the pilot phase of a deployment.

In this chapter, we are going to look at some applications geared toward productivity and a few that have some entertainment value as well. However, there is a lot of fluidity in publicly available applications. They come and go, and traditionally we try not to write about things that are in such constant flux. But then, it doesn't seem as though a book about the iOS would be complete without a survey of pertinent apps, which can be found simply by searching the App Store.

The App Store

The App Store is where users can purchase and/or download applications for their iOS-based device. Application development can be a fairly complicated task. If you are looking for a specific function outside of the default software, it's never a bad idea to see if such a tool is already on the market before committing development resources to the task. The App Store should be the first place you look. To access the App Store, open iTunes and click the iTunes Store listing under STORE. Then click the link for App Store, shown in Figure 10–1.

Figure 10–1. *The iTunes App Store*

As you can see in Figure 10–1, you will now be able to browse, buy, and download applications. The disclosure triangle that appears beside the App Store icon when you hover over it can be used to narrow down a search for categories. As of the writing of this book, there are 2,840 apps for the Business category, nearly 3,700 for the Productivity category, and over 2,000 for the Finance category. This represents over

8,500 applications that could have some impact on your organization. This impact can range from keeping apprised of the performance of your stock options (Figure 10–2) to collaborating with your peers using your organization's messaging platform.

Figure 10–2. *Stocks*

Integrating GroupWise

Not all organizations have the technology for interfacing with their groupware solutions like Microsoft has (see Chapter 4 for more information on deploying Exchange accounts). There is no built-in support for GroupWise on the iPhone. Apple supports a number of other services, but GroupWise has not been high on the priority list, and given its market share, you might not want to hold your breath for a GroupWise client. Having said that, there are several ways to integrate GroupWise.

The first is to buy an application that can be used to interface with GroupWise. This involves using applications such as GW Mail, GW Calendar, and GW Web. These third-party applications, from Ghost Pattern Software, will allow you to use GroupWise, while fixing some of the more common complaints that users have when browsing the site in Mobile Safari. John Nelson's unWise does the same thing, but neither solves the problem of getting data while not on the Internet.

The second and third options are outsourced services that just handle everything for you. Of these, GroupWise Sync is a great option (they have a free version that just grabs mail or pay-per-month for contacts and calendars) as is the monthly version of the CompanionLink GroupWise sync. CompanionLink has a separate desktop client, but much of what it does can be obtained by using GroupWise 6.5 along with Office 2003 and iTunes to synchronize contacts and calendars while cradled.

Security Applications

There are a number of applications available to provide a more secure iOS-based device. More importantly, there are also a lot of promising applications that have not yet been made useful or actually developed. Applications such as Finger Scan Protector, from Li Pu, and Face Recognition Security, from William Sidell, can even make you think that the devices support fingerprint scanning and face recognition. But what you can do is further encrypt data, extend the use of multi-factor authentication mechanisms such as RSA tokens, and even turn your iOS-based device into a security system to guard your hotel room while you're out to dinner.

An emerging standard for security is the VeriSign Identity Protection, or VIP program. VIP generates one-time passwords that change in timed intervals. Verisign has an iPhone application for accessing this information in VIP Access, which can be seen in Figure 10–3.

Figure 10–3. *VIP Access from VeriSign*

For more on the VIP program, visit http://www.verisign.com/authentication/two-factor-authentication/index.html.

RSA

If your users are tired of carrying around that RSA SecurID token thingy from 1994, all beige and chewed on routinely by kids and dogs alike, then RSA now has an app for that. Using the SecurID token, you can have the exact same functionality using the iPhone that you would otherwise have to use a keychain dongle for. If you're like me and have been trying to reduce the items you carry on your person for a long time, this is a fantastic option (Figure 10–4). In a way, RSA is just helping to make a case for using an iPhone in highly secured Enterprise environments (not that they're not helping to make the same case with their Blackberry version of a SecurID application).

Figure 10–4. *Configuring RSA tokens*

The application is free, but your organization will have likely already purchased a seed that costs much more than an iPhone application does. Tokens will need some conversion, and then users will need to click a link to install them,

Good for Enterprise

Using the options discussed in Chapter 6, you can configure an iPhone for connecting to an Exchange environment. You can also remotely wipe the devices if they go missing or if you release an employee. However, what if you don't own the devices? Or, what if you want all of your corporate data secured on the devices? In these cases, you might want to look at Good Enterprise for the iPhone.

Good Enterprise allows you to encrypt the groupware data that is owned by your organization but stored on these distributed devices. If the user of the device then leaves your organization, you can wipe the data that is owned by the organization without impacting the user's ability to access the data that they own. The application appears very similar to the suite of Apple applications, as you can see in Figure 10–5; however, all of the data is stored on an encrypted disk image, making it easily wiped and secured.

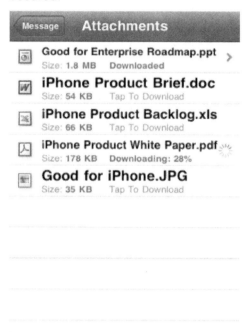

Figure 10–5. *Good Enterprise attachment handling*

Managing Thin Clients

Keeping up with the changing needs of managing a fleet of client computers can be daunting. Managing application updates on a large number of systems, replacing hardware routinely, and securing each system en masse are all part of this equation. Additionally, sometimes you just need to control the screen or look at what an end user is doing on a client computer. For all of these reasons, practically every environment leverages some form of a thin client.

Uses for thin clients range widely. Many environments publish specific applications with Citrix or allow specified users to access an entire Windows session with Microsoft's Terminal Server (using Microsoft's RDP protocol). Other environments use thin client solutions like VNC to control Mac, Windows, or Linux systems. Still others leverage thin clients to allow for remote workers to control their desktop computers or KVM

(Keyboard Video Mouse) switches from home. Among these, the most scalable and centrally managed that we've seen in the wild seems to be Citrix.

Citrix

Custom application development, whether for web portals or for Objective-C and thus native to the iPhone and iPod touch, can result in delays in getting applications to market. If you do not need to access your application while the device is offline, and you already have a Citrix infrastructure in place, then it is possible to leverage the Citrix client for the iPhone and iPod touch to deploy an application store of your own (of sorts). Using the Citrix Receiver application, from Citrix you can access any application that has been published from Citrix's XenApp.

To download the Citrix client for the iPhone and iPod touch, first open iTunes and tap the link for the App Store. Alternatively you can go directly there using the following URL: `http://itunes.apple.com/WebObjects/MZStore.woa/wa/viewSoftware?id=313735334&mt=8`. Once you have downloaded the application, install it on the iPhone or iPod touch and then look for the Citrix application in your list of available applications. When Citrix is first opened, it will prompt you for connection information (Figure 10–6):

- *Description*: Text on what the connection is for.

- *Address*: The host name or IP address of the server you will be logging into.

- *User Name*: The user account that you will be using on the server.

- *Password*: The password for the user logging in.

- *Domain*: The Active Directory domain name on the server.

- *Access Gateway*: Tapping here opens a new screen with the following settings.

  - *Sign in Automatically*: Choose whether to log into the server automatically.

  - *Gateway Type*: Only Standard Edition is supported as of the writing of this book.

  - *Gateway Authentication*: Allows you to select No Authentication, Domain Only, RSA SecurID Only, or Domain + RSA SecurID authentication.

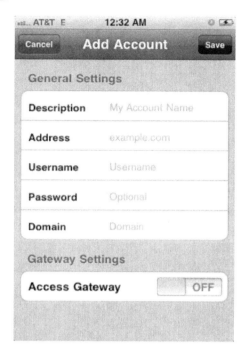

Figure 10–6. *Citrix configuration options*

Once you have selected the appropriate settings, tap Next and the device will attempt to authenticate into your Citrix environment. Citrix has published a fair amount of information regarding iPhone support, and will likely continue to publish more as time goes on and the product matures, at `http://community.citrix.com/iphone`.

NOTE: The negative of deploying applications through Citrix to iPhone and iPod touch devices is that the application will require a constant Internet connection and will not be useful to the end user while he or she is not online—for example, when on an airplane.

Remote Desktop

In addition to the Citrix client, there are a few applications available that will allow you to access standard RDP-based sessions being published from Windows (or AquaConnect for that matter). There are a number of these available as of the time of this writing. These include the following:

- *Jaadu Remote Desktop*: Allows access to most versions of Windows (or at least those that support Remote Desktop). `http://itunes.apple.com/WebObjects/MZStore.woa/wa/viewSoftware?id=299002339&mt=8`

- *Remote Desktop*: Allows access to Windows XP.

- http://itunes.apple.com/WebObjects/MZStore.woa/wa/viewSoft
  ware?id=288362053&mt=8

- *Jaadu VNC*: Allows remote access to Mac and Windows PCs via the
  VNC protocol.

  - http://itunes.apple.com/WebObjects/MZStore.woa/wa/viewSoft
    ware?id=288362053&mt=8

- *Wyse PocketCloud*: Available for iPhone and iPad, and comes with a
  mobile file browser and remote viewing of video.

- http://itunes.apple.com/us/app/wyse-pocketcloud-remote-
  desktop/id326512817?mt=8

- *iTap RDP*: Allows connections to terminal services and remote
  desktop. Available for both iPhone and iPad (Figure 10–7).
  http://itunes.apple.com/us/app/itap-rdp-remote-desktop-
  for/id317062064?mt=8

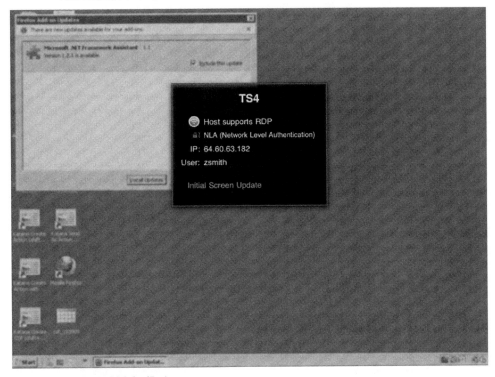

Figure 10–7. *iTap's RDP for iPad*

VNC

Remote Desktop is useful for communicating with Windows computers and servers, but not functional for Mac OS X, Unix, and Linux clients. Therefore, VNC, or Virtual Network Computing is where you will want to turn. The VNC clients come with many options that allow for more granular configurations than the existing rdp applications, as you can see in Figure 10–8.

There are a number of clients available, but one of the more mature is called Mocha VNC, from Jan Frydendal. A quick search of the App Store will net a number of other applications, each with its own set of options compared to price point.

Figure 10–8. *Mocha VNC, from Jan Frydendal*

Contact Management Options

One of the hardest things for any organization to do well is communication. Nowhere is this more true than the modern enterprise; often made up of tens of thousands of employees, it seems rare that disparate groups within an enterprise are able to keep abreast of the goings-on within the organization. In few areas is this more critical than in managing contacts outside of the organization.

CRM, or Customer Relationship Management (or one of the numerous offshoots over the past few years) is the modern answer to managing contacts. If your organization has already invested in SalesForce.com or another solution for CRM, then you will likely want your mobile strategy (as with most aspects of IT) to simply be an extension of your desktop strategy. If you are using SalesForce.com, you will be happy to note that there is a free application on the App Store from SalesForce.com that can allow subscribers to tap into your existing customer data. Many other solutions will also provide an application, so search the App Store and touch base with your vendor before you devise a strategy that does not align itself with the IT vision of CRM.

There are also some gaps that mobile devices can step in to manage. Being a mobile device, you'll find it useful that you can capture those business cards and use OCR (Optical Character Recognition) to import contact information directly into the Address Book application in iOS. The following applications can perform such a task (most are similar in use and functionality):

- iCardManager-HD, from SI Agency

- CardMunch, from CardMunch, Inc.

- CamCard, from IntSig Information Co. Ltd., shown in Figure 10–9

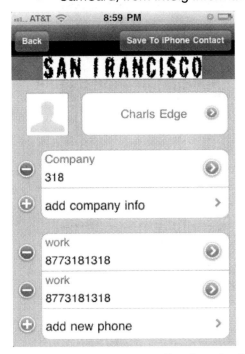

Figure 10–9. *CamCard, from IntSig Information Co. Ltd.*

Tools for Public Speakers

Public speaking is hard for many. Being prepared makes a huge difference, both in giving confidence and showing attendees that you care enough not to waste their time. Technology has been changing the way we give presentations for a number of years, and the iPhone, iPod Touch, and iPad are taking that a step further.

Keynote

Those who have used the Keynote application that is included in iWork on Mac OS X will note that the application for the iPad is very similar. You can create brilliant presentations on your iPad. Sure, when you get ready to do complicated transitions, you will want to move to the desktop application, but writing a standard presentation is straightforward from the iPad, given its mature and flexible Keynote application, from Apple. A sampling of the template presentations (Themes) can be seen in Figure 10–10.

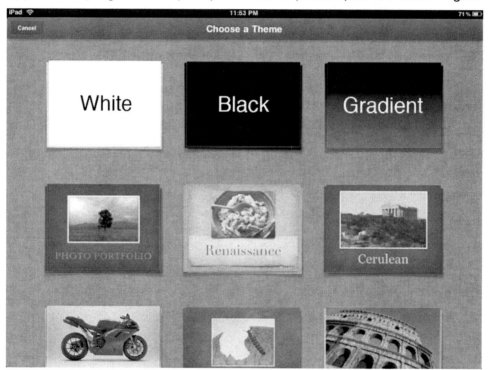

Figure 10–10. *Keynote, from Apple*

Once you have built a slide deck in Keynote, you can then play it straight from the iPad or copy the presentation to a computer and play it from there. If you are playing the presentation on a desktop computer, one of the best tools available is Keynote Remote, also from Apple. Keynote Remote, which is shown in Figure 10–11, allows you to view (and preview) slides and move to the next slide, thus replacing yet another piece of equipment in your arsenal of presentation toys that you need to travel with, the remote control.

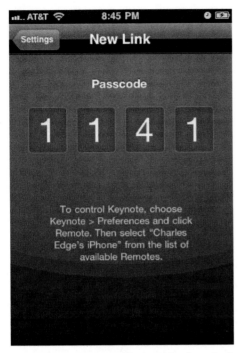

Figure 10–11. *Keynote Remote, also from Apple*

Teleprompters

Public speaking isn't just about a good slide deck, though. You still have to say the words that go along with the slides, something mastered by many a politician. Those politicians will have nothing on you once you start using a teleprompter on your mobile device. Speaking in front of an audience is hard enough, but trying to remember everything on your presentation is just too much. There are a few teleprompter applications that have been developed for iOS:

- Prompterous is a tool that is used to convert an iPad into a teleprompter. Using Prompterous, you put text into the application and it plays the text as you see text on a teleprompter. Prompterous is a simple application that does one task, and does it well.

- i-Prompt (Figure 10–12), from Greenality Limited, is a free application with many of the same features.

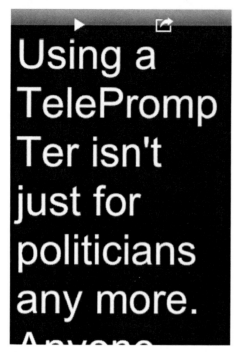

Figure 10–12. *i-Prompt, from Greenality Limited*

Bridging the Gap

The line between personal lives and work lives becomes ever so slimmer year by year. Long gone are the days that you got off work and drove home to your house in the suburbs, not thinking about work until the next morning. These days, we take our work home with us, we check our e-mail on practically a 24 by 7 schedule, we stay later in the office, and we are more connected than ever. But we don't just bring our work home with us. We bring our home to the office too!

NetFlix

These days it seems like many are travelling more than ever. And rather than spend $10 or $20 per night when staying in a hotel room, the iPad can be used to manage your NetFlix queue as can a number of applications developed by other entities. Not only can you manage your queue, though, you can now watch movies when you are on the road, using the official application from NetFlix, called aptly NetFlix (Figure 10–13).

Figure 10–13. *Netflix for iPad*

Facebook

One of the most popular sites on the Internet, Facebook, also has an application for iOS. Using the Facebook application, you can view your profile, view the profiles of others, upload pictures taken from the camera of an iPhone, and manage requests and recommendations. As you can see in Figure 10–14, feeds that you view will be complete with photos and you will be able to comment on them from links on the feed.

Figure 10–14. *Facebook for iPhone*

Yes, Facebook is an application with almost 100% personal uses; however, as we've noted, the line between home and the office is shrinking due to our always-online technology nature.

Twitter

Is Twitter an absolute waste of time? Who knows? But like it or despise it, Twitter has made a fundamental change in the always online personality of the world. Whether your users are marketing professionals trying to use Twitter to brand your organization's products, or people talking about which stall they went to the bathroom in last time they were at Grand Central Station, the Twitter application (shown in Figure 10–15), from Twitter, is now the best tool available for accessing Twitter.

Figure 10–15. *Twitter for iPad*

At the time that this book is being written, that application (Figure 10–15) is very new, and the applications that you have to pay for that link to Twitter are likely to undergo drastic upgrades. But for now, if you want to use Twitter on an iPad, check out the Twitter application.

Finally, Twitter has a lot of uses outside of just general micro-blogging. For example, other applications can post directly to Twitter (such as WordPress), and then those posts can be fed into other social networking sites, such as Facebook and LinkedIn, making Twitter a possible hub for many of your social networking needs.

LinkedIn

Twitter and Facebook are great social networks and great applications for that matter. But they have very different uses than LinkedIn. LinkedIn is more professional and geared toward connecting like-minded professionals. The LinkedIn application can be used to manage messages, invitations, and other features that are traditionally managed in the LinkedIn web portal, as you can see in Figure 10–16.

Figure 10–16. *LinkedIn*

NOTE: There is also an app for MySpace and a number of other social networking sites, but we figure you've basically got the point by now.

Becoming the Informed Traveler

One place where the iPhone and iPad can be incredibly useful is making for a better travel experience. There are a number of applications geared to finding places to eat, locating that cab in a difficult location, tracking expenses, or even finding your coworkers and friends who are also on the road.

Tripit, which can integrate with Facebook and Twitter, is one of the more useful apps. Once you have an account with tripit.com, when your organization gives you a travel itinerary, you can simply forward that e-mail to plans@tripit.com. Those plans then get parsed and placed into a feed that the Tripit app displays, as you can see in Figure 10–17.

Figure 10–17. *Tripit on iPhone*

In addition to just seeing your flight, hotel, and rental car information, you get updated flight times, can find information about airports, and get maps of the area to locate things. This puts a pretty comprehensive way to manage each trip right in the palm of your hand. But Tripit is not (yet) going to show you where to go for food, gas, or a nightcap after a long night writing. Yelp, an application that integrates with Facebook and allows for a comprehensive rating system, can be used to find those things, though (Figure 10–18). Yelp will look at your location and then allow you to select a place nearby. These places show ratings, and you can read reviews as you go.

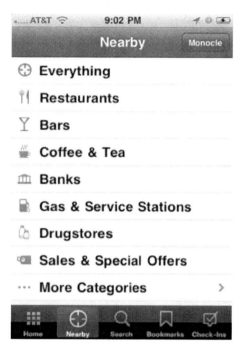

Figure 10–18. *Yelp on iPhone*

During your trip, you are sure to rack up many expenses. This is where an application to track those expenses comes in handy. There are a few expense reporting applications available on the App Store, with iXpenseIt (from FYI Mobileware, Inc) and iReceipt (from Inner Four, Inc.) standing out. Both of these applications allow you to scan expenses and e-mail expense reports back to your organization. But as with many other options for applications, there are a number of different ways that people like to work, so look at each application and find the one that best matches you and your way of working.

Summary

According to the commercials, there's an app for everything. With applications being added every day, the commercials are increasingly accurate. When you are thinking of building your own application, you should typically search the App Store and make sure that you aren't duplicating someone else's work. If you are, then you can review the application (or applications in many cases) and make an informed decision as to whether you would like to build your own custom tools. Additionally, innovation is a key aspect of deploying mobile devices. Organizations tend to want fast returns on their investments, and one of the quickest ways to get that return quickly is to buy rather than build an application.

Most applications are inexpensive and fill a gap. But for many applications, there are a lot of competitors. Before you buy a lot of copies of any application, make sure it works for a group of pilot users and make sure that it works with your organization's workflow.

Given that employees spend more and more time in the office, it is also going to be likely that you allow applications that your organization maybe bans for desktop computers, e.g., while you might ban the Facebook web site for desktops, you might allow access to it for the iPad. Therefore, being informed as to how those tools work (and potential ways to increase productivity for your organization using them) is a key element to supporting the iOS platform both in and out of the office (and it might get you invited to those poker parties you've been trying to get invited to all these years).

Finally, we have showcased a number of applications in this chapter. This is just a small sampling of what is available on the App Store. Practically every application fits a specific niche. They each have a different set of features or something unique that made the developer submit them for approval on the App Store and made Apple accept them for the App Store. These are meant to get you thinking about your own environment and the uses that applications can have in innovating how you do business!

Chapter **11**

Developing A Program For Support

The iPhone, iPad and iPod Touch are very limited operating environments. Users and applications are sandboxed into restricted environments, where little damage can be done to the devices other than physically breaking them. Applications also can do little harm to the device because they are reviewed by Apple before being made available on the App Store. Therefore, the validation, configuration, and documentation of the platform, which we covered throughout the first ten chapters of this book, becomes the first step that an Information Technology department will undertake with regard to these devices.

In the first part of this chapter, we're going to turn our attention to what you need to support iOS. After all, if the end users cannot collaborate and derive value from these devices then whether you are doing a large deployment or a pilot, there will be little reason for any of it.

Then, we're going to spend a little time also looking at Software Update Server in Mac OS X Server. Software updates make running updates on iOS-based devices and computers that commonly run the devices (Apple computers, that is) happen faster. This reduces the network overhead required and provides more control over which updates are released in the organization.

Given the limited risk that the user represents to the devices, much of the support of an iPad, iPhone, and iPod Touch will cover how to configure access to your organization's infrastructure and application support.

What Is Supported?

Many organizations create environments that will limit what applications can be installed on their mobile devices. Others will allow end users to have a choice of what they want on their devices. However, every organization will draw the line somewhere as to what will they support (except for maybe when their CEO walks in). As with other parts of the organization, administrators of environments with large numbers of systems have realized that they can't support everything users want. In fact, many environments have undertaken a process of *application consolidation*, or reducing the number of applications with similar uses, and overall, in the environment.

If you are going to extend policies in place for other platforms to iOS-based devices, you are likely to limit what can be done on the device, most notably restricting users from installing software. Therefore, you will need to build a list of applications that you are going to support in the environment. This may include only a single proprietary application that provides access to data your organization has chosen to expose to the platform, or it may be a bevy of applications both public and private that are geared for collaboration, productivity, and so on. Either way, each application will be considered based on the justification of cost to supporting the application. You might also review security implications of the application and how exposure of data that is at rest on the device might impact the environment.

A common theme throughout this book has been that iOS is different. The applications users install cannot damage the device, and those purchased from the App Store will rarely represent a security threat in the enterprise. If you choose to allow users to install software, it becomes difficult to restrict which software they can install. Therefore, you would simply make a list of applications that you will help users with, and likely indicate that they are to support themselves or look to 3rd party vendors for support of any other tools. Furthermore, if you are going to allow users to interact with assets other than those that you own, like installing and accessing personal mail accounts, you will also need to indicate whether you will support those tasks.

Another theme that has been common throughout this book is the idea of user choice. The iPhone, Blackberry, Android, and other platforms have merit, as do tablets other than iPad. Therefore, when developing applications that communicate with backend systems, most organizations are looking at web portals for all devices (and maybe sizing them for each platform). If you are doing so, you will likely see two sides of the support offering for mobile devices: the first being the infrastructure, wireless, mass deployment, monitoring, change control, and so on, and the second being the application space that includes how to use each of the applications that you have determined is supported, including the custom web portals for the mobile platforms you are running.

Preparing Support Staff

Your support desk receives a phone call from a user who cannot access mail on your servers from an iPad. Have you made the iPad an officially supported device? If so, have you decided to extend support of your groupware environment to the platform? If so, what restrictions have you put in place to provision that access? These questions have hopefully been answered as you worked through the rest of this book, but you should to communicate the answers to the end users.

If you have purchased this book, we're guessing you're allowing iOS-based devices, and maybe you're officially supporting them. While we sincerely hope that you will have approximately 1,000 support staff members that all need a copy of this book, it's not very likely. Therefore, for those individuals to support your end users, they will need to be trained and prepared for doing so. Once you have a list of supported applications, it is time to train the service desk, desktop support, and network teams on supporting the devices.

Training Considerations

If your organization is supplying mobile devices, you will need your staff to know how to activate them. If your network is going to support mobile devices, your network engineering team will need to know the various options that are needed per device.

A sample syllabus for training might be similar to the following:

- Activation
- iTunes
- Basic configuration
- Connecting to the organization's network
    - Configuring wireless connections
    - Configuring proxies (if needed)
    - Connecting to the network from outside (i.e., VPN)
- Accessing documents and other files
- Accessing mail
- Accessing calendars
- Accessing contacts
- Accessing instant messaging clients
- Accessing internal web portals
- Installing and using custom applications
- Using the App Store
    - Installing applications
    - Upgrading applications

You may note how similar to the outline of this book that the sample syllabus is. That's because we modeled this book specifically after managing an enterprise of mobile devices (and specifically an enterprise of iPhones).

Training Materials

When developing your training materials, there's little reason to reinvent the wheel. Apple has a large number of support articles on their knowledgebase at http://www.apple.com/support/iphone that are dedicated to management of the platform. As you can see in Figure 11–1, these include manuals, technical specifications, and online discussion groups.

Figure 11–1. *The iPhone Support portal*

The manuals provided can often be repurposed as training materials, requiring very little work from your team to generate a large amount of information. Additionally, the support site is available using an RSS feed, allowing you to put the feed into an existing intranet such as Microsoft SharePoint or the Mac OS X Server Wiki and Blog services. The RSS feeds (see Figure 11–2) are available at the following URLs:

- *iPhone*: feed://rss.support.apple.com/iphone
- *iPod*: feed://rss.support.apple.com/ipod
- *iTunes*: feed://rss.support.apple.com/itunes

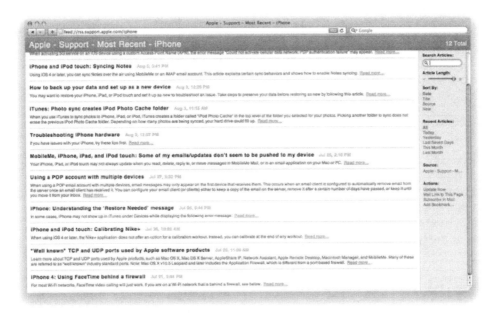

Figure 11–2. *Apple RSS Feeds*

You can also use PDFs provided by Apple to obtain content (making sure, of course, not to infringe on any Apple copyrights). Some of these documents worth noting include:

- *"iPhone in Business"*:
  http://images.apple.com/iphone/business/docs/iPhone_Business.pdf

- *Information on Microsoft Exchange integration*:
  http://images.apple.com/iphone/business/docs/iPhone_EAS.pdf

- *Documentation on the VPN*:
  http://images.apple.com/iphone/business/docs/iPhone_VPN.pdf

- *Connecting to the Wi-Fi environment*:
  http://images.apple.com/iphone/business/docs/iPhone_WiFi.pdf

- *Leveraging certificates*:
  http://images.apple.com/iphone/business/docs/iPhone_Certificates.pdf

- *An introduction to mobile device management (MDM)*:
  http://images.apple.com/iphone/business/docs/iPhone_MDM.pdf

- *Deploying iTunes*:
  http://images.apple.com/iphone/business/docs/iPhone_iTunes.pdf

- *A security overview (for the CISO types)*:
  http://images.apple.com/iphone/business/docs/iPhone_Security.pdf

■   *"The Enterprise Deployment Guide", for the help desk staff to memorize (yes, there will be quizzes):* `http://manuals.info.apple.com/en_US/Enterprise_Deployment_Guide .pdf`

NOTE: While these will provide a good foundation for a knowledge base, you will also need to customize them in most cases.

Finally, when training your users, make sure to be prepared. This is true with all types of training, but nothing destroys confidence in end users (or any other type of trainee) faster than working with a trainer who doesn't understand the subject matter. One of the most important aspects of any new technical initiative is the perception of the users. There is no getting back the first impression, which permanently impacts those perceptions in many cases.

Supporting End Users

After reading this chapter, hopefully you will create materials that support staff can use to troubleshoot problems. The materials that you make available to your support staff can also be made available to end users. If you do not already have a zero-tier, or collaboration solution, you can use the blog, wiki, and Podcast Producer services in Mac OS X Server to supply an ad hoc support portal, especially given that these can easily provide pages formatted especially for iOS-based devices.

As far as written content goes, the *iPhone Users Guide* provides a great starting point for bridging the gap between supporting these devices and training end users. The guide outlines many of the main issues that end users initially have with the iPhone, iPod Touch and iPad. It can be found at `http://manuals.info.apple.com/ en_US/iPhone_iOS4_User_Guide.pdf`.

Once you have assembled a lot of materials, the support staff and end users will need a way to quickly access this content. The Spotlight feature of Mac OS X is a great tool for quickly finding the answer to many support questions. To use Spotlight, you click the picture of the magnifying glass in the upper right-hand corner of your screen, which brings up the search dialog shown in Figure 11–3.

Figure 11–3. *Using Spotlight*

From here, you can search for a term and see all documents that reference that term. Clicking the document will open it. Once open, most applications in Mac OS X support the ability to use the Command+F shortcut to quickly find content within the document, as shown in Figure 11–4.

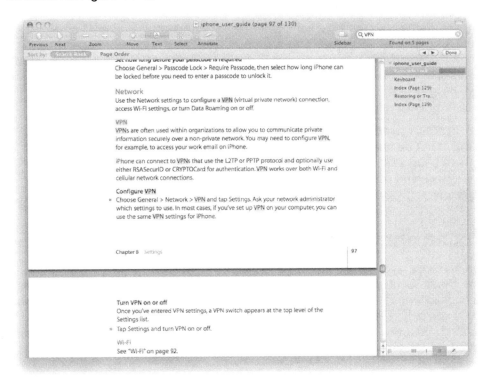

Figure 11–4. *Finding Items in Preview*

Many support environments will have scripts and knowledge base articles as a standard means of supporting any platform. End users often quickly see through scripted responses when support staff spends time looking for information on a given problem and then provides a scripted response. The patience level for basic issues will usually be low (as with all platforms), and users will expect support staff to magically know why they cannot send mail from their hotel rooms. Therefore, training support staff and providing good documentation, including a fast way to navigate through that documentation, are key to success. Having well trained support staff, situated to train others and actually understand what they're talking about is another key element to providing a sturdy support infrastructure. You should also keep devices handy for support staff to use when troubleshooting issues with users.

Considering the Help Desk

Often, the people sitting on the front lines determine a lot about how your IT organization is perceived. An organization serious about supporting a bevy of different operating systems for a mobile initiative would do well to outfit support staff with a wide variety of these devices. For example, if your environment is large enough to have a dedicated team of iPhone specialists, it would be wise for them to use the iPhone for everyday tasks just as end users would.

If your team is not large enough to have dedicated teams for each device operating system, it might not be feasible to outfit every support staff person with one of each. In any case, there should be an iPhone on hand for troubleshooting. In addition to an iPhone, it is possible to use the iPhone Simulator to do a number of tasks, especially when it comes to software that is being developed within the enterprise.

The iPhone Simulator

The iPhone Simulator is an application that Apple provides as part of its development toolset. The iPhone Simulator provides a means of accessing and testing core features or options on the devices. However, the usefulness to support staff members is limited because they can only test web sites in mobile Safari and perform basic troubleshooting. You cannot use the simulator to configure mail clients or calendars or to install software for which you don't have the uncompiled Xcode project files or unstrapped libraries.

While limited as a support tool, the iPhone Simulator is a great tool to use for application testing during the application development process. While writing an application, you can use the iPhone Simulator for testing the appearance and functionality. You can also check whether or not your organization's site and web-based applications appear and function appropriately on an iPhone or iPod touch.

To obtain the iPhone Simulator, shown in Figure 11–5, download the iPhone SDK from `http://www.apple.com/downloads/macosx/development_tools/iphonesdk.html`. Once the SDK is downloaded, install it, browse to the `/Developer/Library/Platforms/iPhoneSimulator.platform/Developer/Applications` directory, and open the iPhone Simulator.

Figure 11–5. *The iPhone Simulator*

NOTE: You cannot simulate the loss of network connectivity with the iPhone Simulator. The device connects through the active network connection of your computer, so it can provide mixed troubleshooting results, even if you disable the network connection on the computer itself.

Using the Software Update Server for Patch Management

In Chapters 8 and 9, we looked at some options for patch management. The thing about patch management that is a hang-up in many organizations is that there is no one watching for and approving patches. For example, the Apple Software Update Server can cache all patches from Apple (or only the ones approved). If you have Mac OS X clients running iTunes, this can help to quickly deploy patches to a large number of systems. A Software Update Server will also help to reduce the amount of bandwidth consumed by downloading these patches (one host downloads the patches, as opposed to having every edge device caching them).

Mac OS X Server can run as a Software Update server and share updates with other Mac OS X clients. The Software Update service mirrors updates from the Apple Software Update service that you use by default when running software update. This helps to keep larger Apple updates for operating systems and Apple software packages from taking up all of your Internet bandwidth when five or five hundred computers go to download that update all at the same time.

The server runs a modified version of Apache and is, therefore, basically just a web server. The updates are synchronized with Apple's updates, and as the administrator, you have the ability to simply mirror or to freeze updates to time frames when you're able to do more comprehensive testing than reading up on Macfixit or Versiontracker to see if anyone else has had an issue.

Before you install the Software Update service, first make sure you have enough hard drive space available. The updates will be stored in the /var/db/swupd directory, along with a number of catalog files in property list format, that instruct the client as to where to find updates. Provided you have enough free space, your first step is to enable the service. To do so, open Server Admin, and click the name of the server where you will be installing Software Update services. Then, click the Settings button in the Server Admin toolbar and the Services tab just below that. As you can see in Figure 11–6, you will then find the Software Update service in the list, and check the box to enable it. Once that's checked, click Save to see the service listed in the SERVERS section of Server Admin.

Figure 11–6. *Adding the Software Update Server service*

Installing the Software Update Service

Now that you have enabled the service, you will want to configure it and start it up. By default, the settings for Software Update are to automatically mirror all Apple updates and essentially act as a proxy for the Apple Software Update services. If this is what you would like to do, you will have little more to configure. Simply click the Software Update entry in the SERVERS list under the server that you are configuring. Then, click the Settings button to see the available settings such as the location that the updates will be cached, as shown in Figure 11–7.

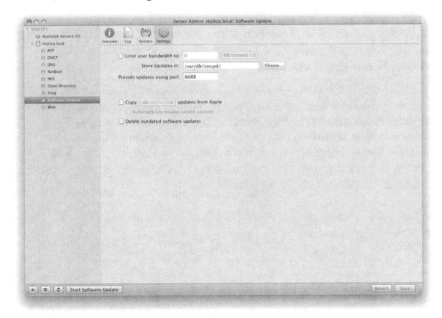

Figure 11–7. *Software Update Settings*

For most environments, the default settings will suffice, but if you choose to customize settings they include the following:

- *Limit user bandwidth for updates to*: Configure per-user bandwidth throttling for the Software Update service.

- *Provide updates using port*: The port setting defaults to 8088 but can be changed if 8088 is problematic for your environment.

- *Copy all Updates from Apple*: Use this drop-down to determine if server is to automatically download all updates from Apple.

- *Automatically enable copied update*: Determine if all files synchronized from Apple will be provided to clients (use this feature and the "Copy all Updates from Apple" feature together if you want to mirror all updates).

- Delete Outdated Software Updates: Choose whether old software updates will be discarded.

Once you are satisfied with your settings, click the Start Software Update button near the bottom of the Server Admin screen and wait. Keep in mind that the server is caching a large number of updates and will possibly take up to eight or nine hours to refresh the updates that are available and fully be ready for client connectivity.

Managing Your Software Update Server

Now that you have installed the Software Update Service, you'll want to get familiar with configuring and managing the server. Luckily, it's one of the easiest services to manage, assuming everything is working as intended. The main things that will need to be done are enabling and disabling updates. For example, if an update to iTunes is released that renders half of your customizations useless, you might want to uncheck the Enable button for that update until you figure out a resolution.

To disable an update that may be problematic for your environment, you can click the Updates tab and uncheck the Enable dialog for the specified update. Or if you have chosen not to automatically enable copied updates, you will be able to enable the updates using the check boxes shown in Figure 11–8 on a per-update basis. In our experience, the maturity of your imaging and patch management environment will dictate whether or not you decide to enable updates automatically. Either way, having a test group vet the updates is recommended at a minimum.

Figure 11–8. *Enable and disable software updates*

Once the server has been configured, you can move on to configuring the clients to use the server for updates.

Configuring Updates for Clients

The easiest way to install clients is to use Open Directory and configure Software Update as a managed preference. However, this is not a luxury everyone will have. Therefore, you can also manually configure each client to use the Software Update service that you have installed from the command line. Or you can use local managed preferences, as described in *Enterprise Mac Managed Preferences* by Edward Marczak and Greg Neagle (Apress, 2010).

To deploy the Software Update services using Open Directory, open Workgroup Manager, connect to an Open Directory server or the appropriate directory service, and click the user, computer, or computer group that you would like to edit the software update information for. Then, click Preferences in the Server Admin toolbar. At the preferences screen, you will see each of the items that you can configure for managed preferences, as shown in Figure 11–9.

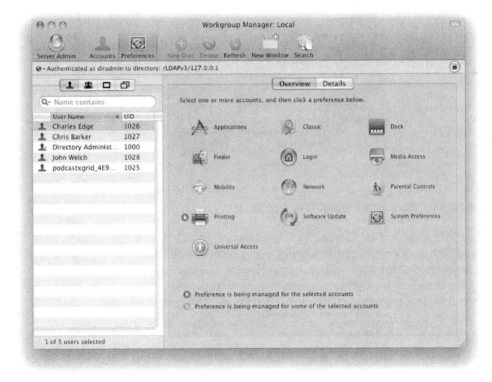

Figure 11–9. *Managed preferences*

Click the Software Update icon to bring up the managed preferences settings for Software Update, which is shown in Figure 11–9. Here, type in the appropriate URL following the format below the box that you are typing in. Assuming that you have not customized the port that you are using, this would be `http://servername.domain.com:8088/index-leopard-snowleopard.merged-1.sucatalog`, where the server name and domain name in the string are replaced with the name or IP address of your server. In the example in Figure 11–10, the server name is `replica.krypted.com`, and the port number has not been customized.

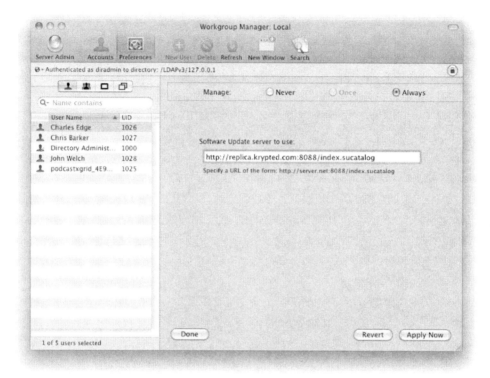

Figure 11–10. *Software Update managed preference settings*

Setting up a Software Update server if you are using Open Directory is a fairly simple task. But what if the system is not managed using Open Directory? That's when you would use a terminal command, or use Apple Remote Desktop (ARD) to send out the command *en masse*. In the following example, we will continue with the previous example, but this time updating client computers from the command line:

```
defaults write /Library/Preferences/com.apple.SoftwareUpdate CatalogURL \
"http://replica.krypted.com:8088/";
```

To use the Software Update server, you first configure the client to run software updates through the Software Update server. Then, you run software updates.

Using Software Update

Once you have configured the client to leverage the Software Update services on your Mac OS X Server, there are two ways to interact with Software Update: through the System Preference pane and through the `softwareupdate` command.

To use the System Preference pane, open System Preferences from the Apple menu. Then, click the Software Update System Preference pane, which will open the Software Update application. Here, you can see when the application was last run, and configure when updates will be run and whether they will be downloaded in the background automatically for the client (see Figure 11–11).

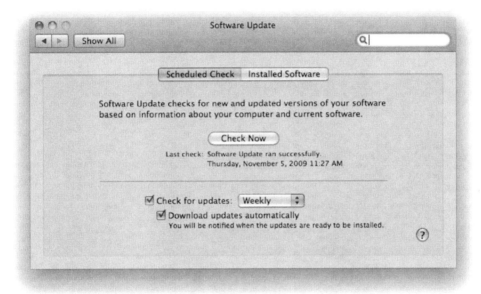

Figure 11–11. *The Software Update System Preference Pane*

When you click the Check Now button, Software Update will check for updates on the server. If updates are found, you will be presented with a list on the client computer to install each update, as shown in Figure 11–12. Here, you can uncheck updates to run them later or click the Install button near the bottom of the screen to install them immediately. Additionally, you can select items and use the Ignore Update menu to tell the system never to run the update or you can use the Go to the Apple Downloads Page button in the Update menu go to the specific web page that explains the update further.

NOTE: In the list of Software Updates you will see an icon with a sideways triangle in it that indicates which updates require restarts.

Figure 11–12. *Checking for updates*

Back at the Software Update screen (see Figure 11–11), you can also click the Installed Software tab to see a list of all of the software updates that have run on that system (see Figure 11–13). Each of these updates can be found in the /Library/Updates directory. Cached updates will be stored in the ~/Library/Caches/com.apple.SoftwareUpdate directory.

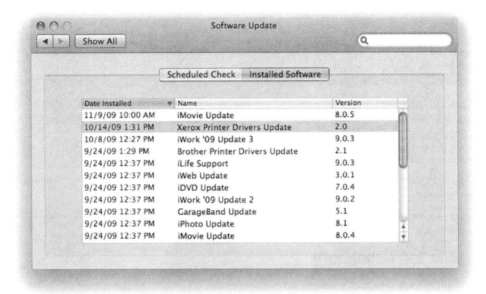

Figure 11–13. *Reviewing installed updates*

Using the softwareupdate Command to Install Software Updates

Mac OS X Server and Mac OS X client use the softwareupdate command to install software updates. To get a list of available updates from the Apple servers (or whichever software update server you may be using), run the softwareupdate command along with the -l option (or -list if you like to type):

```
softwareupdate -l
```

The output should look something like the following, with the bulleted items acting as the label for each update:

```
Software Update found the following new or updated software:
   * iTunesX-9.0.2
      iTunes (9.0.2), 90630K [recommended]
   * HDDUpdate10-1.0
      Performance Update (1.0), 105K [recommended] [restart]
   * iMovie_805-8.0.5
      iMovie Update (8.0.5), 36076K [recommended]
```

To install all of the available updates, simply run the softwareupdate command along with the -all option:

```
softwareupdate -all
```

> **NOTE:** Installing updates via the command line can cause instability of the system for users that are using it. Therefore, we recommend that you do so during the standard maintenance windows kept by most enterprises.

To install specific updates, you can use the `softwareupdate` command along with the `-i` option and the label for an update, which can be obtained using the –list option as described previously:

```
softwareupdate -i <label>
```

For example, to install the iMovie update from earlier in this section, you would use the following command:

```
softwareupdate -i iMovie_805-8.0.5
```

Working with the Repository

You can also browse the update server directly by looking at the `index.sucatalog` file. This is a great step when troubleshooting service related issues. If you are using the default port number of 8088, the URL to do so would be `http://` followed by the name or address of your software update server, followed by `:8088/index.sucatalog`. If the browser successfully opens the page, it will appear as shown in Figure 11–14.

Figure 11–14. *Viewing the Catalog Directly*

Not only can you manage software updates themselves with the command line but you can also manage the server, as we will illustrate in the next section.

Using the Command Line to Manage Software Update Server

The command line options for Software Update services are fairly rudimentary compared to some of the other services in Mac OS X Server. However, you can also configure the server using the `serveradmin` command (as with many other services in Mac OS X Server). These commands will allow for more granular administration of the server to ease the administrative burden once that server is placed into production.

serveradmin

The `serveradmin` command is capable of starting and stopping the Software Update service and of more granularly configuring settings for the Software Update service. When running the `serveradmin` command, you will use the `swupdate` option to specify that the service that you are working with is Software Update. A basic version of this would be to use the following command, which uses the status verb to determine if the Software Update server is running:

```
serveradmin status swupdate
```

In addition, you can use `serveradmin` to look at the critical settings for the service by running it with the `fullstatus` option. For example, consider the following command:

```
serveradmin fullstatus swupdate
```

Querying using `fullstatus` would net the following result, which shows that the server is running along with a number of critical settings:

```
swupdate:state = "RUNNING"
swupdate:lastChecktime = 2009-11-09 03:00:00 -0600
swupdate:setStateVersion = 1
swupdate:syncServiceState = "RUNNING"
swupdate:readWriteSettingsVersion = 1
swupdate:logPaths:swupdateAccessLog = "/var/log/swupd/swupd_access_log"
swupdate:logPaths:swupdateErrorLog = "/var/log/swupd/swupd_error_log"
swupdate:logPaths:swupdateServiceLog = "/var/log/swupd/swupd_syncd_log"
swupdate:pluginVers = "10.6.58"
swupdate:checkError = no
swupdate:updatesDocRoot = "/var/db/swupd/"
swupdate:hostServiceState = "RUNNING"
swupdate:autoMirror = yes
swupdate:numOfEnabledPkg = 290
swupdate:servicePortsAreRestricted = "NO"
swupdate:numOfMirroredPkg = 290
swupdate:startTime = 2009-11-08 14:50:22 -0600
swupdate:autoMirrorOnlyNew = no
swupdate:autoEnable = yes
```

> **NOTE:** You can also just run `serveradmin settings swupdate` for a full listing of all settings, but as the output includes information on each update, it is far too verbose to include here.

Each of theses settings can then be altered using the `serveradmin` command with the settings option, followed by the string with the new content. For example, to change the path of the service log to the same folder on a different drive called LOGS, you would use the following command:

```
serveradmin settings swupdate:logPaths:swupdateServiceLog =
"/volumes/LOGS/var/log/swupd/swupd_syncd_log"
```

The `serveradmin` command primarily gives you the ability to configure the service from the perspective of Mac OS X Server. However, keep in mind that the Software Update service is actually a scaled-down implementation of Apache 1. Therefore, you can also edit the Apache configuration files directly or edit the `/etc/swupd/swupd.plist`, as we will explain in the next section of this chapter.

Multiple Software Update Servers

Software Update services allow your server to cache updates from Apple and redistribute them to clients within your organization. This can greatly cut down on the amount of bandwidth consumed by new software patches. But if you have a very large distributed organization, you might want to have multiple Software Update servers daisy-chained together in a cascade to download updates from each other and provide updates to sets of clients (maybe clients are geographically separated or you just have too many clients to provide updates to for just one server). Cascading the Software Update services would further conserve bandwidth in your environment if you have multiple Software Update servers.

To cascade Software Updates from one server to another, you set up your first Software Update server. Let's say that you set it up as SUS1.krypted.com and set it to run on port 8080. Next, you set up your second server (let's call it SUS2.krypted.com), and edit the `metaindexURL` key (by default, it's set to swscan.apple.com) of the file `/etc/swupd/swupd.plist`. So you would change the key to be SUS1.krypted.com/content/meta/mirror-config-1.plist.

Implementing a Process to Manage Patches

Now that you have a functional Software Update Server, it's time to put in place a process to manage patches. In most cases, there are already going to be processes and procedures in place for managing patches for Windows and other platforms. We recommend mirroring the release of patches for Mac OS X with those of other platforms when possible. Therefore, if you have a patch management schedule that is such that all patches are tested and released to clients within 30 days of release from the vendor, it would be a good idea to retain that same functionality for iOS.

These patches, when cached, need to be pushed to devices. Whether you are using a third-party solution or iTunes, the Software Update Server will help you to get the most recent patches to client computers in environments that use iTunes on Mac OS X client for patch management of iOS-based devices and, when possible, on servers that are used for patch management with solutions such as AirWatch, covered further in Chapter 9.

Summary

Throughout this book, we have looked at configuring profiles, building infrastructure to support iOS, and developing solutions to help automate tasks around this beautiful operating system. But if you cannot support it, you will have a lot of hassle when reacting to end user adoption.

In our experience, once iOS-based devices are ratified as a user choice, they are adopted in a fast and furious fashion. As part of ratification of the platform, before official support is provided, you need to put in place a support mechanism. In this chapter, we have looked at a number of resources for training support staff and end users, and for making information quickly available.

We have discussed patch management throughout this book, with a sharper focus on patch management in Chapters 8 and 9. But keeping machines that will be used to support (and develop patches for) iOS-based devices is another key of supporting them. Therefore, we also looked at leveraging Mac OS X Server as part of your patch management system in this chapter as well.

There are likely already plenty of users in your environment using iOS-based devices. Now it's time to get a pilot going for legitimizing that use and officially supporting iPhone, iPad, and iPod Touch. Good luck!

Acceptable Use Policy

This example of an Acceptable Use Policy was created by the SANS Institute. As is the case with most documents that can contain a legal ramification, you should have the legal counsel for your organization review and approve the document prior to giving it out to your users. The document is not necessarily meant to be handed out as is but is meant to be an example to guide you in the creation of your own. If you have a policy to contribute, please send e-mail to stephen@sans.edu.

InfoSec Acceptable Use Policy

1.0 Overview

InfoSec's intentions for publishing an Acceptable Use Policy are not to impose restrictions that are contrary to <Company Name>'s established culture of openness, trust, and integrity. InfoSec is committed to protecting <Company Name>'s employees, partners, and the company from illegal or damaging actions by individuals, either knowingly or unknowingly.

Internet/intranet/extranet-related systems, including but not limited to computer equipment, software, operating systems, storage media, network accounts providing electronic mail, World Wide Web browsing, and FTP, are the property of <Company Name>. These systems are to be used for business purposes in serving the interests of the company, and of our clients and customers in the course of normal operations. Please review Human Resources policies for further details.

Effective security is a team effort involving the participation and support of every <Company Name> employee and affiliate who deals with information and/or information systems. It is the responsibility of every computer user to know these guidelines and to conduct their activities accordingly.

2.0 Purpose

The purpose of this policy is to outline the acceptable use of computer equipment at <Company Name>.

These rules are in place to protect the employee and <Company Name>. Inappropriate use exposes <Company Name> to risks including virus attacks, compromise of network systems and services, and legal issues.

3.0 Scope

This policy applies to employees, contractors, consultants, temporaries, and other workers at <Company Name>, including all personnel affiliated with third parties. This policy applies to all equipment that is owned or leased by <Company Name>.

4.0 Policy

4.1 General Use and Ownership

1. While <Company Name>'s network administration desires to provide a reasonable level of privacy, users should be aware that the data they create on the corporate systems remains the property of <Company Name>. Because of the need to protect <Company Name>'s network, management cannot guarantee the confidentiality of information stored on any network device belonging to <Company Name>.

2. Employees are responsible for exercising good judgment regarding the reasonableness of personal use. Individual departments are responsible for creating guidelines concerning personal use of Internet/intranet/extranet systems. In the absence of such policies, employees should be guided by departmental policies on personal use, and if there is any uncertainty, employees should consult their supervisor or manager.

3. InfoSec recommends that any information that users consider sensitive or vulnerable be encrypted. For guidelines on information classification, see InfoSec's Information Sensitivity Policy. For guidelines on encrypting e-mail and documents, go to InfoSec's Awareness Initiative.

4. For security and network maintenance purposes, authorized individuals within <Company Name> may monitor equipment, systems, and network traffic at any time, per InfoSec's Audit Policy.

5. <Company Name> reserves the right to audit networks and systems on a periodic basis to ensure compliance with this policy.

4.2 Security and Proprietary Information

1. The user interface for information contained on Internet/intranet/extranet-related systems should be classified as either confidential or not confidential, as defined by corporate confidentiality guidelines, details of which can be found in Human Resources policies. Examples of confidential information include but are not limited to private company data, corporate strategies, competitor-sensitive information, trade secrets, specifications, customer lists, and research data. Employees should take all necessary steps to prevent unauthorized access to this information.

2. Keep passwords secure and do not share accounts. Authorized users are responsible for the security of their passwords and accounts. System-level passwords should be changed quarterly; user-level passwords should be changed every six months.

3. All PCs, laptops, and workstations should be secured with a password-protected screen saver with the automatic activation feature set at 10 minutes or less, or by logging off (Ctrl+Alt+Del for Windows users) when the host will be unattended.

4. Use encryption of information in compliance with InfoSec's Acceptable Encryption Use policy.

5. Because information contained on portable computers is especially vulnerable, special care should be exercised. Protect laptops in accordance with the Laptop Security Tips.

6. Postings by employees from a <Company Name> e-mail address to newsgroups should contain a disclaimer stating that the opinions expressed are strictly their own and not necessarily those of <Company Name>, unless posting is in the course of business duties.

7. All hosts used by the employee that are connected to the <Company Name> Internet/intranet/extranet, whether owned by the employee or <Company Name>, shall be continually executing approved virus-scanning software with a current virus database—unless overridden by departmental or group policy.

8. Employees must use extreme caution when opening e-mail attachments received from unknown senders, because they could contain viruses, e-mail bombs, or Trojan horse code.

4.3 Unacceptable Use

The following activities are, in general, prohibited. Employees may be exempted from these restrictions during the course of their legitimate job responsibilities (for example, systems administration staff may have a need to disable the network access of a host if that host is disrupting production services). Under no circumstances is an employee of <Company Name> authorized to engage in any activity that is illegal under local, state, federal, or international law while utilizing <Company Name>-owned resources.

The following lists are by no means exhaustive, but attempt to provide a framework for activities that fall into the category of unacceptable use.

System and Network Activities

The following activities are strictly prohibited, with no exceptions:

1. Violations of the rights of any person or company protected by copyright, trade secret, patent, or other intellectual property, or similar laws or regulations, including, but not limited to, the installation or distribution of pirated or other software products that are not appropriately licensed for use by <Company Name>.

2. Unauthorized copying of copyrighted material including, but not limited to, digitization and distribution of photographs from magazines, books, or other copyrighted sources, copyrighted music, and the installation of any copyrighted software for which <Company Name> or the end user does not have an active license is strictly prohibited.

3. Exporting software, technical information, encryption software or technology, in violation of international or regional export control laws, is illegal. The appropriate management should be consulted prior to export of any material that is in question.

4. Introduction of malicious programs into the network or server (for example, viruses, worms, Trojan horses, e-mail bombs, and so forth).

5. Revealing your account password to others or allowing use of your account by others. This includes family and other household members when work is being done at home.

6. Using a <Company Name> computing asset to actively engage in procuring or transmitting material that is in violation of sexual harassment or hostile workplace laws in the user's local jurisdiction.

7. Making fraudulent offers of products, items, or services originating from any <Company Name> account.

8. Making statements about warranty, expressly or implied, unless it is a part of normal job duties.

9. Effecting security breaches or disruptions of network communication. Security breaches include, but are not limited to, accessing data of which the employee is not an intended recipient or logging into a server or account that the employee is not expressly authorized to access, unless these duties are within the scope of regular duties. For purposes of this section, *disruption* includes, but is not limited to, network sniffing, pinged floods, packet spoofing, denial of service, and forged routing information for malicious purposes.

10. Port scanning or security scanning is expressly prohibited unless prior notification to InfoSec is made.

11. Executing any form of network monitoring that will intercept data not intended for the employee's host, unless this activity is a part of the employee's normal job/duty.

12. Circumventing user authentication or security of any host, network, or account.

13. Interfering with or denying service to any user other than the employee's host (for example, denial of service attack).

14. Using any program/script/command, or sending messages of any kind, with the intent to interfere with, or disable, a user's terminal session, via any means, locally or via the Internet/intranet/extranet.

15. Providing information about, or lists of, <Company Name> employees to parties outside <Company Name>.

E-mail and Communications Activities

1. Sending unsolicited e-mail messages, including the sending of "junk mail" or other advertising material to individuals who did not specifically request such material (e-mail spam).

2. Any form of harassment via e-mail, telephone, or paging, whether through language, frequency, or size of messages.

3. Unauthorized use, or forging, of e-mail header information.

4. Solicitation of e-mail for any other e-mail address, other than that of the poster's account, with the intent to harass or to collect replies.

5. Creating or forwarding chain letters, Ponzi schemes, or other pyramid schemes of any type.

6. Use of unsolicited e-mail originating from within <Company Name>'s networks of other Internet/intranet/extranet service providers on behalf of, or to advertise, any service hosted by <Company Name> or connected via <Company Name>'s network.

7. Posting the same or similar non-business-related messages to large numbers of Usenet newsgroups (newsgroup spam).

5.0 Enforcement

Any employee found to have violated this policy may be subject to disciplinary action, up to and including termination of employment.

6.0 Definitions

Term Definition

Spam: Unauthorized and/or unsolicited electronic mass mailings

7.0 Revision History

Using Mac OS X Server for Groupware

In this book, we primarily focused on using iOS as a client to other solutions. In this appendix, we cover using an entirely Apple-based groupware solution. This could be an out-of-band environment just to support Mac and iOS-based devices, or it could be a complete walled garden used to test push notifications and other services. iCal Server, Address Book Server, iChat Server, and Mac OS X Mail Server can all act to provide a centralized collaboration-based solution.

There are entire books dedicated to Mac OS X Server. This appendix is not looking to replace those. If you are interested in one after reading the chapter, look into *Beginning Mac OS X Server* by Robert Walters, Grant Fritchey, and Carmen Taglienti (Apress, 2009) or the books on Mac OS X Server from the Apple Training Series (Peachpit Press).

iCal Server

The first step on this journey is using iCal Server to supply shared calendars to users. To do this, you will need an Open Directory environment, or at a minimum, augment records to another directory service. The augments will be created automatically if you set up your Mac OS X Server in WorkGroup mode, bind to your directory service, and use the Server Preferences tool, rather than Server Admin, to perform the setup.

iCal Server uses CalDAV, an extension of the WebDAV protocol that Microsoft Entourage can use to interface with Exchange. CalDAV is a well-defined open standard, so developing around it is in no way a black box. However, it is not as widely dispersed as Microsoft Exchange, so there are fewer tools that integrate with it. Still, nothing is likely to work better with iCal Server than the iCal client itself, included by default with all Mac OS X installations. Alternative clients include open source programs Mozilla Sunbird and the Mulberry email and calendaring application. Additionally, there are several third-party Outlook plug-ins available, though they tend to perform as second-class citizens.

Setting Up iCal Server

To get started with iCal Server, first install the service. On a freshly installed Mac OS X Server that is either running as a directory server or already bound to one, open the Server Preferences application. Server Preferences can be found at /Applications/Server and, when opened, looks far less intimidating than Server Admin (see Figure B–1). This is because Server Preferences is a fairly dumbed-down version of Server Admin.

To enable the iCal service, click the orb just to the left of the iCal icon. Then, as shown in Figure B–2, click the "Limit each calendar event's size to" field and provide a number (in megabytes) for the maximum size of a calendar event, keeping in mind that calendar events can contain attachments. Next, click the "Limit each user's total calendar size to" field, and provide a maximum per user. If you will not be using attachments, you can use a number around one megabyte or smaller, at which point storage becomes a minimal issue. Next, move the slider to the On position, and the service will start up.

Figure B–1. *The Server Preferences application*

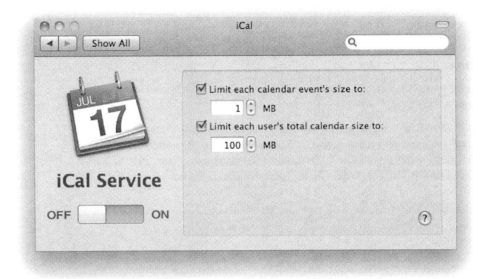

Figure B–2. *Enabling iCal service using Server Preferences*

At this point you might be saying to yourself, "That can't be all there is." Well, you're right. You can use the iCal service in Server Admin to more granularly configure settings, as shown in Figure B–3. To set up the iCal service from the Server Admin tool, click the name of the server in the SERVERS list, and click the Settings icon. Next, click the check box next to the iCal entry, and you should see the iCal service appear in the SERVERS list underneath the name of the servers when you click the Save button.

Now, click the iCal server entry, and you will see a number of options shown in Figure B–3, including:

- *Data Store:* The location on the server's file system for the iCal database.

- *Maximum Attachment Size:* The maximum size of a given attachment (and therefore the maximum size of a given event).

- *User Quota:* The maximum size of a user's calendar.

- *Authentication:* The authentication method used—Digest, Kerberos or Any Method (forcing to Kerberos or Digest can be useful in troubleshooting or to enforce encryption policies).

- *Host Name:* The DNS name of the server (or service if you have multiple records pointing to the host).

- *SSL:* Allows you to select a certificate that has been installed on the host. Even if you are using a self-assigned certificate on the Mac OS X Server, you should use SSL when possible.

■ *HTTP Port Number:* The port number that the HTTP iCal service's listener uses.

■ *SSL Port Number:* The port number that the SSL iCal service's listener uses.

■ *Log Level:* The verbosity with which you want the iCal server to write events into logs.

■ *Push Notification Server:* By default, this will list the current server, but it can be used to select another host in high-volume environments. The push notification server enables the most seamless interaction between iPhone and Mac OS X Server's groupware services offerings.

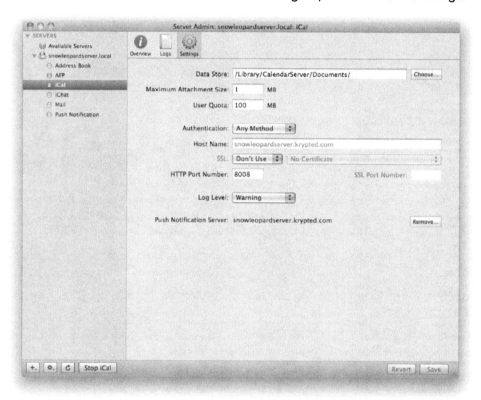

Figure B-3. *Configuring the iCal service using Server Admin*

Once you are satisfied with your settings, click the Save button to start up the service. If you're now thinking that these can't be all the options, again, you'd be correct. In addition to the two GUI panels developed by Apple, a host of other options can be accessed using the serveradmin command. To see the available settings, use this:

```
serveradmin settings calendar
```

You will then see the following items:

```
calendar:SudoersFile = "/etc/caldavd/sudoers.plist"
calendar:DirectoryService:params:restrictEnabledRecords = no
calendar:DirectoryService:params:restrictToGroup = ""
calendar:DirectoryService:params:cacheTimeout = 30
calendar:DirectoryService:params:node = "/Search"
calendar:DirectoryService:type = "twistedcaldav.directory.appleopendirectory.↩
OpenDirectoryService"
calendar:Aliases = _empty_dictionary
calendar:BindSSLPorts = _empty_array
calendar:EnablePrincipalListings = no
calendar:DocumentRoot = "/Library/CalendarServer/Documents/"
calendar:EnableDropBox = yes
calendar:SSLPrivateKey = ""
calendar:ServerStatsFile = "/var/run/caldavd/stats.plist"
calendar:ProcessType = "Combined"
calendar:UserName = "calendar"
calendar:BindHTTPPorts = _empty_array
calendar:EnableAnonymousReadRoot = yes
calendar:HTTPPort = 8008
calendar:ServerHostName = ""
calendar:PIDFile = "/var/run/caldavd.pid"
calendar:Authentication:Digest:Algorithm = "md5"
calendar:Authentication:Digest:Qop = ""
calendar:Authentication:Digest:Enabled = yes
calendar:Authentication:Kerberos:ServicePrincipal = ""
calendar:Authentication:Kerberos:Enabled = yes
calendar:Authentication:Wiki:Enabled = yes
calendar:Authentication:Basic:Enabled = no
calendar:ReadPrincipals = _empty_array
calendar:EnableTimezoneService = yes
calendar:FreeBusyURL:AnonymousAccess = no
calendar:FreeBusyURL:Enabled = yes
calendar:FreeBusyURL:TimePeriod = 14
calendar:UserQuota = 104857600
calendar:MaximumAttachmentSize = 1048576
calendar:MultiProcess:ProcessCount = 0
calendar:EnableProxyPrincipals = yes
calendar:DefaultLogLevel = "warn"
calendar:EnableMonolithicCalendars = yes
calendar:ErrorLogFile = "/var/log/caldavd/error.log"
calendar:SSLCertificate = ""
calendar:EnableSACLs = no
calendar:Notifications:CoalesceSeconds = 10
calendar:Notifications:Services:XMPPNotifier:Host = "snowleopardserver.krypted.com"
calendar:Notifications:Services:XMPPNotifier:JID = "com.apple.notificationuser@↩
snowleopardserver.krypted.com"
calendar:Notifications:Services:XMPPNotifier:Enabled = yes
calendar:Notifications:Services:XMPPNotifier:Service = "twistedcaldav.notify.↩
XMPPNotifierService"
calendar:Notifications:Services:XMPPNotifier:Port = 5222
calendar:Notifications:Services:XMPPNotifier:ServiceAddress = "pubsub.↩
snowleopardserver.krypted.com"
calendar:EnableAnonymousReadNav = no
calendar:DataRoot = "/Library/CalendarServer/Data/"
calendar:BindAddresses = _empty_array
```

```
calendar:AdminPrincipals = _empty_array
calendar:RedirectHTTPToHTTPS = no
calendar:RotateAccessLog = no
calendar:GroupName = "calendar"
calendar:EnablePrivateEvents = yes
calendar:AccessLogFile = "/var/log/caldavd/access.log"
calendar:Scheduling:CalDAV:EmailDomain = ""
calendar:Scheduling:CalDAV:HTTPDomain = ""
calendar:Scheduling:CalDAV:AddressPatterns = _empty_array
calendar:Scheduling:iSchedule:Servers = "/etc/caldavd/servertoserver.xml"
calendar:Scheduling:iSchedule:Enabled = no
calendar:Scheduling:iSchedule:AddressPatterns = _empty_array
calendar:Scheduling:iMIP:Receiving:Server = ""
calendar:Scheduling:iMIP:Receiving:UseSSL = yes
calendar:Scheduling:iMIP:Receiving:PollingSeconds = 30
calendar:Scheduling:iMIP:Receiving:Username = ""
calendar:Scheduling:iMIP:Receiving:Type = ""
calendar:Scheduling:iMIP:Receiving:Password = ""
calendar:Scheduling:iMIP:Receiving:Port = 995
calendar:Scheduling:iMIP:MailGatewayServer = "localhost"
calendar:Scheduling:iMIP:Enabled = no
calendar:Scheduling:iMIP:MailGatewayPort = 62310
calendar:Scheduling:iMIP:AddressPatterns = _empty_array
calendar:Scheduling:iMIP:Sending:Server = ""
calendar:Scheduling:iMIP:Sending:Username = ""
calendar:Scheduling:iMIP:Sending:Address = ""
calendar:Scheduling:iMIP:Sending:UseSSL = yes
calendar:Scheduling:iMIP:Sending:Password = ""
calendar:Scheduling:iMIP:Sending:Port = 587
```

Many of these settings appear fairly cryptic, but you'll find they allow for very granular configuration of the service. You can customize these items by using the same command and pasting the particular setting on to the end of it, along with the desired value. For example, if you want to force all users who can authenticate into the iCal service to have an account in the directory services, you would use the following command:

```
Serveradmin settings calendar:DirectoryService:params:restrictEnabledRecords = yes
```

> **TIP:** You can further reduce the maximum attachment size to the bytes level using the `calendar:MaximumAttachmentSize` setting.

Managing Calendars

Once you have enabled the iCal service, you will want to provide access to calendars for your users. To do so, you can enable the service for an account, again using the Server Preferences tool. Simply open Server Preferences and click the name of a user you'd like to configure, and you'll see a listing of services the user can access on the right side of the screen as in Figure B–4.

NOTE: You can also use Server Preferences to configure Groups as well.

Figure B–4. *Enabling services for users*

Once access has been enabled, you can easily add the account on your mobile device. Simply open the Preferences application, and tap "Mail, Contacts and Calendars". Then tap Add Account. From here, provide the server name or IP address, the username and password to authenticate to that server, and optionally, a short description about your account (see Figure B–5).

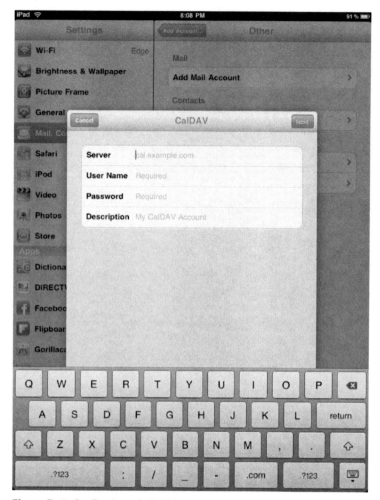

Figure B–5. *Configuring a CalDAV Account*

Subscribing to Calendars

The CalDAV service has a number of features for allowing multiple users to access a single repository of data in a highly collaborative fashion. But not all environments need iCal Server. You can save an iCal file on a server and allow only a single user to edit the file. When you do so, additional users can subscribe to the file. This is useful for a number of scenarios such as booking a conference room through a single person, having one individual manage a schedule, and publishing calendars to the general public. To create the calendar, simply create an ICS file on a server using iCal. Once the calendar is published, browse to it from your mobile device by visiting Preferences, selecting the "Mail, Contacts and Calendars" preference, and tapping Add Server. At the Subscription screen, tap the Server field, and provide the name or IP address of your ICS file (Figure B–6).

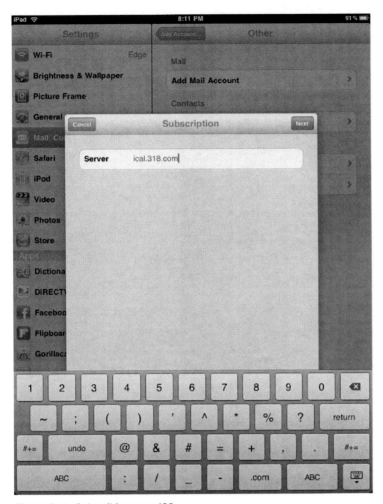

Figure B–6. *Subscribing to an ICS*

Once you are satisfied with the address, tap on the Next button and provided that the server can access the file, you can then provide a username and password (if required). As shown in Figure A2-7, you can also provide a description and indicate whether the connection should use an SSL certificate and whether you would like to disable the use of alarms (which are alerts that inform you when a calendar event is about to come due). Once you are satisfied with your selections, tap the Save button to complete the setup of the subscription.

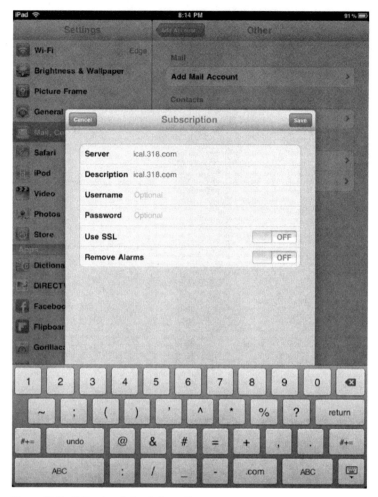

Figure B–7. *Full subscription information*

Delegating Access

Using iCal Server, it is possible to delegate access to a user's calendar from another user. Once your account has been configured in iCal on a desktop Mac OS X system, you can access delegation capabilities through the Accounts tab of iCal preferences, as shown in Figure B–8. With iCal open, select Preferences under the iCal menu, and then select Accounts. From here, highlight your account, and select the Delegation Tab. Now, you can click the Edit button at the bottom of the window to access the delegation tab, where you can add users and grant them read-only or write privileges as desired.

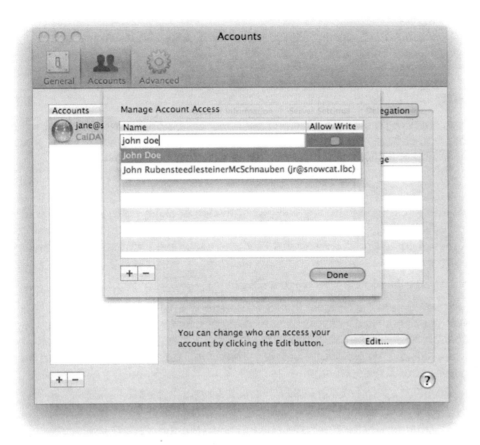

Figure B–8. *Delegating calendar access*

Backing Up Calendars

The calendar file itself is located by default in the `/Library/CalendarServer/Documents` directory. You can customize this folder, so when you're going to back it up, be careful that no one has changed the default location. Simply backing up the contents of this directory with standard software will provide an archive of the data, provided that backup also includes metadata. You can verify the directory used by your Calendar store by running the command:

```
serveradmin settings calendar:DocumentRoot
```

However, you may choose to back up the settings for the service as well. To do so, you can use the `serveradmin` command and list all of the settings as shown earlier in this chapter. But this time, we will push the contents into a file by adding the greater-than symbol > at the end of the command, followed by the file name. For example, the following will back up the service settings to a file called icalbak in the /backups directory:

```
serveradmin settings calendar > /backups/icalbak
```

Finally, also back up /etc/caldavd/caldavd.plist, and verify that you have a good backup of Open Directory as well.

Clustering CalDAV

Assuming you are using a storage medium capable of supporting multiple writes on the same volume, you can use the iCal service in a clustered fashion. Clustering iCal Server can provide an active-active solution, giving users a performance boost if the connections on your server are saturated and providing high availability.

To cluster the iCal service, you configure two iCal servers in an identical manner. To do this, you can configure the settings as you just did when backing up the iCal server to the /backups/icalbak file. To configure the same settings on the second host, use the same serveradmin command but swap the > for a <, assuming that the icalbak file has been copied to the same location on the second server:

```
serveradmin settings calendar < /backups/icalbak
```

After running this, update the SSL settings on the second host to ensure a proper SSL certification is specified. Next, we'll move the calendar files to the server in a shared directory location. In this case, we'll copy the /Library/CalendarServer directory to the /volumes/Xsan/ volume we previously created. Then, we'll point the directories for the calendar server at our shared storage:

```
serveradmin settings calendar:DocumentRoot = "/Volumes/Xsan/CalendarServer/Documents/"
serveradmin settings calendar:DataRoot = "/Volumes/Xsan/CalendarServer/Data/"
```

When you are comfortable with the settings, stop and start the iCal service:

```
serveradmin stop calendar
serveradmin start calendar
```

How you distribute the load across the two servers is up to you. Load balancers are the most obvious choice in many environments, but operating in a shared namespace and using round robin DNS will work as well, and using round robin DNS will not usually incur additional hardware or software costs (beyond, of course, having two or more copies of the Mac OS X Server software).

Web and Wiki Integration

Not all users are going to have a Mac OS X–based desktop on which to run iCal. Therefore, users are also able to view and manage calendars through the Mac OS X Server's web services, provided the web service is enabled. To do so, simply turn on Calendar Services through the Web pane of Server Preferences, as shown in Figure B–9. The web interface, also shown in Figure B–9, allows users full read and write access to their calendars; they can create new calendars, schedule events, send invitations, and view free/busy schedules. Notable limitations include the inability to access delegated calendars; to-dos do not register, and you can't attach files to events.

Figure B–9. *Configuring Calender Web Services in Server Preferences (front), Web Calender Interface (back)*

Troubleshooting

So you installed your new server and you're having a few problems. Let's look at the common issues and a few simple fixes for them.

If iCal will not start, there are a few things you can try. As always, consult the log entries. In many cases where the service simply won't start, your log entries may indicate that the service is unable to create a virtual host. This is typically a DNS-related problem, so check your host name. iCal needs the host name to be correct in order to start. Use `scutil -get HostName` or `changeip -checkhostname` to verify DNS resolution. Next, make sure that the host name listed in the iCal Server settings is identical to this value. If you prefer to use the `serveradmin` CLI to control your services, you can also use this command:

`serveradmin settings calendar:ServerHostName`

Then, you can configure the setting using the following:

`serveradmin settings calendar:ServerHostName  = "SomeHostName"`

You can also use the `calendar:HTTPPort` to change the port number you are using for connectivity.

If the service is reportedly running, but you still don't have connectivity, you can verify that your iCal server is running by visiting it in a web browser at `http://icalserver.myco.com:8008/`.

If the server is up and running, you should be presented with a generic web page that lists various XML configuration settings used by the Python-based twistd engine that iCal server is based on. If the service is not running, verify proper settings of the service, paying close attention to the document root. Verify that there is a data store at this location, which will be nested inside of two folders: Data and Documents. Verify that the calendar user _calendar is the owner of these directories and has full read/write/execute access.

Here's another common problem with the iCal server: you set up a user, check the box in Workgroup Manager to enable calendaring, and then save your settings—but you get the following error in your logs:

```
Jul10 10:21:56 cedge Workgroup Manager[2282]: +[WPUser userWithGUID::] returned nil!
```

In this case, you are probably enabling a calendar for a local user. Make sure you are using an OD-based user and see if you get the same error. Likewise, you can navigate to the user calendar URI in a web browser:

```
http://icalserver.myco.com:8008/principals/users/snowcat
```

If you receive a 404 when browsing to this address, the calendar server is not properly resolving the user record.

Here's another issue you may run across: everything is configured and the account has been created for the user, but when you add the account in iCal, it fails to connect. If you find yourself in this situation, verify that the port specified at the end of the hostname in the http:// URL is correct. Verify that you can connect to the remote server port via telnet if necessary, or by using a web browser as previously discussed. When you connect to the server this way, you will be prompted to authenticate. If you can authenticate as the user whose calendar you are trying to set up, you can use the information in this screen to determine ACL information and other security settings that could be keeping the calendars from working. Pay attention as well to the authentication method you are using. If you have selected Kerberos authentication only, your client will need to be able to directly contact the Key Distribution Center (KDC) to receive the proper service principal. Also, keep in mind that while your default port might generally be 8008, if you are using SSL, your default port is actually 8443.

Once you get this far, you should be able to create an event and see data listed in the Overview tab for iCal. If so, you should be able to find out about anything you want in the iCal server.

Address Book Server

The Address Book service is new in Mac OS X Server 10.6 and is based on the emerging CardDAV standard, a specification that defines the exchange of vCard information via the WebDAV protocol. Also based on the twistedcaldav engine, the Address Book Server setup and configuration will be much the same as with iCal: you can use Server Preferences to get the job done easily; you can use Server Admin if you require more options; or you can use the command line for optimal granularity. The

Address Book Server maintains its own data store but also allows the option to search Open Directory for User or Contact information.

Setting up Address Book Server

To set up the Address Book service on Mac OS X Server, open the Server Preferences application from /Applications/Utilities, then click the button for Address Book. When it opens, uncheck the option to limit each user's total book size if you'd like to disable user Address Book quotas, as shown in Figure B–10. Next, move the slider from the OFF to the ON positions, and wait for the service to complete installation and fire up.

Figure B–10. *Server Preferences Address Book pane*

Once the service has started, click the Show All button (Figure B–11) to get back to the main Server Preferences screen. Click Users, and] check the box for the Address Book service per user who you would like to enable the service.

Figure B–11. *Server Preferences Users pane*

As with the iCal Server service, you can also use Server Admin, located in /Applications/Server to more granularly configure the Address Book Server service. When you click the Address Book entry for your Address Book Server in Server Admin, you'll see the screen in Figure B–12.

- Enable Secure Sockets Layer (SSL): Enables SSL (requires a certificate to be accepted).

- *SSL Port Number*: If SSL is enabled this option allows for the customization of the port that the listener will run on.

- *Certificate*: Allows you to choose an SSL certificate that will be used when serving out SSL encrypted traffic.

With all services, if SSL is an option, it is strongly recommended that you use it. The stock configuration of Mac OS X Server comes with a self-assigned SSL certificate, and it is a fairly straightforward task to use it to secure your services. Alternatively, you can obtain a certificate from a third-party, as those are often easier to deploy. If your organization has an internal certificate authority, you can use its services to sign certificates for your Mac OS X host.

Once you are satisfied with your settings, click the Save button in the lower right-hand corner of the screen, and restart the service using the Server Admin utility or from the command line. To restart the service from the command line, you can use the following two commands in sequence:

```
serveradmin stop addressbook
serveradmin start addressbook
```

If you need more granularity for your Address Book Server configuration, you can also use the serveradmin command with the settings option to view all of the settings that can be changed:

```
serveradmin settings addressbook
```

This would result in the following list:

```
addressbook:SudoersFile = ""
addressbook:DirectoryService:params:restrictEnabledRecords = no
addressbook:DirectoryService:params:cacheTimeout = 30
addressbook:DirectoryService:params:restrictToGroup = ""
addressbook:DirectoryService:params:node = "/Search"
addressbook:DirectoryService:type = "twistedcaldav.directory.↵
appleopendirectory.OpenDirectoryService"
addressbook:BindSSLPorts = _empty_array
addressbook:EnablePrincipalListings = no
addressbook:DocumentRoot = "/Library/AddressBookServer/Documents"
addressbook:SSLPrivateKey = ""
addressbook:ServerStatsFile = "/var/run/carddavd/stats.plist"
addressbook:ProcessType = "Combined"
addressbook:UserName = "_calendar"
addressbook:BindHTTPPorts = _empty_array
addressbook:EnableAnonymousReadRoot = no
addressbook:DefaultLogLevel = "info"
addressbook:HTTPPort = 8800
addressbook:ServerHostName = ""
addressbook:PIDFile = "/var/run/carddavd.pid"
addressbook:ReadPrincipals = _empty_array
addressbook:UserQuota = 104857600
addressbook:MultiProcess:ProcessCount = 0
addressbook:EnableProxyPrincipals = no
```

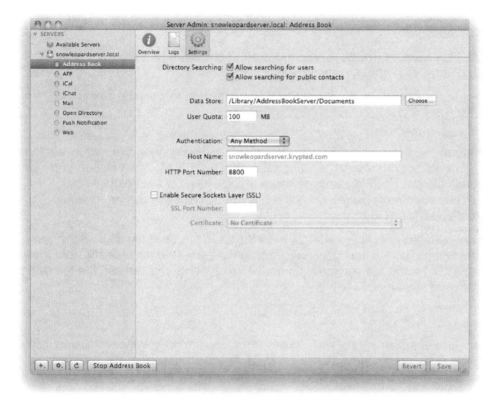

Figure B–12. *Configuring Address Book Server in Server Admin*

Here, you have the following options:

- *Directory Searching*: Allows for searches against the address book server to optionally query Open Directory for LDAP-based users (cn=users,dc=myco,dc=com) and/or public contacts (cn=people,dc=myco,dc=com).

- *Data Store*: The path to the Address Book database.

- *User Quota*: Maximum size per user for the Address Book database in megabytes.

- *Authentication*: Allows you to choose Digest or Kerberos authentication (or both).

- *Host Name*: By default, this value is dynamically generated based on the determined host name of the server; it can also be overridden.

- *HTTP Port Number*: The port that the HTTP service will listen on for Address Book traffic.

```
addressbook:Authentication:Digest:Algorithm = "md5"
addressbook:Authentication:Digest:Qop = ""
addressbook:Authentication:Digest:Enabled = yes
addressbook:Authentication:Kerberos:ServicePrincipal = ""
addressbook:Authentication:Kerberos:Enabled = yes
addressbook:Authentication:Basic:Enabled = no
addressbook:MaxAddressBookMultigetHrefs = 5000
addressbook:ErrorLogFile = "/var/log/carddavd/error.log"
addressbook:SSLCertificate = ""
addressbook:EnableSACLs = yes
addressbook:AB_EnabledGroups = _empty_array
addressbook:EnableAnonymousReadNav = no
addressbook:DataRoot = "/var/run/carddavd"
addressbook:BindAddresses = _empty_array
addressbook:AdminPrincipals = _empty_array
addressbook:MaxAddressBookQueryResults = 1000
addressbook:RedirectHTTPToHTTPS = no
addressbook:EnableSearchAddressBook = yes
addressbook:DirectoryAddressBook:params:queryUserRecords = yes
addressbook:DirectoryAddressBook:params:liveQuery = yes
addressbook:DirectoryAddressBook:params:cacheQuery = no
addressbook:DirectoryAddressBook:params:peopleNode = "/Search/Contacts"
addressbook:DirectoryAddressBook:params:fakeETag = yes
addressbook:DirectoryAddressBook:params:ignoreSystemRecords = yes
addressbook:DirectoryAddressBook:params:queryPeopleRecords = yes
addressbook:DirectoryAddressBook:params:dsLocalCacheTimeout = 30
addressbook:DirectoryAddressBook:params:queryAllAttributes = no
addressbook:DirectoryAddressBook:params:userNode = "/Search"
addressbook:DirectoryAddressBook:params:cacheTimeout = 30
addressbook:DirectoryAddressBook:params:maxDSQueryRecords = 150
addressbook:DirectoryAddressBook:type = "twistedcaldav.directory.↵
opendirectorybacker.OpenDirectoryBackingService"
addressbook:RotateAccessLog = no
addressbook:AnonymousDirectoryAddressBookAccess = no
addressbook:GroupName = "_calendar"
addressbook:AccessLogFile = "/var/log/carddavd/access.log"
addressbook:ResponseCompression = yes
```

Backing up Address Books

Backing up the Address Book Server data store is similar to backing up the iCal Server information store. The path to the database can be found through Server Admin or using the following command:

```
serveradmin settings addressbook:DocumentRoot
```

Once you know the path, you can back up the data store as you would most other directory structures, making sure to keep extended attributes backed up as well. The service runs with the _calendar username as the default owner, although the root account will provide access as well. The default location to the information store is /Library/AddressBook/.

NOTE: When restoring data, you may have to reset the permissions on the files.

iChat Server

The iChat application in Mac OS X is a fantastic tool for instant messaging. It supports video, conferencing video, file transfer, and even sharing screens over an iChat session. These capabilities make it a great support tool for the service desk, as well as an excellent communication platform that can enhance an organization's intracompany communications. If you like, iChat can also be leveraged to extend communication externally (though it is primarily intended for internal communications).

To set up the iChat Server, the steps you perform are roughly the same as those for other services. For a simple server setup, use the Server Preferences tool (shown in Figure B–13), which allows you to configure serverwide logging and archiving of chat transcripts and to enable server-to-server communication, which allows Extensible Messaging and Presence Protocol (XMPP) federation between hosts.

Figure B–13. *Server Preference iChat pane*

Once you have a functional iChat service, chances are you'll be interested in pushing the boundaries of what it can do beyond the default two options in Server Preferences. Just as with iCal and Address Book, you can also access the service from within Server Admin. To do so, click the iChat service under the SERVERS list and then under the General tab (as shown in Figure B–14) to configure the appropriate settings:

- *Host Domains*: Indicates the DNS domain names (or IP addresses) that will be used by the Jabber server.

- *SSL Certificate*: Integrates the service with SSL. Once selected, choose the appropriate certificate.

- *Authentication:* Sets the method of authentication to Digest, Kerberos, or both, which will attempt Kerberos first and then fail back to Digest.

- *Enable XMPP server-to-server federation*: Allows you to federate the server with other servers, which means that users of one host can establish chat sessions with users from another host. This can be useful if you have multiple servers in multiple locations, or if you want to extend your server to communicate with third-party hosts.

- Require secure server-to-server federation: Forces XMPP federation to use SSL.

- Allow federation with all domains: Allows all other XMPP-compliant servers to communicate with yours.

- Allow federation with the following domains: Configures other servers (by IP or DNS) that are federated to this server.

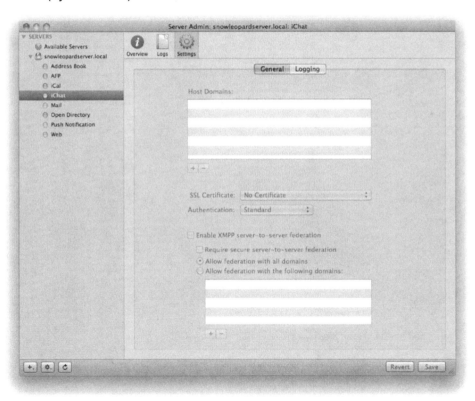

Figure B–14. *Configuring iChat settings in Server Admin*

Transcripts

You can also configure message archival (transcript storage) options using Server Admin. To do so, click the Settings tab shown in Figure B–15. Enable the "Automatically save chat messages" features, which will store a centralized copy of all instant messaging chat sessions for each user on the server. Next, click the Choose button to select a location and then use the "Archive saved messages every" field to configure how long messages are kept before they are moved into a compressed archive file. Unfortunately, this function is limited to text-based transcripts. Audio and video chats, once initiated, are peer-to-peer and, as such, the server never sees the data.

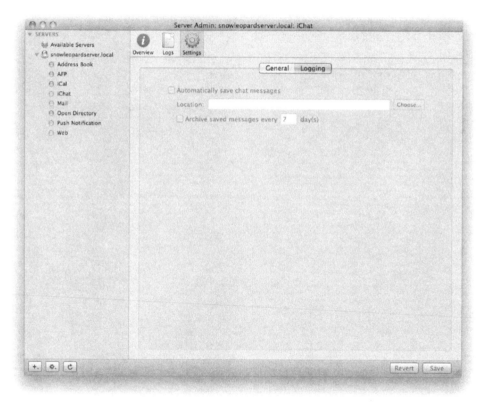

Figure B–15. *Saving and archiving chat messages*

The serveradmin command can again be used to list additional configuration settings for the service:

```
hax.lbc:~ hunterbj$ sudo serveradmin settings jabber
jabber:enableAutoBuddy = no
jabber:s2sAllowedDomains = _empty_array
jabber:requireSecureS2S = no
jabber:sslCAFile = "/etc/certificates/hax.lbc.chcrt"
jabber:sslKeyFile = "/etc/certificates/hax.lbc.crtkey"
jabber:hosts:_array_index:0 = "hax.lbc"
jabber:authLevel = "ANYMETHOD"
```

```
jabber:s2sRestrictDomains = no
jabber:savedChatsArchiveInterval = 7
jabber:eventLogArchiveInterval = 7
jabber:savedChatsLocation = "/var/jabberd/message_archives"
jabber:enableSavedChats = yes
jabber:enableXMPP = no
jabber:logLevel = "ALL"
```

Once you have configured your iChat server, you can use a number of Jabber clients available for iOS-based devices to communicate through that server. For more on these, see Chapter 10.

Mac OS X Mail Server

While most enterprises will already have a stable messaging and groupware infrastructure, Mac OS X Server can also be leveraged for much of the same type of functionality. We have already extolled the virtues of the Address Book, iCal, and iChat; Mail rounds out the groupware offerings quite nicely and also enables Push Notification to handheld devices. In environments where an incumbent solution exists for mail, the Mac OS X mail service can provide ancillary messaging services, such as supplemental or archival mail storage, listserv functionality, and virus and spam filtering before mail goes into a separate solution, or it can act as a relay.

While the Mac OS X Server's mail service doesn't provide as many services for other platforms as it could, it's not because the services that make up the Mac OS X Server mail service are immature. Mac OS X Server uses Dovecot for the message database (POP and IMAP), Mailman for listservs, and Postfix for mail services (SMTP). These tools, deeply rooted in Unix, go back sometimes decades and are as stable, when used for the appropriate environments, as Microsoft Exchange.

Setting Up a Mail Server

Setting up Mac OS X Server to be a mail server is much like setting up the other services that have been described, although the messaging ecosystem includes basic networking, message hygiene and other aspects that aren't directly related to the mail server itself. To enable the service, you can use the Server Preferences application. Click the Mail icon, and you will see some simple settings that can be configured for the Mail service (see Figure B–16). Use the check boxes to enable a few features, and then move the slider to the ON position to fire up the service:

- *Relay outgoing mail through ISP*: Enables all mail being sent from or through the server to be routed through the organization's ISP, which, among other benefits, eliminates the need for reverse DNS.

- Reject email from blacklisted servers: Use spam blacklist server (DNSBLs): Enables Spamhaus blacklist servers (default is zen.spamhaus.org).

■   *Enable junk mail and virus filtering:* Enables ClamAv for virus filtering
    and SpamAssassin for antispam and allows you to set how
    aggressively it filters e-mail.

Figure B–16. *Mail Service Server Preferences settings*

The features available in Server Preferences are minimal, and it is highly likely that any
substantial user base will require far more configuration. As usual, you can also use
Server Admin to configure the Mail Server, with much more granularity.

Configuring Mail with ServerAdmin

To configure mail services with the Server Admin tool, you must first enable the service
in the server overview pane, as described with other services. You can then configure
numerous details, as shown in Figure B–17. Here are the general global settings you can
configure:

■   *Domain name:* The domain name of the primary mail domain.

■   *Host name:* The host name of the mail server (defaults to the name
    entered at the time the server was setup if it has not since been
    altered).

■   *Push Notification Server:* Allows the server to be used with the push
    notification service to provide iPhone compatibility.

■   Enable SMTP: Enables the SMTP service and daemon.

■   Allow incoming mail: Enables inbound mail acceptance for configured
    users.

■   *Hold outgoing mail:* Do not send outgoing mail until it is manually
    released.

- *Relay outgoing mail through host*: Relays all mail not destined for local storage through specified server. This option enables a Mac OS X mail server to operate as an intermediate Mail Transfer Agent (MTA), which can be used to route local email to a centralized company SMTP server or to an ISP's SMTP server. The extensibility of the postfix MTA engine means you can use it to provide customized e-mail filtering, which can ultimately be integrated into existing business systems.

- Authenticate to relay with user name: The username for the SMTP server specified in the previous field.

- Password: The password for the SMTP server.

- *Copy undeliverable mail to*: If an e-mail address is specified, it will be copied on all nondelivery reports (NDRs), a good measure for proactive admins.

- *Copy all mail to*: Allows for a backup account to store a copy of each incoming and outgoing e-mail that routes through the SMTP daemon. A good measure for the guy who has the "I read your e-mail" bumper sticker and means it.

- *Enable IMAP with maximum of*: Enables the IMAP service and allows you to limit the maximum number of connections to it.

- *Enable POP*: Enables the POP service but does not allow you to throttle the number of connections.

- Deliver to "/var/mail" when IMAP & POP are disabled: Stores messages as flat files in the /var/mail directory if no services have been enabled to route mail to.

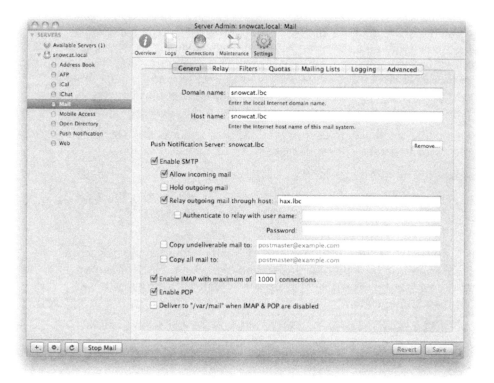

Figure B–17. *Configuring Mail in Server Admin*

You can also configure the supported authentication mechanisms. To do so, click the Advanced tab, where you will be able to configure authentication options for SMTP and for POP/IMAP services, as shown in Figure B–18. Of these options, login, PLAIN, and Clear all actually utilize cleartext passwords, so you should think twice about enabling them without SSL configured. CRAM-MD5 is the preferred authentication method, and all popular mail clients support it. However, there will be times when your best (or only) option is SSL plus cleartext authentication. Notably, if you are using an Active Directory backend for authentication, you will likely need to use this option.

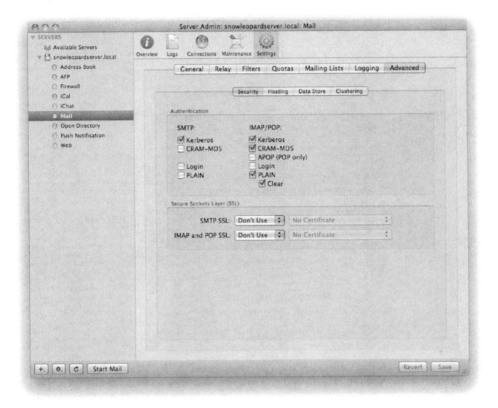

Figure B–18. *Mail service authentication settings*

Protecting the Mail Servers

Once the settings are configured, click the Relay tab, shown in Figure B–19. Here, you can configure how the server manages attempts to relay SMTP traffic through it. Using the "Accept SMTP relays only from these hosts and networks" option, you can configure which IP addresses (and ranges) are able to relay mail through the SMTP service. With "Refuse all messages from these hosts and networks", you can also configure a blacklist of IP addresses that you will never accept mail from (for example, those you feel are abusive). Finally, you can configure the "Use these junk mail rejection servers (real-time blacklist)" option to indicate multiple RBL servers that your SMTP server will use when checking the source server that is attempting to relay mail through yours.

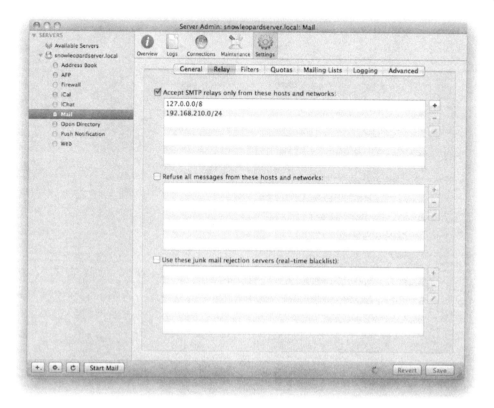

Figure B–19. *Mail Service relay configuration*

It is worth noting that in the "Accept SMTP relays" option, the networks and IP addresses listed specify *unauthenticated* external relay only. "Relay" in the context of SMTP means that the mail is destined for a different mail exchanger. Messages destined for a mail user stored locally on the mail server are messages requiring not relay but, rather, delivery. E-mails bound for local users will be accepted from hosts that are not explicitly listed in the "Refuse all messages" list or designated as a spammer by a specified RBL. Be particularly careful when configuring IP address relays, as a poorly planned relay configuration can result in your e-mail server being flagged as an *open relay*, meaning that your server has been determined to be delivering SPAM. For this reason, it is recommended that you leave the allowed relay list relatively sparse and, instead, require your users to authenticate in order to relay mail.

You can also configure junk mail and spam filters by clicking the Filters tab (see Figure B–20). Here are options you can set:

- *Enable junk mail filtering*: Enables the spam filter, which is based on the open source spam filter SpamAssassin

- *Minimum junk mail score*: When junk mail filtering is enabled, each message is assigned a score that identifies the likelihood the message is spam. You can use this field to identify the score that a message would need to exceed before it is flagged as spam and the appropriate action to be taken (defined in the "Junk mail messages should be" field).

- *Accepted languages*: Allows you to configure acceptable languages for incoming mail. All mail determined to be not on the list will be marked as junk, and the appropriate action will be taken.

- *Accepted locales*: Defines acceptable geographical regions that mail will be accepted from.

- *Junk mail messages should be*: Defines the appropriate action that will be taken with regard to mail identified as being junk mail.

- *Attach subject tag*: Can be used to augment the subject line of incoming mail flagged as spam.

- *Encapsulate junk mail as MIME attachment*: Moves mail flagged as spam into an attachment, which requires user interaction before the mail client will attempt to parse and present the message.

- Enable virus filtering: Enables ClamAv scanning for incoming messages.

- *Infected messages should be*: Defines the appropriate action to be taken on e-mail identified as containing a virus.

- Send notification to: Allows infected mail to be sent to a specified mailbox.

- *Notify recipients*: Sends an e-mail advising the receiver of an infected message without sending the message itself.

- *Update the virus database*: Updates the virus database on a timed interval, defined in number of times per day.

- Enable server side mail rules: Enables preprocessing of rules for all mail coming into the server.

NOTE: If you choose any option other than Delivered for junk mail messages, the recipient will never see them, and the sender will never know they were deleted. Only the e-mail address you specify will be notified, which means that you, the administrator, will have to deal with the message. keep in mind that "from" addresses are almost always spoofed on actual spam messages, and you could end up flooding legitimate email addresses with delivery notices.

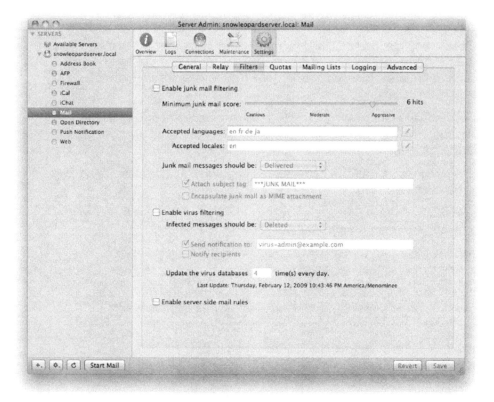

Figure B–20. *Mail service filtering options*

Another way to protect the mail server is to keep users from abusing resources. Not that anyone will do so on purpose, but storage in many environments is a finite resource, while consumption typically is not. Therefore, you can configure how mailbox quotas are handled globally using the Quotas tab, shown in Figure B–21 (quotas themselves are set for each mailbox using the Quotas tab on a per-account basis in Workgroup Manager). Here, you specify settings that match your organization's business logic:

■ *Refuse messages larger than*: Identifies the maximum attachment size for incoming mail to the organization.

■ Enable quota warnings: Warns users when their mailbox exceeds a specified size.

■ Disable a user's incoming mail when they exceed 100% of quota: Blocks a user's mail if the mailbox is full.

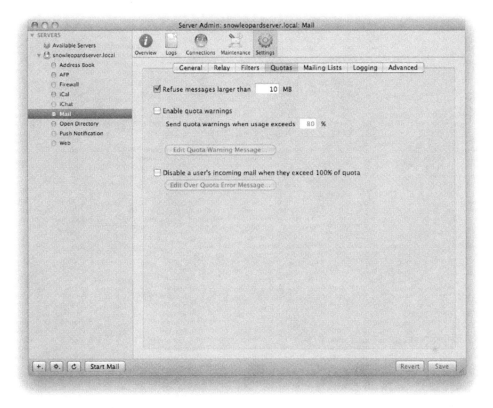

Figure B–21. *Configuring Mail service quotas*

Mailing Lists

Mac OS X Server comes with a fully functional listserv. To configure it, click the Mailing Lists tab in Server Admin, and check the box for "Enable server group mailing lists" (see Figure B–22). You can then use the "Enable mailman mailing lists" check box to enable actual lists. Use the plus icon (+) to create mailing lists and the Users & Groups button to drag users to the list.

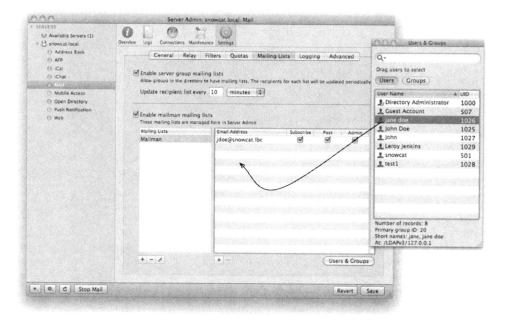

Figure B–22. *Enabling mailing lists in Server Admin*

Mailman is a far more complex solution than this simple screen seems to imply. The configuration files provide an abundance of further options that can be used to tailor the system to your liking, including full support for automated subscription and unsubscription via e-mail. Mailman is a tried and true solution and is pretty much the same beast on Mac OS X as in other environments.

Logging

Mac OS X Server, by default, logs events from the mail server. You can customize these events on the Logging tab. Here, you can customize the log levels for SMTP and IMAP/POP, as well as for junk mail and viruses (see Figure B–23). Additionally, you can set logs to be compressed on a timed schedule by using the "Archive logs every" field, which specifies the number of days logs are stored before they are compressed.

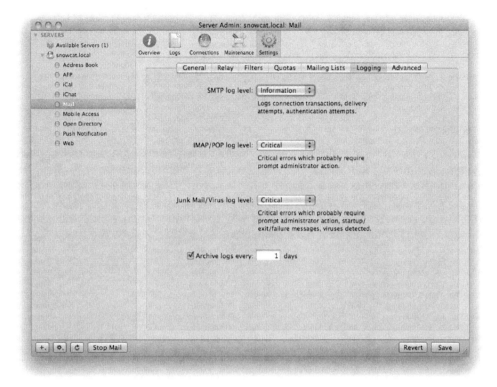

Figure B–23. *Mail service logging options*

The Command Line

The Mac OS X Mail service is one of the most feature rich, with pages of options that can be configured using `serveradmin`, as described in previous sections. The following command will display a list of settings:

```
serveradmin settings mail
```

You can also leverage the various configuration options provided by each of the Mac OS X mail server's underlying packages. Postfix, for instance, is robust and highly extensible and can be made to work with many plug-ins. For instance, you may wish to inject your own filtering code into the MTA process to watch for e-mails with particular criteria. To inject your own filter into the MTA pipeline, you would modify the Postfix master process configuration file found at `/etc/postfix/master.cf`. The `main.cf` file is another one that controls the overall behavior of Postfix. While the administration GUI in Server Admin provides a decent amount of configurability, it exposes only a small subset of Postfix's capabilities. Through the direct modification of these files, much, much more flexibility can be wrangled out of the system.

While we're on the topic of Postfix, there are numerous command line-binaries that can assist in the day-to-day management of your mail server. For instance, the `postqueue` command can be used to manage basic delivery queuing. The following command will output a list of all queued massages:

```
postqueue -p
```

Messages in the queue can be flushed (resent) either by specifying the -f flag to flush all queued mail, or by specifying the -i flag and a queueid to resubmit just a single email:

```
postqueue -f
postqueue -i B8EB9C6BDBD
```

If you have queue problems, sometimes the only solution is to delete certain messages from the queue altogether. Malformed messages can certainly cause problems. To delete a message from the queue, postsuper must be used. The postsuper command is very similar to postqueue, but it includes (and requires) superuser access to utilize it. This command also provides the only supported way to delete particular mail messages from the queue. For instance, to delete a specific queued message, use the following command:

```
sudo postsuper -d 308AE53AF9
```

or to release all messages on hold, use this one:

```
sudo postsuper -r hold
```

It is also extremely easy to send an e-mail using postfix's sendmail compatabilty features. For example, the following single line of shell code will send an e-mail to user jdoe@myco.com:

```
printf "To:jdoe@myco.com\nFrom:myserver@myco.com\nSubject:This is the subject\n\n↵
This is the message body.\n"  | sendmail -t
```

Choosing Mailbox Locations

The internal storage of a Mac OS X Server is often not where you'll want to store the database of the mail service. Instead, if you have spacious and fast external storage, you will often use that (obviously, the number of users and intensity of use would define the storage requirements). If you want to move the mail database, click the Advanced tab of the Mail Settings and then the Data Store subtab, where you will see the location of the default mail store, as shown in Figure B–24. The default store can stay here, or it can be moved to external storage by using the Choose button to select an alternate location. The key point, however, is that you can create multiple mail stores at multiple locations, allowing you to use different storage for different tiers of users depending on speed, department, or other requirements you put in place to determine whose mail goes where.

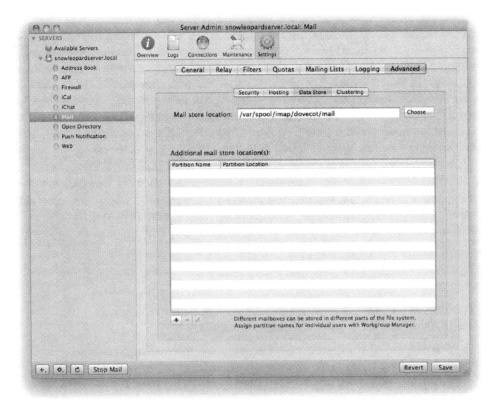

Figure B–24. *Advanced mail service settings*

If you are satisfied with your settings, click the Save button, and restart the Mail service. Once you have created additional mail partitions, you assign individual users to each in Workgroup Manager, under the user's Mail tab.

The Dovecot Mailstore

Starting with Snow Leopard, Mac OS X Server uses the Dovecot mailstore as the storage mechanism for mail. The Dovecot mailstore, by default, exists at /var/spool/imap/dovecot. This folder contains two subdirectories, sieve-scripts, which holds third-party sieve scripts, and mail, which contains subdirectories with user data, named after the respective user's GeneratedUID value. To determine a particular user's GeneratedUID, you can use the dscl command:

```
dscl /Search read /Users/jdoe GeneratedUID | awk '{print $2}'
```

which generates the following output, which will be the name of our folder:

```
C3C4E3BB-1FE8-4A6E-B445-5474CC4E3223
```

Each user folder is owned by the respective user and contains index and cache files, mailboxes, and e-mail messages. For e-mail message storage, Dovecot uses a flat-file system. That is, every message is represented by an associated file that contains the e-mail's contents, including any attachments in a standard MIME-encoded format. Each of a user's mailboxes is represented by dot-prepended directories. Thus, for the mailbox Sent Messages, a folder called .Sent Messages is created. Each of these mailboxes contains a number of files and directories for storage. For each mailbox, e-mails are stored in a subdirectory named cur. These files are stored with a standardized file name that includes a unique identifier, the message size, and the message flags. The user's IMAP inbox is represented by that user's root folder on the file system. Specifically, user jdoe's inbox is represented by e-mails existing in the folder /var/spool/imap/dovecot/C3C4E3BB-1FE8-4A6E-B445-5474CC4E3223/cur, using the GeneratedUID value found earlier. To optimize mail listings, Dovecot creates index files for each inbox, and these are used to provide accelerated access to commonly queried data, though the index files themselves do not contain any otherwise unrecoverable data. Dovecot utilizes the following cache files:

- *dovecot.index*: The main index file that contains mailbox summary information, including number of messages and size of and pointer to message cache file

- *dovecot.index.cache*: Cached mailbox data, including message headers, sent date, and other message information

- *dovecot.index.log*: A transaction log file used to improve performance in situations where there are multiple concurrent connections

- dovecot.index.log.2: A rotated transactional log file

Rebuilding a mailbox in Dovecot is pretty straightforward. To rebuild the index for any Dovecot user's mailbox, you can simply remove the cache and index files mentioned previously. The index file will be automatically re-created, and the cache file will begin to repopulate with data as it is requested. If you want to rebuild all index files for a user, the command is fairly simple:

```
find /var/spool/imap/dovecot/mail/C3C4E3BB-1FE8-4A6E-B445-5474CC4E3223 -name
"dovecot.index*" -exec rm {} \;
```

This command will delete all index files for the user, and these files will subsequently be rebuilt. While this can be done on a live system, you are deleting files that contain synchronization data, so it's probably a good idea to ensure that there are no active connections to the user's mailstore. Upon reconnecting to the server, there may be slight a delay for the user as the index files are rebuilt, although message flags (read versus unread) should be in tact.

Setting Up Public folders

Public folders in Dovecot can be configured a few ways. The easiest way is to simply use symlinks. A dot prefixed symbolic link to external directories will be properly resolved by Dovecot and will be presented to the user as a standard mailbox. When setting up such a public share, it is important to note that Dovecot operates within the user context. Thus each user who is granted access to the public folder via symlinks must also have the appropriate file system permissions, designated via either standard POSIX or ACL management. To set up a shared folder in this manner, you can run the following commands:

```
## cd into the mail store so we can use relative paths
cd /var/spool/imap/dovecot/mail

## create our shared folder and mailbox
mkdir -p Shared/.MySharedFolder

## setup POSIX and ACL privileges on the mailmox for our users
chgrp -R staff  Shared/.MySharedFolder
chmod -R g+rwx Shared/.MySharedFolder
chmod +a "staff allow
list,add_file,search,delete,add_subdirectory,delete_child,readattr,writeattr,readextattr,↵
writeextattr,readsecurity,file_inherit,directory_inherit" Shared/.MySharedFolder

## create our symlinks for our users. We first cd into our user's folder so that we can use
## relative paths on our links
cd C3C4E3BB-1FE8-4A6E-B445-5474CC4E3223
ln -s ../Shared/.MySharedFolder .MySharedFolder
```

> **NOTE:** The ../ portion of the above path references the parent directory. Thus, inside of user jdoe's email folder, we are creating a link to the Shared folder in the parent folder. Using a relative symlink like this allows us to move the entire mail store to a different directory or volume without breaking the paths.

At this point, user jdoe will have full access to the mailbox MySharedFolder. We could then symlink the same directory to another user, say janedoe. The beauty of file-system–level permissioning here is that you can do all kinds of cool stuff with ACLs. For instance, you could prevent janedoe from deleting items, leaving her only with the ability to add new items to the store.

Backing Up Mail

With the introduction of Dovecot in Mac OS X Server 10.6, backing up mail got quite a bit easier. In 10.5, the Cyrus database risked potential for corruption when backed up live. Though this was far less of an issue than with earlier versions of Mac OS X, the reality was that Apple still recommended taking the system offline to back it up. No longer! Now, mail can be backed up by your standard backup program, be it Netvault, TiNa, rsync, or even Time Machine. Because each message is stored as its own file system entity, granular message-level or mailbox-level restores are possible.

To perform a restore, just replace the appropriate e-mails or directories into the user's mail root. You can restore entire mailboxes simply by placing the respective dot-prefixed folder there; alternatively, you can create your own restore mailbox, using the following command (here, we use jdoe in the mail paths; it is necessary to use the user's GeneratedUID, as discussed previously):

```
## create the new Mailbox Restored, and it's cur subdirectory, which holds the mail
files
mkdir -p /var/spool/imap/dovecot/mail/jdoe/.Restored/cur

## copy our backed up email files into our restore mailbox's cur/ directory.
rsync -avu /path/to/my/backupemaildir/ /var/spool/imap/dovecot/mail/jdoe/.Restored/cur/
## make sure the new user is the owner
chown -R jdoe /var/spool/imap/dovecot/mail/jdoe/.Restored
## Delete our index file, forcing them to be rebuilt
rm /var/spool/imap/dovecot/mail/jdoe/.Restored/dovecot.index*
```

You can also copy individual e-mail messages into preexisting mailboxes without much fanfare, though it is once again recommended that you remove the index file.

There are other notable mail-related configurations and database files that you may want to back up, though it's not strictly required:

■ /var/amavis: Contains filtering information, including the SpamAssassin Bayes database (all learned junk mail)

■ /var/clamav: Contains the latest virus definitions

■ /etc/freshclam.conf: ClamAv configuration file

■ /etc/amavisd.conf: Amavisd configuration file

■ /etc/mail/spamassassin: SpamAssassin configuration files

If you are running a Mac OS 10.5–based mail server, you should back up its Cyrus database without the service running. An excellent tool named mailbfr can be found at http://osx.topicdesk.com. It is a free utility and manages the backups of the Mac OS 10.5 database, including stopping and starting the services as necessary.

Clustering Mail Services

As mentioned previously, the Mail service provided by Mac OS X Server can be clustered, provided you have shared storage with file-level locking. Currently, the only supported means to implement mail clustering is through Xsan.

To set up a cluster, you must first run the Service Configuration Assistant, found by clicking the Change button on the Mail services Clustering tab. Once the assistant fires, you will be presented with the option to create a new cluster or join an existing one, provided that the system detects an available Xsan volume, as shown in Figure B–25.

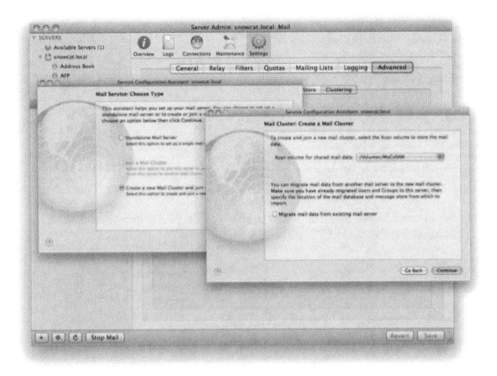

Figure B–25. *Changing the Mail clustering setting*

Once a cluster is established, it will be stored in a hidden directory, .MailCluster, at the root of the volume. The Mail service cluster will be managed by the first host that is added to it. Inside of the .MailCluster folder, you will find a directory named after the name of the Xsan volume, and inside of it reside configuration files, files that are locked, and the mail datastore:

```
bash-3.2# ls /Volumes/MyCoSAN/.MailCluster/MyCoSAN/
```

The preceding command would result in the following output, showing the directories with the configuration and backup data within them:

```
MailClusterConf.plist    config                data                    lock_files
```

Inside the config folder, you will find both standard Dovecot and Postfix configuration files. The data folder contains the mail store, SMTP spool, Mailman datastore, and server-side e-mail rules (vacation messages, server-side filters, and sieve scripts). Worth mention in this folder is the MailClusterConf.plist file, which contains data relevant to the configuration of the mail cluster, including a list of member servers:

```
<?xml version="1.0" encoding="UTF-8"?>
<!DOCTYPE plist PUBLIC "-//Apple//DTD PLIST 1.0//EN"
"http://www.apple.com/DTDs/PropertyList-1.0.dtd">
<plist version="1.0">
<dict>
        <key>cluster_name</key>
```

```
            <string>MyCoSAN</string>
            <key>cluster_path</key>
            <string>/Volumes/MyCoSAN</string>
            <key>cluster_type</key>
            <string>combined</string>
            <key>members</key>
            <array>
                    <string>snowcat.lbc</string>
            </array>
            <key>name</key>
            <string>MyCoSAN</string>
            <key>path</key>
            <string>/Volumes/MyCoSAN</string>
</dict>
</plist>
```

Once the cluster is configured, you can verify in the Mail service's overview that clustering is enabled, as shown in Figure B–26.

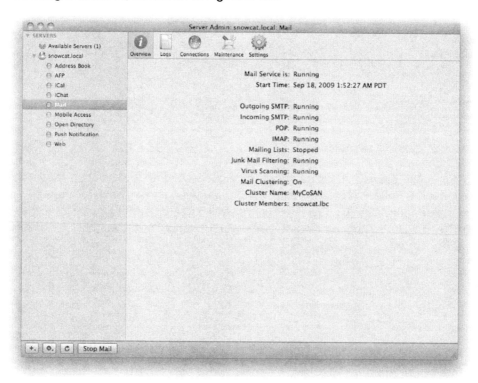

Figure B–26. *Mail service overview with clustering*

Index

Special Characters

- button, 199
$EMAIL variable, 244
$USERNAME variable, 244
%@ variable, 246
+ button, 199

A

about.html file, 184
Accept Cookies setting, 41
Accept SMTP relays option, Server Admin tool, 344
Acceptable Use Policy, 311–316
    definitions, 316
    enforcement, 316
    general use and ownership, 312–313
    purpose of, 312
    security and proprietary information, 313
    unacceptable use, 314–316
        e-mail and communications activities, 315–316
        system and network activities, 314–315
Accepted languages option, Server Admin tool, 345
Accepted locales option, Server Admin tool, 345
access, controlling, 162–163
Access Gateway option, 273
Access icon, Server Admin toolbar, 162
Access option, 162
Account Description field, 201, 204, 206
Account Hostname and Port field, 206
Account Hostname field, 204
Account Name field, 201
Account Name setting, 203
Account setting, 142, 144
Account Type field, 201

Account Username field, 204, 206–207
Accounts tab, iCal, 326
Activate Plugin button, 174
activating. See also purchasing
    devices, 19–22
        synchronization options, 21–22
        synchronizing, 20–21
    managing, 17–19
        StoreActivationMode, 17–18
        StoreGeniusMode, 18–19
Activation mode, iTunes, 17
ActiveSync, configuring iOS for, 79–83
activities, e-mail and communications, 315–316
Add Account option, 96, 323
Add Account screen, 48–49, 96
Add App from App Store screen, JSS, 256
Add App icon, JSS, 254
Add Bookmark option, 43
Add Configuration screen, Settings application, 141, 143
Add Mail Account button, 51
Add Profile button, JSS, 242
Add Server option, Server Preferences tool, 324
Add Server screen, 114
Add Server wizard, 115–116
Add VPN Configuration button, Settings app, 140–141
Address Book framework, 210
Address Book Host Name setting, Address Book service, 158
Address Book Host Port setting, Address Book service, 158
Address Book proxy, configuring, 157–158
Address Book Server, 330–335
    backing up address books, 335
    setting up, 331–335
Address field, 51
Address option, 273
administrative users, setting up, 223–224

T

 U

You Need the Companion eBook

Your purchase of this book entitles you to buy the companion PDF-version eBook for only $10. Take the weightless companion with you anywhere.

We believe this Apress title will prove so indispensable that you'll want to carry it with you everywhere, which is why we are offering the companion eBook (in PDF format) for $10 to customers who purchase this book now. Convenient and fully searchable, the PDF version of any content-rich, page-heavy Apress book makes a valuable addition to your programming library. You can easily find and copy code—or perform examples by quickly toggling between instructions and the application. Even simultaneously tackling a donut, diet soda, and complex code becomes simplified with hands-free eBooks!

Once you purchase your book, getting the $10 companion eBook is simple:

❶ Visit **www.apress.com/promo/tendollars/**.

❷ Complete a basic registration form to receive a randomly generated question about this title.

❸ Answer the question correctly in 60 seconds, and you will receive a promotional code to redeem for the $10.00 eBook.

233 Spring Street, New York, NY 10013

Breinigsville, PA USA
26 November 2010
249956BV00005B/23-76/P